Blake and Modern Literature

Blake and Modern Literature

Edward Larrissy

First published in 2006 by
PALGRAVE MACMILLAN
Houndmills, Basingstoke, Hampshire RG21 6XS and
175 Fifth Avenue, New York, N.Y. 10010
Companies and representatives throughout the world.

PALGRAVE MACMILLAN is the global academic imprint of the Palgrave Macmillan division of St. Martin's Press, LLC and of Palgrave Macmillan Ltd. Macmillan® is a registered trademark in the United States, United Kingdom and other countries. Palgrave is a registered trademark in the European Union and other countries.

ISBN-13: 978–1–4039–4176–3 hardback
ISBN-10: 1–4039–4176–9 hardback

This book is printed on paper suitable for recycling and made from fully managed and sustained forest sources.

A catalogue record for this book is available from the British Library.

Library of Congress Cataloging-in-Publication Data

Larrissy, Edward.
    Blake and modern literature / Edward Larrissy.
      p. cm.
    Includes bibliographical references and index.
    ISBN 1–4039–4176–9 (cloth)
      1. Blake, William, 1757–1827 – Influence. 2. Literature,
    Modern – 20th century – History and criticism. 3. English literature –
    20th century – History and criticism. I. Title

PR4148.I52L37 2006
821'.7—dc22
                                            2006042625

10 9 8 7 6 5 4 3 2 1
15 14 13 12 11 10 09 08 07 06

Transferred to digital printing in 2007.

Contents

Acknowledgements

An earlier version of Chapter 2 appeared in *Myth and the Making of Modernity: The Problem of Grounding in Early Twentieth-Century Literature*, ed. Michael Bell and Peter Poellner (Amsterdam and Atlanta GA: Rodopi, 1998); Chapter 6, in *David Jones: Artist and Poet (Warwick Studies in the European Humanities)*, ed. Paul Hills (Aldershot: Scolar, 1997); and Chapter 7 in *Palgrave Advances in William Blake Studies*, ed. Nicholas Williams (Basingstoke: Palgrave Macmillan, 2005).

This book was supported by the AHRC. The AHRC funds postgraduate training and research in the arts and humanities, from archaeology and English literature to design and dance. The quality and range of research supported not only provides social and cultural benefits but also contributes to the economic success of the UK. For further information on the AHRC, please see the website www.ahrc.ac.uk

 Arts & Humanities
Research Council

1
Introduction: Blake Between Romanticism, Modernism and Postmodernism

Blake is the Romantic writer who has exerted the most powerful influence on the twentieth century. Indeed, the more one looks into the matter, the more surprised one may be by the extent and pervasiveness of that influence. He figures here as an important example of the way in which Romantic currents may feed into Modernist and Postmodernist ones – but by no means a straightforward one. On the one hand, he is now regarded as one of the great canonical literary artists of the Romantic period, and he is rightly seen in relation to then current modes, such as the sublime. On the other hand, Blake's popularity may have much to do with qualities which are supposed to differentiate him from other Romantics. In any case, if he were without any ado to be an example of Romantic influence, we would have to have a clear, essential idea what Romanticism is or was – and we do not. This book will attempt to offer an account of Blake's afterlife which shows that he was central in the retrospective construction of a Romanticism that was acceptable to the twentieth century, that he assisted in the gestation of innovative writing in the modern period, and that this kind of centrality is continuing into the twenty-first century. In the process, it will seek to be sensitive to the theoretical difficulties involved in describing canon-formation.

Blake was not especially well known at the time of his death in 1827, although the tendency to assume that nobody had heard of him in those later years has never been accepted by scholars. He was known in the sense that many would have heard of him as an interesting minor poet and eccentric visionary artist. The ascent to his current exalted status has been a gradual but steady process. But already, by the 1840s, he was posthumously exhibiting his uncanny capacity to attach himself to the current avant-garde, for his influence is significant in the development of pre-Raphaelitism, *via* the patronage of the Rossetti brothers. Swinburne's book on him (1868) shows remarkable understanding. It is true that Swinburne helps to transmit to Oscar Wilde that decadent reading of Blake which sees in *The Marriage of Heaven and Hell* the sweets of sin. How Swinburne could have associated Blake's Hell with the discipline he solicited and received at 7, Circus Road, St John's Wood, is a question that reminds one how alien the past can be. But when Wilde avers in his commonplace book that 'In modern times Dante and Dürer, Keats and Blake are the best representatives of the Greek spirit', this is one of his purer references to Greece, as well as being the highest praise he can accord.[1] He seems to have in mind both clarity of outline (he possessed drawings by Blake) and an ardour which Blake would have called Energy. Blake himself, as Wilde probably knew, was capable of thinking of this combination of clarity and Energy as Greek, at least in his earlier years. But the subversive Blake has also left his mark, I think, on the aphorisms at the beginning of *The Picture of Dorian Gray*.

However, the greatest tribute the Nineties paid to Blake was the three-volume annotated edition, with lithographic reproductions of a fair number of the illustrations, by Edwin Ellis and W. B. Yeats.[2] This edition benefited by the knowledge both shared of occult philosophies. However much their own interests have to be seen in the context of a late nineteenth-century fad for the occult, they are to a significant degree illuminating about Blake; whose own knowledge, however, can partly be explained by the eclecticism of antinomian Protestantism. In any case, Blake's conviction that 'Without Contraries is no Progression' has left its mark everywhere on Yeats's poetry and his esoteric writings. It is customary to compare Yeats's juxtaposition of 'The Song of the Happy Shepherd' and 'The Sad Shepherd', at the beginning of the *Crossways* grouping, with the pairs of poems in *Songs of Innocence and of Experience*. Indeed, one of the notable things about Yeat's shepherds is the unbridgeable gulf that separates their states of mind. The Happy Shepherd laments the passing of a world where dreams fed poetry and its replacement by modernity. But he is confident that telling one's story into an echo-harbouring shell will bring comfort. The Sad Shepherd tries the advice – but it doesn't work for him:

> Then he sang softly nigh the pearly rim;
> But the sad dweller by the sea-ways lone
> Changed all he sang to inarticulate moan
> Among her wildering whirls, forgetting him.[3]

If one should be tempted to adduce Spenser, or Milton's 'L'Allegro' or 'Il Penseroso' as better sources, one should first go on to ponder Yeats's other contraries: 'The Rose of Peace' and 'The Rose of Battle'; Self and Soul; *Hic* and *Ille* (even though the proximate source here is William Morris's 'Hapless Love'); He and She; Aherne and Robartes – or whole volumes: *The Tower* versus *The Winding Stair*, the former representing a proud, bitter, masculine assertiveness, the latter something inward, ruminative, which Yeats thought of as more 'feminine'. And then, of course, there are moon and sun in *A Vision*, the great symbolic antinomies which represent what he sometimes calls Subjectivity and Objectivity. These two are indebted to Blake's Energy and Reason – and to later formulations like Imagination and Nature. But the indebtedness is no mere borrowing of scaffolding: Yeats's tinctures are not only opposites, but move in opposite directions, as do Blake's contraries in his poem 'The Mental Traveller'.[4]

Unlikely as it might seem, Yeats also thinks of his use of Irish mythology, and romance, in relation to Blake's half-invented mythology; the explanation is this: Blake could not work with an over-used classical system and also needed to root his mythology in what he knew. So he created his own system and saw visions of its personages among the stones of Clerkenwell or the fields 'from Islington to Marybone'; or near mournful, ever-weeping Paddington. Yeats, on the other hand, could revive a mythology which was not over-used and which had the merit of being rooted by tradition in the hills, lakes, coppices and bogs of Sligo and Galway:

> The host is riding from Knocknarea
> And over the grave of Clooth-na-Bare;
> Caoilte tossing his burning hair,
> And Niamh calling *Away, come away*. (*YP*, 55)

Yeats's plays to do with the matter of Ireland, not least those which dramatise the Ulster cycle, must in part be seen in the light of Blakean archetypes and Blakean psychomachia. Nor are even stylistic matters immune from influence, however unlike Blake Yeats may seem. The poems of the Nineties must be seen not just in relation to Symbolism, or the influence of William Morris's poetry, but also in relation to that view of Blake – very influential from the Nineties and right into the 1930s – which sees his lyric poetry in terms of symbolist suggestiveness and musicality, compare, for instance, the views of Yeats's friend Arthur Symons, author both of *The Symbolist Movement in Literature* and of an Introduction of *William Blake*. By an apparent paradox, when Yeats becomes dissatisfied with the style of his Nineties poetry, he speaks in terms of a desire for firmer form, outline and energy, which suggests that he was attempting to rectify a mistaken interpretation of Blake and orient his own new style in relation to those many utterances of Blake which praise definiteness. In later years, Yeats was to proclaim that 'Measurement began our might' – the might of Western art. This sounds a trifle like Urizen, Blake's tyrannical patriarchal deity, half false Jehovah, half iron-hearted Jupiter, who divides and measures the universe. Yet Blake depicts a sublime as well as an erring figure, and Yeats's proclamations can be seen as deriving from his life-long dialogue with his mentor. As age descends upon him, Yeats sees himself as one of Blake's old men: in particular, the tattered coat upon a stick in 'Sailing to Byzantium' is a direct reference to this image, one of Blake's designs for Blair's *Grave*. Or this is what the old man is, 'unless soul clap its hands and sing and louder sing/ For every tatter in its mortal dress'. So, the soul grows young as the body grows old – contraries moving in opposite directions again. And clapping of the hands also derives from Blake – from his story, that is, about how, when his brother Robert died, he saw his soul rising from his body, clapping its hands.

I referred earlier to the way in which the Nineties could see Blake's technique in his lyrics in relation to symbolism. There is a tradition of seeing Blake's meanings as ineffable. Quiller-Couch in *On Reading* (1920) implies that Blake's poetry provides examples of the way in which true poetry is *apprehended* rather than *comprehended*. It is illuminating to note that Quiller-Couch sees Celtic poetry as apprehended poetry *par excellence*, for this sheds further light on Yeats's valuation of Blake and may help to explain why he expressed the conviction that Blake's family came from Galway, on no discernible evidence. The *reductio ad absurdum* of apprehended Blake, though, is to be found in A. E. Housman's 1933 lecture, *The Name and Nature of Poetry*:

> For me the most poetical of all poets is Blake. I find his lyrical note as beautiful as Shakespeare's and more beautiful than anyone else's; and I call him more poetical than Shakespeare, even though Shakespeare has so much more poetry, because poetry in him preponderates more than in Shakespeare over everything else, and instead of being confounded in a great river can be drunk pure from a slender channel of its own. Shakespeare is rich in thought, and his meaning has power of itself to move us, even if the poetry were not there: Blake's meaning is often unimportant or virtually non-existent, so that we can listen with all our hearing to his celestial tune.[5]

The effect such a view might have on the interpretation of a reasonably clear use of symbolism by Blake may be illustrated from Housman's eccentric handling of Blake's brief lyric, 'To the Accuser who is the God of this World':

> It purports to be theology: what theological sense, if any, it may have, I cannot imagine and feel no wish to learn: it is pure and self-existent poetry, which leaves no room in me for anything besides.[6]

As it happens, this provides a good example of the extremes to which such an attitude might be taken, since the symbolism of the poem is not at all obscure. This false god remains the Son of Morn (i.e., Lucifer) in weary Night's decline (i.e., fallen). He appears in a vision to the traveller (or pilgrim) when that traveller is 'lost' or deluded. He is Christian's vision of Apollyon.

It will be recalled that Housman's lecture was the one in which he described good poetry as interfering with shaving, because it caused the skin to bristle. It is also the one in which he offers a hint on how to get a poem started:

> Having drunk a pint of beer at luncheon – beer is a sedative to the brain, and my afternoons are the least intellectual portion of my life – I would go out for a walk of two or three hours. As I went

along, thinking of nothing in particular only looking at things around me and following the progress of the seasons, there would flow into my mind, with sudden and unaccountable emotion, sometimes a line or two of verse, sometimes a whole stanza at once, accompanied, not preceded, by a vague notion of the poem which they were destined to form a part of.[7]

The inadequacy of this account of poetry does make one far more aware of how necessary and understandable were the efforts of Richards and Empson, contemporaneously in train in the Cambridge of Housman's day. Housman's lecture, however, is in part a reaction against those efforts. It is a pity that such ideas, which still linger in popular theories of literature, should ever have helped slightly to tarnish by association the work of poets of exacting rigour such as Baudelaire and Mallarmé. Furthermore, Housman's remarks hint at the way in which Blake might also be regarded as a precursor of surrealism, as it seems that he was by David Gascoyne, whose poems exhibit a debt – for instance, in 'The Diabolical Principle' or 'Innocence and Experience'.[8]

Whatever one may think of Housman's jejune theorising, it may serve to underline the fact that as much as anything else, Blake in the early twentieth century, and just before, is considered as an arresting aesthetic phenomenon and one that is hard to categorise, and this is true for more sophisticated critics than Housman and true as much – if not more so – for comment on his graphic art. Roger Fry canonised Blake's paintings for Bloomsbury and the art world and introduced him into their Elysium where Giotto as much as Cézanne is praised for line, form and the relationship between masses of colour. In his article for the *Burlington Magazine* (1904), Fry fastens on Blake's anti-illusionism in some characteristically equivocal formulations:

Blake's art indeed is a test case for our theories of aesthetics. It boldly makes the plea for art that is a language for conveying impassioned thought and feeling, which takes up the objects of sense as a means to this end, owing them no allegiance and accepting from them only the service that they can render for this purpose [...] The theory that art appeals solely by the associated ideas of the natural objects its imitates is easily rejected when we consider music and architecture [...] But in pictorial art the fallacy that nature is the mistress instead of the servant seems almost inadvisable.[9]

The equivocation to which I refer is to be found in the phrase about 'conveying impassioned thought and feeling'. This might appear to imply that the subject-matter of painting is still entertained, albeit in some ancillary role. In practice, Fry thinks only of what he calls 'form'. Thus is Blake enlisted in the service of that critical spirit which was preparing the taste which would accept abstraction. While Housman could scarcely be said to be doing the same thing, he looks a bit like Fry if you contrast the view of Blake offered by our own critical consensus – something not far from E. P. Thompson's perhaps. The early twentieth century values something ardent, forceful and eloquent in Blake's aesthetic, and while there is no shortage of those who do understand that Blake had something to say – Yeats, Symons, and, as we shall see, Shaw and Joyce – it is perhaps the perceived aesthetic qualities of this work which were decisive in raising the estimate in which he was held. They were qualities which, in their directness, as much as their suggestiveness, appeared to set him apart from the other Romantic poets: made him seem 'pre-modern'. This is the guise under which he began his ascent to his current eminence.

Mentioning E. P. Thompson offers a convenient way into an obvious question: were there not those who were interested in the political and ethical aspects of Blake's aspects of Blake's work? – Shaw certainly was, in one of his *Three Plays for Puritans, The Devil's Disciples*, first performed in New York in 1897 and in London in 1899. His Preface reveals an assured understanding of the provenance of Blake's religious, political and ethical ideas, something which seems to have been of scant interest to so many other commentators. This understanding is hinted at in the word 'Puritans'; for in the Preface he leads in to the topic of Blake via John Bunyan:

> Two and a half centuries ago our greatest English dramatizer of life, John Bunyan, ended one of his stories with the remark that there is a way to heaven even from the gates of hell. A century ago William Blake was an avowed Diabolonian: he called his angels devils and his devils angels. His devil is a Redeemer. Let those who

have praised my originality in conceiving Dick Dudgeon's strange religion read Blake's Marriage of Heaven and Hell, and I shall be fortunate if they do not rail at me for a plagiarist.[10]

Shaw's story and its setting are cogent in supporting his understanding of Blake, for the play is set in New Hampshire in 1777, when the passions of the American colonies, as Shaw puts it, were 'roused to boiling point' inspired by defence of liberty, resistance to tyranny, and self-sacrifice on the altar of the Rights of Man'.[11] The play, as befits its classification as a *Play for Puritans*, presents different versions of Protestantism: there is the life-denying rancour of Mrs Dudgeon whose 'face [...] is grimly trenched by the channels into which the barren forms of a dead Puritanism can pen a bitter temper and a fierce pride'.[12] Contrasted with this is her son, the Diabolonian Dick, a reputed reprobate who shows his true mettle by seeking to take the place on the scaffold of a man about to be hanged by the British. Dick is given great chunks of slightly transformed Blake to speak (this is Shaw, after all): 'I was brought up in the other service; but I knew from the first that the Devil was my natural master and captain and friend.' To the minister, Anderson, Dudgeon asserts: 'there is something in you that I reflect, and that makes me desire to have you for my enemy' – compare Blake's 'Opposition is True Friendship'. Shaw's play is an attempt to be discerning about the inheritance of Protestantism: to reject those aspects of it which deny the Life Force and to suggest that its combative questioning and egalitarian spirit was an essential component of the age of the Rights of Man; and further, that Blake, an unusually radical and corrosive embodiment of that spirit, could still be an inspiration as the twentieth century approached.

Political Blake is also present in the thirties. For Auden, Spender and MacNeice, references to Blake are taken for granted: they are sometimes the more telling simply by virtue of the fact that they are not self-conscious – like MacNeice's epitome of the relationship between Northern Irish Catholics and Protestants in *Autumn Journal XVI*, 'one read black, where the other read white', which he doesn't even bother to attribute to Blake. MacNeice's account of W. B. Yeats shows an easy understanding of the relationship to Blake, one which it is harder for contemporary specialists to muster. It is from Spender, though, that my favourite anecdote derives; it is the famous scene from *World Within World* when the hearties at Oxford decide to break up the rooms of the newly arrived aesthete:

> I was sitting in a chair reading Blake when about a dozen of them trooped in, equipped with buckets and other clanking instruments of room-breakers and throwers-into-rivers. I could not decide on the most suitable way of receiving them, so I went on reading, very conscious of course that I was reading *poetry*. They were embarrassed as I. They stood about in an awkward semi-circle. One of them said: 'What's the big idea Spender?' For reply I read *aloud* a few lines of Blake. I achieved the result: they simply changed their minds and left the room, shrugging their shoulders as though to indicate that I was too crazy for their treatment.[13]

Yet Blake can hardly be described as important to an understanding of Spender. The same is not the case with Auden: I've already referred to Blake's habit of trying to haunt the best company, and this turns out to be proved in the case of Auden, too. Blake is essential to the working out of the socio-political-psychoanalytic theory of the Airman: the neurotic, homosexual outsider, surreptitiously under-mining society from within; while at the same time renouncing the impossible task of trying to understand infection by the enemy, the forces of repression, bourgeois morality and the capitalist system. One must accept that infection will occur: as Auden says in *The Orators*, 'The power of the enemy is a function of our resistance – Conquest can only proceed by absorption of, i.e. infection by the conquered.' Now the broad outlines of *The Orators* do owe something to the *Marriage of Heaven and Hell*; which it resembles in its dramati-zation of opposed contrary principles, its impromptu and irreverent mythologising, its proffer of proverbs and outrageous aphorisms and its blend of prose and verse. But Auden's comments are more learned in Blake studies than these broad outlines would suggest. The idea of accepting infection by the system to which one is opposed is strongly Blakean. Blake calls it striving with systems to redeem individuals from these systems. It explains why Blake will employ terms derived from Descartes or Newton in the services of his own anti-rationalist ideas. But one has to be quite well versed in Blake, including the more challenging later works, before one grasps this idea. Interestingly, the quotation about 'continuous annihilations of the self by the Identity' derives from the later Prophetic Books, not from *The Marriage of Heaven and Hell*: it contrasts the closed and tyrannical 'Selfhood', as Blake himself called it, with the openness and creativity of true human Identity. Sometimes, the hardened self, as in Blake, is depicted as a father who accuses, as in the parodies of school hymns from *The Orators*.

The Marriage of Heaven and Hell remained a key text for Auden, and, as with Yeats, re-thinking his own beliefs required re-thinking, rather than rejecting Blake. From May to September 1939, disenchanted with the political infatuation of a low dishonest decade, and increasingly sympathetic towards Christianity, he enlists Blake in his revisionism, labouring at a prose work called the *Prolific and the Devourer*, the title of which is one of the contraries from Blake's *Marriage*.[14] (For Blake, the Prolific are the Artists, who produce, while the Devourers are those reasoners and theorisers who are parasitic on the conception produced by the imagination, by the Prolific.) Auden makes the Prolific the artist and the Devourer the politician – a suggestion of the disillusionment to which I referred. The work is peppered with Blakeisms: 'There are two and only two philosophies of life, the true and the false', or: 'There are not "good" and "evil" existences [...] everything that is is holy [...] Evil is not an existence but a state of disharmony between existences'; ' "Hell" is a state of being one may leave at any time. Worship of Jesus in churches has made him into a "false idol" '; and so on. (A number of these ideas end up in *New Year Letter*, by the way.) Once Auden's conversion was complete, he came to regard the thinkers he admired in the thirties – Blake, Lawrence, Freud and Marx – as preparing the way for it. Of these four figures, there is one who falls outside the customary purview of contemporary courses on Modernism, and it is not Shakespeare, Milton, Wordsworth or Shelley, but Blake. But note the assumption that Blake would naturally be a guiding light to any middle-class intellectual of his generation. That would certainly include Aldous Huxley whose interest predates *The Doors of Perception* and *Heaven and Hell* and makes itself felt in *Eyeless in Gaza*.

It scarcely needs saying that the most obvious example of political Blake is that which is to be found in the British Sixties variant of Beat poetry, exemplified in Michael Horovitz's *Children of Albion: Poetry of the Underground in Britain* (1969), the 'Afterwords' for which begin with the suggestion that Blake was revived in 1957, two hundred years after his birth.[15] Alongside the name 'Albion', the cover, with its reproduction of 'Glad Day', is explicit enough about the debt. Adrian Mitchell, whose poems find generous representation in the anthology, shares the debt, as in 'Lullaby for William Blake', which ends with a declaration of love for the master.[16] Mitchell was also the author of the play *Tyger: A Celebration Based on the Life and Work of William Blake*, first performed at the National Theatre in 1971. (London: Jonathan Cape, 1971). In this, Blake fights the influence of Sir Joshua Reynolds, who, however, is here known as 'Sir Joshua Rat'.[17] He is also enlisted in the libertarianism and anti-Vietnam politics of the period. Fittingly enough, Blake appears to come to these poets via Ginsberg. Yet Ginsberg, who figures in a later chapter, though he shares similarities with Mitchell, is far more aware of the ambivalence of Blake's response to power, perhaps because he shares in it himself. This permits Ginsberg, in creations such as his Moloch, to glimpse the suggestiveness of Blake's myth in ways that Mitchell cannot. Indeed, Blake as myth-maker is an important subject for many modern writers.

I mentioned Joyce as one who understood his Blake. Certainly, Blake is referred to often enough in *Ulysses*. It seems to me that Blake's importance for Joyce lies in an acute awareness of the time-bound, historical character of the artist's productions, even as he lauded Poetic Genius and the Visions of Eternity. The deferrals, the partial apprehensions, the loss of vision and the struggles with current artistic convention imposed by the world of Time are a source of anxious meditation in Blake; and it might be claimed that the burden of this meditation falls particularly on one character in his invented mythology, namely Los, who represents poetic inspiration. The third episode of *Ulysses*, 'Proteus', has Stephen walking along Sandymount strand and opens with that ringing phrase: 'Ineluctable modality of the visible' – that is to say, the inevitable fact of apprehending the world only under modes or conventions, modes or conventions that are shaped by and saturated with language. The next line is 'Signatures of all things I am here to read': modality is written, and is written in the difference and deferrals of time. Stephen's walking on the strand with his eyes closed allows Joyce to emphasise the novelist's passage through real time in the sound of his boots 'crush[ing] crackling wrack and shells'. It is then that he thinks of *Los Demiurgos*, Los the Demiurge, that title given to the artificer in Plato's *Timaeus*, who, though not the one, yet creates the universe. This conception is itself one which bespeaks creation at a remove from Eternity. So far from simply being a reference which takes us away from the time-bound, and towards a bardic yearning for Eden, the reference reveals Joyce's intimate, but on the whole not surprising, familiarity with Blake's system: Los is time; he 'kept the divine vision in time of trouble'; he it was who 'must create a system or be enslaved by another man's'. In this way, Joyce is a pioneer in his indebtedness to Blake, as in so much else. For the self-consciousness about the constructedness of myth that one finds in him is to be found in postmodernist writers such as Carter, Rushdie and Sinclair.

But unlikely as it may seem, it may be worth pausing on Ted Hughes, for the connection with Blake opens up a way of apprehending the post-*Crow* Hughes, who is still not as well known as the writer of the early bestiaries. *Crow*, like *The Book of Urizen*, can be seen as a kind of Bible of Hell. Furthermore, the famous dust jacket illustration by Leonard Baskin is arguably intended to function as a kind of 'illumination'. This argument is reinforced by the consideration of a closely connected subsequent volume, a poem series called *Cave Birds: An Alchemical Cave Drama* (1978), for the crows and other birds who figure in it are depicted in engravings again by Leonard Baskin on facing pages. Towards the end we are shown an alchemical marriage of contrary principles; and this idea is an obvious influence on Blake's *Marriage of Heaven and Hell* – though Hughes is entirely devoted to the idea of these contraries as masculine and feminine – something they could always be in the tradition of philosophical alchemy, mind you. Blake gives his contraries a wide array of meanings, so as to encompass his ideas about Body and Soul, about political revolution, about poetic genius and what obstructs it; Hughes, on the other hand, with help not just from Blake, but from Jung, from Lawrence and from Graves's *White Goddess*, believes that he has suffered, as his culture does, from a disastrous failure to value those qualities traditionally termed 'feminine'. In *Crow* he convicts himself of error in this regard; in *Gaudete* (1977) and in *Cave Birds* (1978) he unveils the solution in a renewal of understanding and love between the sexes. In the poem to which this is an illustration, for instance, we are told that the bride and groom lie hidden for three days, after which they ensure each other's resurrection: 'She gives him his eyes, she found them / Among some rubble', and 'He gives her skin / He just seemed to pull it down out of the air'.[18] This narrative of their progressive re-creation of each other's bodies is the positive inversion of the creation of the body in Blake's *The Book of Urizen* where there is a dwelling on the ghostliness of anatomy and an emphasis on overtones of limitation. For Hughes, just as *Crow* itself is a placing and analysis of the earlier animal poems, *Cave Birds* is designedly a going-beyond *Crow* – a gradual rediscovery of a full humanity, and a transcendence of the melancholy (in the sense of depression) symbolised by *Crow*. (The alchemists sometimes referred to melancholy by reference to the *caput corvi* or 'head of the crow'). Knowing Hughes as we do now, we can also posit the likelihood of his being aware of a link between Blake's Urizen and Saturn and Melancholy. The Ted Hughes we should be thinking about, then, is not the one who is supposed to be almost a Movement poet, but one who was starting to write in an age still dominated by the legacy of Dylan Thomas, and who, furthermore, like Auden, is adopting Blake for a study of diseased sexuality, a typically modernist concern.

One thing, then, that continues into the twentieth century is the desire – or the need – to create a system in a universe without agreed symbolism. But recently this desire has been encompassed with the help of postmodernist irony by Iain Sinclair, the author of *White Chappell: Scarlet Tracings*, which was runner-up for the Guardian Fiction prize in 1987, and more recently of a strange, dark exploration of London, *Lights Out for the Territory*. He is also a Blakean poet, not just in the sense of embodying in his work certain Blakean structures and ideas and images, but also in the sense of using figures from Blake's system – Albion, certainly, but also the evil Hand and Hyle and Kotope. In *Lud Heat* (1975) he produces a map of London which shows certain nodal points of malignant power, mostly Hawksmoor churches, linked by sinister lines of force. Sinclair finds traces of Egyptian forms, such as pyramids, which (he pretends) convince him of the role of this malignity, for in Blake Egypt is evil, reflecting a venerable Christian typology. Israel in captivity in Egypt is the soul in bondage. The map owes a good deal to Blake's rooting of his mythology in London. But the whole of *Lud Heat* makes clear the paranoid lunacy of Sinclair's map. Aspects of the book are patent parodies of meretricious popular occultism – the kind of thing that Sinclair comes across in his other life as a second-hand book dealer. As we shall see later in the book, Sinclair, like his friend Angela Carter, is troubled by the notion that all myths are lies, even as he seeks to build his own myths in a way that emphasises their emanation from a particular, individual point of view. The postmodern age shares the modernist fascination with the construction of myth, but inflects it with a paranoia which is also indebted to the tradition of Gothic romance. Those who admire Blake are able to draw on his own Gothic imagery of spectres and dark sublimity – and this is precisely what Sinclair and Carter also do.

None of this is bad going for a poet not one of whose poems was included in the first edition of Palgrave (1861). My tale so far has been one of inheritance, of course, and this is not the only kind of account that critics and scholars offer of the after-life of Romanticism: it's long been taken for granted that even High Anglo-American modernists such as Pound and Eliot owe more to Romantic modes and conceptualisations than they liked to admit. See Frank Kermode or George Bornstein or C. K. Stead. An influential development of this idea is offered by Maud Ellmann, in an account which draws both on psychoanalysis and Deconstruction: what is seen as Romantic – and therefore, to quote Pound, liable to 'slither' and 'mush' – is projected on to the bad feminine, or the homosexual, but asserts itself nevertheless in a lyric plangency and indefiniteness which undermines the hardness and objectivity to which the Modernist poet aspires.[19] They end up singing from the sirens' song sheet even as they try to stop their ears.

But I should like to return to the old question what we mean by Romanticism in any case. Of course, nobody has ever been able to offer a definition that worked for all the writers grouped under that heading; but that is not what I mean. You can lay out a plausible story about influence by going back through Arthur Symons's impressionistic poems, taking in Pater and Ruskin, and not omitting Arthur Hallam on Poetry. But in order to claim that these are links in a chain that goes back to Romanticism you have to forget all the writers that were in the process of being forgotten in the nineteenth century. You have to forget that the best-selling and most widely read poem of the 1790s was Samuel Rogers's *The Pleasures of Memory* – a conventional poem in heroic couplets. You have to forget the influence within the Romantic period of Charlotte Smith, a poet of sensibility. Who now reads the poems of Walter Scott? Who reads Moore's *Lalla Rookh* or *Irish Melodies*, phenomenal best-sellers of their day? All these writers that a historically conscious criticism is helping us to remember. 'Romanticism' as we have known it until recently comes into being barely before modernism does; in the late nineteenth century, one was moulded as the other came into being. This is all one process. The linear idea of Romantic influence is irredeemably incoherent. As for Blake, I suggested the possibility that he was seen by moderns as an exception to Romantic badness. But more importantly, the case seems to be that he is that kind of Romantic artist who appeals in an age when these developments and re-definitions are taking place and (which is possibly an even more arresting fact) is co-opted into that process himself. Central to his usefulness are his perceived directness of method, a concomitant reliance on suggestion rather than state-ment, an attempt to give voice to unconscious forces, a belief that myth could represent those forces, a sense that myth was neverthe-less constructed, and an oppositional stance. In some or all of these ways, Blake has the potential to be harnessed to the modern or postmodern writer's projects.

Of course, we may be in danger of being mesmerised by another 'ism', 'modernism' itself. It should never be forgotten that many writers – and critics – did not learn their lesson: thou shalt not read Shelley with his weak grasp upon the actual. There was no revolution. Again, we forget: consider the case of Herbert Read, who has some-how clung on into Peter Porter's revision of *The Faber Book of Modern Verse*. In 1947 he published *The True Voice of Feeling: Studies in English Romantic Poetry*. And who are the true Romantics? Coleridge, Wordsworth, Keats, Hopkins, Whitman, Lawrence, T. E. Hulme, Pound and Eliot. More important than this list are the major categories of voice and feeling upon which Read draws, and the associated ideas of organic form and intensity, which he feels no qualms about associat-ing even with Hulme and Pound.

The situation, then, is in reality quite fluid, and what are thought of as 'Romantic' literary traits, imagery or themes may be mustered in the service of some attempt to recover the bardic voice in an urban wilderness; to suggest by Gothic imagery that we may be haunted by a dark future, as much as a dark past; to adopt the Byronic pose, but in leather on a motorbike, like Thom Gunn, or his Elvis Presley, whose pose is generation of the very chance it wars on; like Denise Levertov, to offer a renewed sense of the possibilities of writing with the idea of organic form. And of course there are dangers: working with certain models of Romanticism can produce some very bad writing, as Marjorie Perloff points out in an essay at the end of a volume I edited on *Romanticism and Postmodernism*, so many of our poets and literary clichés are debased pieces of Romanticism. Thinking of oneself as trying to do something clear of such cliché can still be an enabling point of departure for the writer. On the other hand, anti-Romanticism of the kind that still finds its last home in nooks and crannies of this puritanical island can harm the possibilities of writing by the unwarranted and entirely ideological prohibitions on the language of feeling in poetry: a prohibition paralleled by those on ornamentation, or rhetoric, or abstraction. In the work of some male poets their blithely unconscious talk of hard lines and accurate perception, the exhibitionist wielding of violent metaphor, rehearses all the gender sub-texts of modernist anti-Romanticism. This seems to me to be connected to the reason why the gay poet John Ashbery in his early work flaunted a deliberately sonorous, sententious and florid post-Romantic language. So the after-life of 'Romanticism' is really a series of dispositions and strategies partly defined against other tendencies which think of themselves as anti-Romantic. Why people should still be writing Gothic narrative, still be inventing mythologies, still be talking about organic form (occasionally), still be gesturing, however ironically, at their possible discovery of the transcendent in their own experience, still posing as prophets and visionaries, I am not sure. But I cannot help thinking that we still have to look back towards the period of the bourgeois revolution.

Nevertheless, even when one has allowed, as I think one has to do, for the continuation of Romanticisms, Blake occupies a central and distinctive place in the very development of modernism, and has done so in that of postmodernism as well, for reasons that I have been sketching here. This is not something one can say of Wordsworth or Shelley or any other writer of Blake's period. Perhaps for this reason, one feels in his case that Bloom's model of influence does not ring entirely true for his relationship with twentieth-century writers. This is not to say that creative misprision does not occur, but rather that (with some exceptions, such as T. S. Eliot) writers are responding to Blake as a mentor and friend, and experience their differences from him without anxiety. Except in the case of Eliot, my method has been guided as much by a reading of authors such as Jonathan Bate or

Michael O'Neill, who explore the enabling character of 'influence'. At the same time, I have attempted to remain sensitive to the horizon of understanding of modern authors rather than risk subduing them to Blake, since part of the interest of this subject resides in the way Blake has encouraged so much new and innovative writing.

2
Zoas and Moods: Myth and Aspects of the Mind in Blake and Yeats

This chapter takes a fresh look at the oft-compared couple, Blake and Yeats, comparing and contrasting their use of myth to convey aspects of the mind, and relating the differences between them not only to changing conceptions of the mind, but also to their different political assumptions. It should, of course, go without saying that Blake can figure in a discussion of modernism and mythopoeia, and not just because of Yeats's clear indebtedness to him. One of the more dispiriting effects of the resurgence of historicism has been a tendency to revert in practice, though perhaps not in theory, to simple models of temporality which lend a spurious ease to talk of historical periods. But Blake is merely one of the more acute examples of a textual history which renders such talk inadequate. In point of his reception he is in many ways a poet of the modern period. Among his first serious readers was Swinburne, whose influence extends well ahead; and he is important to the understanding of Joyce, Auden, Ted Hughes and Allen Ginsberg. Roger Fry seems to have regarded him as an exponent of 'significant form'. The first serious edition of his works was the great three-volume edition by Edwin Ellis and W. B. Yeats in 1893.

Of course, this is not to deny that Blake exhibits many of the signs of 'Romantic Ideology': the idea of the prophet-poet; the cultivation of the sublime; the value placed on 'Imagination'; the drive to the unity of the *Gesamtkunstwerk* exhibited in his 'composite art', which seeks to integrate text, design and decoration in a complex, contrapuntal mode. But it is not only his emergence in the late Victorian and modern periods that complicates Blake's presence in the list of romantic artists; there is also the perspective backwards: his inheritance of radical Protestant traditions that go back at least to the seventeenth century, and alongside which one may include an interest in the spiritual interpretation of alchemical symbolism.[1] This inheritance conditions not only his sense of the political import of his myths but even, as we shall see, colours their iconography. And here we find a point of difference between him and other romantic mythographers or *bricoleurs* of myths such as Shelley or Nerval. For when Blake says, in *the Marriage of Heaven and Hell* (Plate 11), that 'all deities reside in the human breast', he is not only referring to the idea that myths represent psychic realities, but also declaring his indebtedness to a radical Protestant understanding of revelation and the inner light which allows him a few lines later to converse with Isaiah and Ezekiel (Plate 12).

My initial point, then, was to reiterate that Blake is peculiarly congenial to, and influential in, the modern period. My second point was that some of his sources show him to be the inheritor of a politically radical Protestant tradition. But it is not chiefly to rehearse Blake's peculiar provenance, nor simply for the sake of source-hunting, that I shall here say something about the places from which he drew associations for use in his mythology. For these sources help to give a sense of the role myth plays in his work and help to sharpen a contrast with Yeats. Nor do these sources comprise only those that might be expected from a radical Protestant, for they also include Christian iconography of a kind that was common to Christian poets from other traditions and the iconography of the classical gods as studied by a poet such as Keats.

Blake and the iconographical tradition

In a world that is 'fallen', Blake seeks to find a mythological language for the psychic and sexual conflict he sees as inseparable from a system of political oppression and alienated religion. To do so he draws not just upon his reading of comparative mythology – for instance, in the work of Jacob Bryant – but also interweaves resonances drawn from those iconographies and discourses which might be claimed as psychological. I mean in particular the theory of humours, philosophical alchemy and the tradition of personification of virtues, vices and passions in English poetry, especially that of the eighteenth century. The fact that Blake goes to such sources has occasionally been noted. But the significance of the fact has not been thoroughly studied. What it means is that Blake makes a far more decisive, because more motivated and identifiable, shift towards the human breast, and away from Olympus or the heavens, than do other mythopoeic poets of the period. Like these other poets he sees the mind as a crucial arena of political conflict: the 'mind-forg'd manacles' are forged in the mind. The use of this phrase in 'London' represents a considerable equivocation in the earlier work about whether the real battle is only in the mind or also outside it. (Significantly the phrase replaces an earlier one referring to the Hanoverian soldiery: 'german forg'd manacles'.) In the later work, in any case, the chains can only be removed by 'mental fight'. Unlike with these other poets, however, the tradition of valuing revelation and of finding a symbolic language for spiritual process gives extraordinary ambition and incisiveness to Blake's myth; yet, unlike in Yeats's poetry (as opposed to his occult system), Blake's use of myth retains a fixed and iconic quality: only relatively fixed, of course, subject to variation and indeterminacy, but still recognisably of an age when poets are seeking to return to the origins of the mythopoeic faculty by re-making mythology in their poems, thus providing something that could vie in its narratives and its structures with the pagan myths and the stories of the Old Testament.

The best place to start, then, may not be with what I have called psychological iconographies and discourses, but at the most obvious place, with the gods themselves. A figure such as Urizen famously constitutes a parody of images of God to be found in the Christian tradition, notably in Raphael's designs for the Vatican *Loggie*, which Blake had studied carefully in engravings. But Blake's figure is a composite. Thus the related figure of Death in the *Night Thoughts* engravings clearly draws upon images of Jupiter to be found in such Renaissance manuals as Vincenzo Cartari's *Imagini delli Dei de gl'Antichi* (Venice, 1556). It is possible to find designs in Blake which ostensibly illustrate a Biblical or Christian theme, but draw their iconography from Renaissance manuals displaying the gods.[2] In some of these manuals the gods can look quite unexpected. Jean Seznec, in *The Survival of the Pagan Gods*, for instance, looks at an engraving of Jupiter in the 1571 edition of Cartari, where the deity is shown in a white mantle covered with stars, holding a nine-stringed lyre and two globes. 'Who,' asks

Seznec, 'would recognize Jupiter with these accoutrements?'.[3] Seznec remarks that 'our mythographers sum up and continue a syncretistic tradition; they turn for information above all to the last adherents of paganism – that is, to a period when all the cults were being merged and all the gods amalgamated'.[4] It may be worth remarking by the way that a consideration of Renaissance manuals leads to the suggestion that the origins of comparative mythology and romantic mythmaking should be traced back well before the Enlightenment.

In any case, Blake's sources agree with Jacob Bryant 'and all antiquaries', as he puts it, that *All Religions are One*. The effect of syncretism within those sources is to breakdown the differences between similar deities within different cults, and also to blur the differences between similar gods within the same tradition, for instance the difference between Saturn and Jupiter. The iconography of Saturn-Kronos is traditionally confused with that of Chronos, the latter influencing his depiction of Time in the *Night Thoughts* illustrations. Urizen is an amalgam of iconographical hints taken from the depiction of God the Father, of Jupiter, of Saturn and of Old Father Time. Of particular interest to Blake was the association of Saturn with Melancholy, which provides a background to the mournful aspect of Urizen. And this topic leads on to the more psychologically oriented traditions upon which Blake was drawing.

From melancholy to moods

Melancholy had an important place in spiritual or philosophical alchemy. Blake claims allegiance to this tradition, the tradition of 'Paracelsus and Behmen' (Jakob Boehme), at a couple of places in his writing (*The Marriage of Heaven and Hell*, Plate 22, and Letter to Flaxman, 12 September 1800). Without going into the bizarre and florid ramifications of that subject, I want to get straight to the point about my example of Urizen. At the stage where the alchemist's mixture is about to be purified over the fire, it may be symbolized as an old man, often a king, who is sickening and is finally killed by the heat. This is the symbol held by philosophical alchemists to represent Melancholy. But this old man aspect is actually only one element in the original mixture, which comprised Mercury and Sulphur. These were regarded as 'contraries', analogous to water and fire; 'and what Northrop Frye calls the 'Ore-cycle' in Blake the opposition and alteration of Reason and Energy, or Urizen and Orc, is partly modelled on this alchemical opposition. Blake amalgamates this opposition with the traditional psychology of humours. For the Orc-cycle also derives from the well-established notion of the manic-depressive cycle. Quite apart from the romantic interest in texts such as Burton's *Anatomy of Melancholy* evidenced in Keats's 'Ode', for instance, this notion was receiving new confirmation at the end of the eighteenth century in empirical studies, of which Robert James offers a digest in his *Medicinal Dictionary*, where he refers to observations of patients:

> [...] melancholic patients, especially if their Disorder is inveterate, easily fall into Madness, which, when removed, the Melancholy again discovers itself, though the Madness afterwards returns at certain periods [...][5]

He is insistent on the point that Mania and Melancholy are two facets of the same disorder:

> There is an absolute Necessity for reducing Melancholy and Madness to one species of Disorder.[6]

The cause of this malady is 'an excessive Congestion of the Blood in the Brain'.[7] Blake is probably thinking in terms of this kind of psychology when he says that one of the mythological figures or 'Zoas' (more on that word in due course) representative of passion 'flew up from the Human Heart! Into the Brain' (MS, 10, British Library).

On the basis of this internal disorder, Morton Paley has suggested that we should think of Blake's *Vala* as influenced by a subtle form of 'psychomachia' to be found in Spenser's *Faerie Queene:* 'It is of course, the mind (and body) in which the events of the poem take place, and the quests and battles are episodes in the making of that mind.'[8] But Blake draws not only on Spenser's allegorised virtues, passions and vices, but on the tradition of personification in eighteenth-century poets such as Gray, Young and Collins.[9]

That Urizen (to stay with 'our main example) mythologises repressive facets of the mind is clear, and the sources, as we have seen, are appropriate ones. But there is another consideration, that of the historical allegory: how much does it matter that Urizen is also George III? Or that he draws on contemporary radicals' depiction of a malign alliance between Priest and King, such as one may find in the works of Paine, or in Shelley's 'Ode to Liberty'? It clearly matters a great deal. But though Blake's mythology is used to represent political realities, the fact that it also represents psychic ones, combined with the belief that 'All deities reside in the human breast', puts the origin of political corruption and conflict in the human mind, as the kind of equivocation we saw earlier, in the case of 'London', also indicates. Blake's mythology maintains the iconic quality natural to an age seeking a re-authentication of faith in terms of an original poetic faculty. But he is far more radical than any of his contemporaries in shifting the locus and origin of myth into the realm of mental process, and this fact can be gauged quite concretely in an examination of the iconographies and discourses to which he turns. The word 'Zoa', used to denote the faculties and personages of Blake's developed mythology, is expressive of this shift. It is a misunderstanding of the plural of the Greek *zoon*, which translates the Bible's 'living creatures', as in Ezekiel. The reference pushes the origin of mental faculties far back into proximity with the Godhead, while the connotations of the word itself impart a sense of relation to living mental process.

It is arguable that one fact verifying this conclusion is precisely Blake's prestige with a growing number of radical poets, painters and critics from the pre-Raphaelites onwards. That is to say, the serious study and emulation of Blake begins in that period of pre-modernism when the fluidity and tentativeness of states of mind is being increasingly emphasised. Yeats himself finds it easy to assimilate Blake's Zoas to his own tentative concept of 'mood', a word that finds increasing currency in the discussion of mental states at the end of the nineteenth century.[10] The more iconic aspect of Blake's mythology is relegated. Indeed, what is striking about Yeats's work, if one approaches it with the very plausible comparison with Blake in mind, is how very little it corresponds to that world of 'titanic forms' to be found in Blake's prophetic books.[11] Of course, Blake's influence is not merely theoretical, a matter of commentaries in the Yeats–Ellis edition. A number of the structures to be found in *A Vision* have their correlates in Blake's thought. For instance, the interpenetrating and opposed gyres include Blake's 'The Mental Traveller' among their many sources. And Yeats's abiding interest in 'antinomies', which was nursed on Blake's 'contraries' and *Songs of Innocence and of Experience*, finds its expression in poems expressing opposed states of mind – 'The Song of the Happy Shepherd' and 'The Sad Shepherd' – or even in books that do the same thing: *The Tower with* its bitter, masculine assertiveness, as against the next volume, *The Winding Stair*, with its cultivation of sweetness and labyrinthine internality, seen by Yeats as feminine. This aspect of Yeats's work has been studied by Hazard Adams in *The Book of Yeats's Poems*.[12] Nevertheless, it could be claimed that Yeats chooses to emphasise those aspects of Blake's mythology which relate to states of mind.

The most obvious bare word to appear in Yeats's terminology as summing up something more tentative in his representation of mental states is the word 'mood'. In the Blakean-sounding volume of essays, *Ideas of Good and Evil*, there is a brief paragraph, dating from 1895, called 'The Moods':

> It seems to me that these moods are the labourers and messengers of the Ruler of All, the gods of ancient days, still dwelling on their secret Olympus, the angels of more modern days ascending upon their shining ladder.[13]

Later in the passage he speaks of discovering 'immortal moods in mortal desires'. It will be noted that where Blake thinks of mental states as identifiable with his Zoas, Yeats thinks of them as ancillary: as labourers or angels of the gods, connected with them by a ladder. This conception can be seen as paralleled in the later one of *Anima Mundi* and must be included in any general account of the connections between mental states, mythopoeia and politics in his work.

In the poem from *The Wind Among the Reeds* that bears the same title as that little essay, there is none of the definiteness of a pantheon, even of so dynamic and shifting a pantheon as one finds in Blake:

> Time drops in decay,
> Like a candle burnt out,
> And the mountains and woods
> Have their day, have their day.
> What one in the rout
> Of the fire-born moods
> Has fallen away
> ('The Moods'[14])

In his *A Genealogy of Modernism*, Michael H. Levenson has fastened on the use of the word 'mood' in early modernist texts, seeing in it an index of a typical tension between the desire to represent the immediacy of experience and to reveal its deeper structure at the same time, a tension he finds in the Preface to Conrad's *The Nigger of the Narcissus* (1897) where the author wants 'above all to make you *see*' but at the same time to reveal 'what is kept out of sight'. In pursuit of this dual aim Conrad wants the artist to hold up a fragment of life 'in the light of a sincere mood'.[15] The parallel with Yeats's conception of moods as messengers of the 'secret' Olympia is clear. But both Yeats and Conrad are inheritors of a Victorian criticism which concentrated on developing an associationist theory of poetry and of the 'moods of character' (the phrase is Arthur Hallam's) to be found there. Yeats's early work is full of injunctions to capture the livingness of life and its eternal aspect at the same time. Thus in 'To the Rose upon the Rood of Time' he seeks to find 'In all poor foolish things that live a day / Eternal beauty wandering on her way'. Typically he then balances this desire with concern lest, in going too near the Rose of Beauty, he forget to hear 'common things that crave'. Even after, perhaps especially after, Yeats increasingly adopts the strong voice from about 1907 onwards, the tentative and provisional is everywhere to be found. Stan Smith has republished an essay on 'Yeats and the Structure of Forgetting' in his recent book on *The Origins of Modernism*, in which he fastens on lines such as these from 'The Tower', from which he develops an argument about the importance of forgetting and of a sense of unfinished narrative in Yeats:[16] 'Hanrahan rose in frenzy there / And followed up those baying creatures towards, / O towards I have forgotten what – enough!' ('The Tower', *YP*, 196). These lines are inserted into an inventory of memories, and Yeats left them there, where they serve to impress upon us the fact that this inventory is, as it were, dashed off in a casually associative flow of remembrance. Cairns Craig in his *Yeats, Eliot, Pound and the Politics of Poetry* stresses the part that association and memory play in Yeats's conservative ideology, hallowing beloved remembrance, and insists that their role had been prepared even in the early poetry and in, for instance, Yeats's formulations of symbolist doctrine.[17] Not that anyone would maintain that associationism is in itself inimical to symbolism. Craig discusses a passage from 'The Philosophy of Shelley's Poetry' (*EI*, 89–90) in which Yeats describes how 'ancient symbols' occur to us in fantasy and dreams, adducing a 'vision that a friend of mine saw when gazing at a dark blue curtain'. Yet this passage cannot be entirely concerned with contingency, casual or otherwise, if it shows that our associations end in ancient symbols from the Great Mind. For Yeats's ladder is still there, and it still leads, by means of association, to the same place. Of course, whether remembering the value he himself invested in fictional characters such as Hanrahan, or the heroic acquaintances whose portraits adorn the walls of 'The Municipal Gallery Revisited', or lamenting the absence of Major Robert Gregory from the landscape he had loved, ridden over and painted ('In Memory of Major Robert Gregory'), this is a poetry where memory and loved association sanction a world where 'all's accustomed, ceremonious'. But what Yeats gives us, it seems to me, is an even more profoundly conservative political position than Craig suggests: he offers us a world where not only do loved associations have to be accepted with the heart rather than dissected by 'opinion', but also one where those associations, when properly construed, exhibit the faint (but to the Irish Ascendancy occultist, definite enough) outlines of a world of eternal forms – and, indeed, values, for Yeats is not neutral in the great antagonism between the objective and the subjective. These eternal forms have some of the shape and something of the cyclical and antithetical character of Blake's myth, but empty it of the capacity for final redemption not only by making its cyclical character inescapable, but by giving it the character of eternality. In 'Sailing to Byzantium' it could even be said that the eternal appears as a static golden wall on the outer margin of existence. Instead of being at one with the heart, then, as in Blake, myth is to a degree alienated from it. The heart remains the locus of the associative and organic, yearningly connected to the eternal, but also remote from it.

This is suggested by 'The Circus Animals' Desertion' (*YP*, 346–47) where ladders yet again figure the poet's relationship to his myth-making, and the heart, instead of being a place of unified origin, is a scene of multiplicity and disjunction.[18] To be precise, Yeats's 'circus animals' are his works, and the calculatedly demeaning phrase suggests a show from which the poet feels distance. The second section of the poem, in which the poet proceeds to 'enumerate old themes', obviously shows how the dreams embodied in his works took their origin from the desires of the heart, but also how these desires were sublimated and misrecognised. In the third part he briefly honours the dreams with the phrase 'masterful images', which demonstrates that he is assimilating them to the realm of archetypal image and myth in the *Anima Mundi*. And indeed, he asserts that they 'Grew in pure mind'. But they begin in the heart, which is not only described as a 'foul rag and bone shop', but is provided with an inventory of contents: 'Old kettles, old bottles, and a broken can, / Old iron, old bones, old rags, that raving slut / Who keeps the till'. This is not a very prepossessing picture of the relationship between the eternal forms and the merely associative and organic ones. But these are the underlying terms, already familiar from Yeats's earlier work, even though he is here giving them a different emphasis. Blake, on the other hand, would assimilate both terms – the heart as well as the image – to his mythology: what Yeats refers to as the heart, Blake would comprise at various times in the figures of Vala (sometimes equated with Nature) and Luvah (sometimes equated with Passion). There would be no tendency to separate what could be represented in myth, on the one hand, from the natural and the passionate on the other. These observations give further depth to the description of Blake's myth-making as possessing a more 'iconic' quality than that of Yeats.

It has often been said that Yeats attempts to recover a sense of the supernatural reference of symbols by using some of the tools of a symbolist technique which had been devised in a more or less sceptical frame of mind. The combination of archetype and associationism described here would seem to bear witness to the truth of that claim. Blake, on the other hand, although he feels the need to recover the original force of myth, is still sufficiently confident that archetypes imbue every aspect of experience.

3
Eliot Between Blake and Yeats

Most people recognise that however genuine was Eliot's admiration for many aspects of Blake's work, this is probably outweighed by the powerful and trenchantly expressed reservations. In this connection, almost as interesting as what Eliot has to say about Blake is the fact that he chose to say it and then to give his thoughts further prominence in *The Sacred Wood* (1920) alongside such innovative theoretical essays as 'Tradition and the Individual Talent' or 'Hamlet and his Problems'. Like all Eliot's critical work in this period (these essays were written between 1917 and 1920), this piece has a strategic aspect. Eliot, with studied disingenuousness, dismisses the idea that Blake is merely 'a wild pet for the supercultivated', thereby recognising part of the threat posed by Blake's influence while suggesting one way in which he is going to deflect it (not at all dishonestly, of course).[1] What is good about Blake is going to be shown to derive from his hospitality to 'the impersonality of the artistic process' – that famous and highly significant phrase from 'Tradition and the Individual Talent'. At first it might not seem as if this were really the case, for Eliot's first piece of concessive praise is formed from the idea of Blake's 'peculiar honesty' which is 'peculiarly terrifying' (*SW*, 151). One might be tempted to interpret this concession as going all the way in incorporating Eliot among those who look to poetry for the expression of truth and sincerity. But the concession is soon qualified, while it offers admirers of Blake the guarantee that he can understand their point of view. For not only is this honesty 'a peculiarity of all great poetry', but it 'never exists without great technical accomplishment' (*SW*, 151).

This accomplishment Blake learnt as a boy through his 'immense powers of assimilation' (*SW*, 152). As Christopher Ricks points out, the description sounds a little bit like Eliot himself.[2] It is indeed 'important that the artist should be highly educated in his own art'; but it is not necessarily of the essence that he be educated in ideas 'by the ordinary processes of education which constitute education for the ordinary man' (*SW*, 154). At which point Eliot adds a rather unexpected explanation: 'For these processes consist largely in the acquisition of impersonal ideas which obscure what we really want, and what really excites our interest' (*SW*, 154). What is unexpected about this is the word 'impersonal': of course, it has a positive meaning in Eliot's critical vocabulary. But the Blake essay reveals a distinction between the 'impersonality of the artistic process' (good) and 'impersonal ideas' (bad).

However, we soon discover that not all impersonal ideas really are that bad. On the contrary, it seems that what is wrong with Blake has much to do with the fact that he invented his own personal philosophy: 'Blake did not have that more Mediterranean gift of form which knows how to borrow as Dante borrowed his theory of the soul' (*SW*, 156). As David Goldie remarks, 'Eliot distrusted the "impersonal ideas" of public opinion that caused Tennyson to squander his talents or Swinburne's vacuous "impersonality", yet he celebrated Dante's ability to absorb a whole impersonal belief system and wrote approvingly that "the emotion of art is impersonal".'[3] Part of the explanation for this apparent confusion lies hidden in the rather strange phrasing of the remark about Dante quoted above, for it suggests that a 'gift of form' consists in knowing how to borrow a 'theory'. In other words, Eliot seems to be probing an uncertainty in the handling of ideas such that the form is vitiated. This bears in particular on the question of Blake's mythology. Eliot asserts that Blake is a kind of 'resourceful' Robinson Crusoe, putting his philosophy together from 'odds and ends about the house', but swiftly moves on to the question of the mythology which provided the framework (*SW*, 156). Blake's mythological creations illustrate 'the crankiness, the eccentricity, which frequently affects writers outside of the Latin tradition' (*SW*, 157). It is as if this tradition is better able to embody ideas with subtlety, complexity and conviction, and from a true unity of self.

This is an opportune point at which to reflect on the question how far Eliot's judgment is relevant to the case of Yeats, who, though he does not merit an essay in *The Sacred Wood*, was nevertheless present to Eliot's mind in the period; and it is worth remembering that Yeats was strongly associated with the claims of Blake. Yeats's Celtic gods and goddesses must have seemed rather like the 'trolls and pixies' and 'the major Saxon deities' which 'were perhaps no great loss in themselves' (*SW*, 157). But we do not need to speculate on these lines if we turn to Eliot's essay on 'The Modern Mind' in *The Use of Poetry and the Use of Criticism*, where he says of Yeats,

> He was very much fascinated by self-induced trance states, calculated symbolism, mediums, theosophy, crystal-gazing, folklore and hobgoblins. Golden apples, archers, black pigs and such paraphernalia abounded.[4]

Eliot seems especially to have in mind Yeats's symbolist masterpiece, *The Wind Among the Reeds* (1899), to judge by the references to 'The Song of the Wandering Aengus' and 'The Valley of the Black Pig', reprinted six times in London, up to and including the year 1911, in its first and now unfamiliar form – a form, however, which affected Eliot's view of Yeats. Very nearly half of this original version is taken up with notes explaining the mythological personages and events referred to in the poems; the meaning of the myths is explained partly in anthropological terms, the name of Frazer being invoked.[5] And the poems are often given the 'different voices' of a number of mythological or fictional characters: Aedh, Mongan, Michael Robartes. In the revised version, which was available from 1906 in the first volume of the *Poetical Works*, these facts are obscured. In 1906 the characters' names are removed from the titles and the notes are not included. Later, as in the familiar collected edition, the notes are included in a reduced form at the back of the volume, many pages away from *The Wind Among the Reeds*. But given the widespread knowledge and availability of the original version, and given Eliot's singling out of the subject-matter of the volume, it is an unavoidable conclusion that *The Waste Land* is, in its adoption of notes, its reference to Frazer, and its conscious deployment of 'Different Voices', passing a comment on *The Wind Among the Reeds*. The comment is on the lines of replacing eccentric Celtic myth and folklore with the more centrally European classical mythology. In a concession to northern Europe, the Arthurian legend is admitted to possess universal relevance as well.

However, Eliot's Tiresias and Fisher King, while their locations may not be entirely definite, appear to sojourn significantly in London. Yeats has said of Blake,

> He was a symbolist who had to invent his symbols; and his counties of England, with their correspondence to tribes of Israel, and his mountains and rivers, with their correspondence to parts of a man's body, are arbitrary [...]. Had he been a Catholic of Dante's time he would have been well content with Mary and the angels; or had he been a scholar of our time [...] have gone to Ireland and chosen for his symbols the sacred mountains, along whose sides the peasant still sees enchanted fires, and the divinities which have not faded from the belief, if they have faded from the prayers, of simple hearts.[6]

The point is that however 'arbitrary' the choice from a symbolic point of view, it is not arbitrary from the point of view of the poet's context. Indeed, what is revealed is the poet's innate desire to animate the world around. There are many passages from Blake which illustrate the point:

> From Golgonooza the spiritual Four-fold London eternal
> In immense labours & sorrows, ever building, ever falling,
> Thro Albions four Forests which overspread all the Earth,
> From London Stone to Blackheath east: to Hounslow west;
> To Finchley north: to Norwood south.[7]

Eliot has no Golgonooza, nor, at least by name, does he have an Albion. But named places in London he does have in *The Waste Land*: 'Highbury bore me. Richmond and Kew / Undid me [...]. // My feet at Moorgate, and my heart / Under my feet.'[8] The idea of a large mythological figure (in this case feminine), whose parts are symbolically dispersed across London, hovers behind these lines. If one asks who before Eliot apart from Blake has written lines like this, the answer must be, nobody. In sum, Eliot appears to be offering an implied rebuke to Yeats and Blake by adapting myths which in his estimation are central to European tradition. But he has borrowed Blake's tactic of setting a myth within his own place. There is a logic about this within the terms elaborated in Blake's essay on Blake: the poet should work within a coherent and impersonal tradition, but great value is nevertheless placed on the poet's particular experience.

At the same time, however, Eliot is concerned to distinguish clearly the tradition he invokes from that dabbling with esoteric traditions he saw as vitiating Yeats's work and he appears to have regarded Blake as constituting an esoteric tradition all of his own. Connected with these thoughts is the passage about Madame Sosostris, her wicked pack of cards and her horoscope. Yet Helen Gardner has pointed out that the passage from *Burnt Norton* about 'the still point' and 'the dance' was indebted to Charles Williams's description of the magical dance of the Tarot in his *The Greater Trumps*. *Burnt Norton* is of course a later work, but the interest predates its composition.[9] More recently, Leon Surette has laid bare just how keen was Eliot's interest in occult traditions, and how strong was the occult background to Jessie L. Weston's *From Ritual to Romance*.[10] It seems that Eliot was happy to extract from esoteric traditions those elements that could be harnessed to, or seemed to be implicated in, a centrally European tradition. In a parallel manner, Eliot wants to separate out a Blake who responds in an individual way. Leaving the question of mythology to one side, the experience of the city owes something to Blake as well. As Bernard Bergonzi points out, Blake's lines about the city encounter can be seen as an influence on a number of Eliot passages from 'Prufrock' to *The Waste Land*.[11] He quotes the first stanza from Blake's 'London':

> I wander thro' each charter'd street
> Near where the charter'd Thames does flow.
> And mark in every face I meet
> Marks of weakness, marks of woe.
>
> (*E*, 26)

The lines from Eliot most reminiscent of these are the ones about the crowd that flowed over London Bridge: 'Sighs, short and infrequent, were exhaled, / And each man fixed his eyes before his feet.'

The Waste Land suggests that Eliot's writing could indeed be influenced in a significant way by Blake: a way that was reflected in part of the larger conception of the poem. There are other examples, and perhaps the most striking is to be found in *Gerontion*, a fact which is given further piquancy by the knowledge that Eliot's first thought had been to make it an opening or introductory section of what became *The Waste Land*. The lines in question are 'in the juvescence of the year / Springs Christ the tiger' and 'These tears are shaken from the wrath-bearing tree', the latter of which, as Hugh Kenner pointed out, has echoes of Blake's 'The Poison Tree', which was 'water'd' with 'tears'.[12] The other reference, to Blake's 'The Tyger', is no mere playing with associations, but is profoundly Blakean. Blake's paired contrary poems, 'The Lamb' in *Songs of Innocence* and 'The Tyger' in *Songs of Experience*, present contrary aspects of the divine: 'Little Lamb who made thee' and 'Did He who made the Lamb make thee?' But 'The Tyger' is not simply to be equated with the symbol of a wrathful God the Father, for Blake's contemporaneous work, *The Marriage of Heaven and Hell*, which Eliot knew very well and admired in his qualifying way, equates Christ with a fiery and wrathful principle, in a work which also contains the Proverb of Hell, 'The tygers of wrath are wiser than the horses of instruction' – wrath again. Blake's conception of Christ is inimical to insipid notions of humility and certainly to those who posture as humble, as it might be said that the speaker of *Gerontion* does. It comprises indignant wrath against evil and the courage to confront it. Blake is emphatic upon this point, as can easily be seen from a work such as 'The Everlasting Gospel' with its questions 'Was Jesus humble' and 'Was Jesus gentle' (*E*, 518, 523). Thus, when Eliot's speaker exclaims 'The tiger springs in the new year / Us he devours', he aligns himself with a state akin to Blake's Experience. He is bereft of 'Energy' and spontaneity. In this new year, the harbinger of spring, which, as in *The Waste Land*, is a time which awakens memory and regret, a harsh and fiery judgment is passed on the weary and cowardly soul who has never fought at 'the hot gates' and has allowed the bitter fruits of Experience – tears – to gather in the poison tree. This is a process which is bound to elicit 'wrath': Experience is a place of mutually dependent wrath and cowardly pretence: the wrath of the Tyger chastising the cruel stratagems of characters such as the Nurse in 'Nurse's Song'.

As I have suggested, this passage shows an influence from Blake that is far more than superficial. And the proximity of the thinking to be found in *Gerontion* to that of *The Waste Land*, together with hints of Blake's London to be found in the latter, make it clear that Blake's concept of Experience is a significant influence on Eliot in this period. What is not true, of course, is that Eliot accepts even the rudiments of a 'system' to be found in Blake's earlier work – which is the period to which, nevertheless, we are referring.

Eliot's early concern with tradition merges, as the 1920s progress, with his increasing concern with Christian orthodoxy. One aspect of this is his insistence on an orthodox definition of 'mysticism'. In a 1927 review of Blake books in *The Nation & Athenaeum*, referring particularly to Helen C. White's *The Mysticism of William Blake*, Eliot applauds the author's discrimination in pointing out that 'Blake is not a mystic', but rather a 'visionary'.[13] White's distinction is an orthodox one, in that it reserves the word *mysticism* for the encounter with God, and means by *visionary* simply the capacity to see visions. If one accepts this distinction, it appears that Eliot and White are substantially correct: there are very few examples of mysticism in Blake. One example might be the great Job engraving (Illustration IX), 'Then a Spirit passed before my face, the hair of my flesh stood up.'[14] But precisely by virtue of being a representation of an episode from The Book of Job, it cannot prove more than that Blake recognised the existence of mystical experience. But arguably, as we shall see, there is evidence of mysticism in *Milton* of a kind that might have influenced Eliot.

However, staying for a moment with the reasons why Eliot wished to rebut the notion that Blake was a mystic, in brief, his motivation derives from the desire to attack the supposed pretensions of Romanticism to offer a surrogate for religious orthodoxy. For Eliot, there can be no true mysticism that is not grounded in the apprehension of a god whose nature is at least adumbrated by tradition. Eliot has in his sights not only Blake and the Romantics, but also the work of a neo-Romantic critic such as John Middleton Murry, who saw Blake as an 'authentic mystic' and also asserted 'the necessity of [Blake's] obscurity' as the price of his authenticity.[15] In the context of Murry's other work, one can see that Blake is for him the supreme Romantic artist, of a kind who must come into existence after the Renaissance. This is a conception which Eliot feels he must quash.[16]

Oddly, though, it seems that Eliot may indeed have been thinking about at least one aspect of Blake's later work as mystical in *Four Quartets*. We know that Eliot was aware of the influence of Blake when he wrote *East Coker*, since he said Blake 'kept getting into' it, but it is probable that Blake is also an influence on the mysticism of *Four Quartets* in general, from their inception.[17] For while it may be true that Blake's conceptions and visionary mythology are not truly mystical at most points, since they do not embody the direct encounter with the divine being, there is a conception of timelessness in *Milton* which is similar to the idea of the timeless often to be found in writers Eliot would recognise as true mystics and similar to the idea of the timeless he clearly intends to associate with the mystical experience in *Four Quartets*. The first explicit appearance of Eliot's concept is in *Burnt Norton*, in the lines about 'the still point of the turning world'. This paradoxical place is 'neither flesh nor fleshless'; and while it is 'still', it is 'neither arrest nor movement'. Nevertheless, identifiable movement does depend upon it: 'Except for the point, the still point, / There would be no dance, and there is only the dance.' The dance is a form of what Eliot, later in the poem, calls 'the form, the pattern'. It is time and history which reveal that they possess significant pattern in the illumination cast by the timeless moment. At the same time, the timeless moment is the human experience of the divine, so it is also that which actually imparts meaning.

This moment can be compared to a concept in Blake's *Milton*. The irruption of timeless inspiration is described in a passage near the climax of the poem which is intended to explain the transformative power of imagination:

> There is a Moment in each Day that Satan cannot find
> Nor can his Watch Fiends find it, but the Industrious find
> This Moment & it multiply. & when it is once found
> It renovates every Moment of the Day if rightly placed
> (William Blake, *Milton*, 35: 42–45; *E*, 136)

The suggestively ambiguous locution 'Watch Fiends' refers to vigilance, but also to the time that runs like clockwork. This moment is outside such time. In being so radically opposed to Satan it is also divine. Furthermore, like Eliot's conception, while it is not itself of the same order as the other moments, it has the capacity to irradiate them all with a sense of renovation, and this capacity is precisely dependent on the fact that it belongs to a different order: on its timelessness.

The complete picture of Eliot's indebtedness to Blake is far larger than has been realised. It encompasses a range of topics which are central to his work: the experience of the city, the handling of mythological materials in the modern world, the self-deceiving states of mind to be found in experience, the challenge of Christ to those states of mind, the idea of the timeless moment. Yeats is a partner in this relationship, present as a measure of the wrong way of responding to Blake in the modern world: the fact that Yeats is present in this way is yet another reminder of the importance to Eliot of assessing what is possible in the contemporaneous conjuncture. But Eliot's indebtedness to Blake is partially masked by qualification and criticism. Of all the writers in this volume, it is Eliot who corresponds most of all to the Bloomian model of the anxiety of influence where Blake is concerned. Appropriately enough, Bloom's categories are quite illuminating about the relationship. However, just as one feels that Bloom is too prone to insist on one-to-one relationships – there is only one precursor poet or poem – so he naturally tends to ascribe only one type of relationship to the successor's struggle with the predecessor. But Eliot's relationship to Blake bears strong resemblances to two of Bloom's six 'revisionary ratios', '*Tessera*' and '*Daemonization*'. The former is 'completion and antithesis', the latter a 'movement towards a personalized Counter-Sublime' which opens itself to 'a power in the parent-poem that does not belong to the parent proper, but to a range of being just beyond that precursor'.[18] Indeed, one can see these two ratios, where the Eliot–Blake relationship is concerned, as continuous with each other, for the completion Eliot offers is dependent on the power which lies just beyond Blake: on sources such as Dante, admired by them both (and Eliot's knowledge of Blake's admiration for Dante is itself a factor in his reaction to Blake). While Bloom's agonistic conceptions may be too violent for all accounts of influence, they certainly sharpen one's sense of what is involved in a reaction as ambivalent as that of Eliot. But the ambivalence, and the suggestive Bloomian description of it, need to be understood in context: Eliot wishes to learn from Blake, while tactically, and from conviction, rejecting Yeats's late Romanticism and Murry's continuation of it. This means rejecting their understanding of Blake.

4
Blake and Oppositional Identity in Yeats, Auden and Dylan Thomas

It is not an exaggeration to say that Yeats was one of the first serious scholars of Blake. The three-volume annotated edition (1893) he prepared with Edwin J. Ellis (1848–1916) was far more detailed and comprehensive than predecessors offered by W. M. Rossetti and others. The annotations, although they might seem unbalanced to a contemporary scholar in the weight they accord to occult traditions, are still useful. And not only does the edition give full representation to the longer prophetic books, it also attempts to convey a much better idea of the role of the illuminations than would be available from any other source in the period. Of course, Yeats had the assistance of Ellis, who had been something of a mentor.[1] But Yeats's study of Theosophy, Cabbala and Swedenborg had already been undertaken independently of Ellis, and it now 'came into its own'.[2] So the impression Yeats gives in *A Vision* that he and Ellis were genuine collaborators is undoubtedly quite accurate.

This, then, is an important influence on early, Romantic, Yeats, whose date of birth (1865) was only 38 years after the death of Blake. There are other influences, and one of the most important, that of Shelley, pre-dates his immersion in Blake. In fact, R. F. Foster puts it well when he states that Yeats's own ideas of poetry 'as a reflection of 'immortal moods', or archetypal emotions, which he had derived from Shelley, were reinforced by Blake'.[3] But it is a mistake to think that Blake's influence evaporates with Yeats's renunciation of his early style in the opening years of the twentieth century. On the contrary, in this case, as in that of Auden, one finds that a change of attitude necessitates not the rejection of Blake, but the need to re-interpret him and harness him to the change, so that where he was for Yeats in the Nineties happily associated with 'wavering rhythms', he later becomes, by means of his statements about Energy and firm outline, associated with the new emphasis on clarity and definiteness of poetic style. As a result, since Yeats never renounced his passionate interest in occult philosophy, Blake was still there to be drawn upon for illumination in this area, too. Indeed, Blakean ideas play an important role in *A Vision* and in the imagery associated with concepts, such as 'measurement', which occur across the whole range of Yeats's later work. Most of all, though, the theme of 'contraries', Yeats's antinomies – which is intimately bound up with the concept of the 'antithetical' – makes itself felt in all phases of his work.

Blake's concept is, of course, to be found in *The Marriage of Heaven and Hell*, Plate 3: 'Without Contraries is no progression. Attraction and Repulsion, Reason and Energy, Love and Hate, are necessary to Human existence.' There are many possible sources of this concept in the traditions of occult philosophy, including the Kabbalah, with its opposed sides of the Tree of Life, and in alchemy, where the Great Work of finding the philosopher's stone, with which gold could be created, consists of finding a resolution, or 'marriage', of the contrary principles represented by Mercury and Sulphur, which may themselves (confusingly) be symbolised by silver and gold. The tradition of philosophical alchemy influenced Jakob Boehme, whom Blake refers to as 'Behmen', partly crediting him with the inspiration of *The Marriage of Heaven and Hell* in the pages of that very work, where he also refers to another philosophical alchemist, Paracelsus. The phrase 'Without Contraries is no progression' is clearly indebted to one of Boehme's best-known formulations. Yeats's prior knowledge of the tradition of philosophical alchemy would have made it especially easy for him to apprehend the outlines of these ideas in Blake.

Blake's belief in the fundamental character of contraries is the foundation for the very structure of *Songs of Innocence and of Experience*, which bears the legend 'Shewing the two Contrary States of the Human Soul' on its title-page. This idea is developed by Blake in such a way that a song from *Innocence* may well have its opposite counterpart in *Experience*. Thus 'The Lamb' in *Innocence* is 'paired' with 'The Tyger' in *Experience*, 'The Chimney Sweeper' in *Innocence* is 'paired' with 'The Chimney Sweeper' in *Experience*, who evinces a very different point of view, and so on. Yeats adopts a similar strategy, both as between individual poems and, to some extent, between groups of poems or whole books. When the reader of Yeats first opens the old Macmillan *Collected Poems* he or she will come upon 'The Song of the Happy Shepherd', and this is immediately followed by 'The Sad Shepherd'. Go a few pages deeper into the book and in the section called *The Rose* (it was never originally published as a separate volume) one finds 'The Rose of Peace' and 'The Rose of Battle' (*YP*, 37–38). The same section begins with a poem called 'To the Rose upon the Rood of Time' (*YP* 31), where the rood, or cross, is equated with the Tree of Life, the branches of which are termed 'the boughs of love and hate'. The idea of the Tree of Life is substantially derived from the Kabbalah, which itself has opposing aspects of 'sternness' and 'mercy'. In 'To the Rose', the rather Shelleyan personification of Eternal Beauty is said to be 'wandering on her way' beneath these boughs, and the allegory implies that mortal humanity can only encounter this eternal principle through the contrariety and unevenness of the created universe. 'The Two Trees', a poem from the same section, represents the two sides of the Tree of Life as two different trees, and Yeats takes the opportunity here to give full symbolic treatment to the two principles he himself sees as being the fundamental antinomies: subjectivity, understood as faith in the heart and its inspiration, and objectivity. In the first stanza, the beloved is told to gaze into her own heart because '[t]he holy tree is growing there', but in the second she is enjoined to '[g]aze no more in the bitter glass / The demons, with their subtle guile, / Lift up before us when they pass'. The reflecting character of the 'glass' symbolises a secondariness, an externality, a self-consciousness, which are at odds with the direct inspiration of the heart. Accordingly, in the first stanza the tree is beautiful, but in the second it possesses '[b]roken boughs and blackened leaves'. Although the point is made in relation to amorous love, it is a development of a more general view already expressed in 'The Song of the Happy Shepherd' and 'The Sad Shepherd'. In the former poem, we are warned to seek '[n]o learning from the starry men, / Who follow with the optic glass / The whirling ways of stars that pass' – astronomers, standing in for science in general, and sounding not unlike Blake's hostile characterisation of Newtonianism. They cannot be trusted, for 'there is no truth / Saving in thine own heart'. They, however, have destroyed this precious source, for 'the cold star-bane / Has cloven and rent their hearts in twain'. With cloven hearts, and looking outside themselves with an 'optic glass', they are not unlike the demons of 'subtle guile' who hold up a glass to life in 'The Two Trees'. In all of this, one can already see the outlines of the major antinomies of *A Vision*: the 'primary' and the 'antithetical', which Yeats identifies with objectivity and subjectivity.

It will perhaps be seen that, as in Blake, the contrast of contrary states can be quite sharp. Thus, the happy shepherd confidently advises us to gather by the sea some 'twisted, echo-harbouring shell, / And to its lips thy story tell, / And they thy comforters will be'. Rather obviously, this is a metaphor for the poetry that takes its origin from the inspiration of the human heart. Unfortunately, though, it appears that not everyone is in a position to take the advice. This is the predicament of the Sad Shepherd, who does take the advice. But everything he sings changes 'to inarticulate moan'. Some settled disposition or mood keeps him in a state of sadness so disabling to the heart's inspiration that his song is formless and meaningless.

As we have already suggested, even groups of poems or even whole books may stand in contrast to each other. Thus the early group which Yeats came to call *Crossways* contrasts with the immediately subsequent one called *The Rose*. This becomes clearer when one remembers that both terms refer to the 'Rosy Cross' of Rosicrucianism, the syncretist tendency of occult thought which was at the centre of Golden Dawn speculations. The cross, in its very name, represents the contrariety and conflict to be found in the Tree of Life (which, as we have seen, may be figured as a 'rood'). The rose, on the other hand, represents the flowering of the Tree of Life, the temporal blooming of Eternal Beauty, and carries connotations of the transitory unity and harmony which we may occasionally encounter in the world of time. In Yeats's later work one is being asked to contrast the assertive connotations of *The Tower* with those of its successor volume, *The Winding Stair* (the title refers to the stairway inside the tower) which is intended to be more ruminative.

None of this means that there can never be a place for the reconciliation of contraries in Yeats's thought. An obvious exception is provided by the love of man and woman. Here, in his poetry as in his life, Yeats promotes the idea of a true marriage. In the poetry, he draws upon the idea of an alchemical marriage, the very notion upon which Blake also draws, though emphasising contrariety rather than reconciliation, in *The Marriage of Heaven and Hell*. The most memorable representation of the idea of a true marriage – of the right relationship of man and woman – is to be found in the well-known lines which conclude 'The Song of Wandering Aengus', in which the speaker swears that he will find his beloved in a land beyond time, 'And pluck till time and times are done / The silver apples of the moon, / The golden apples of the sun.' Thus he will bring together the alienated polarities of feminine and masculine, lunar and solar. These are also the cosmic polarities around which the whole universe is structured, and in this way Yeats implies that the true marriage will bring about an integration of the different principles operative in the psyche, above all, Reason and Imagination.

Nevertheless, a more noticeable emphasis in Yeats's handling of contraries lies precisely in his appreciation of their value as fundamental concepts, an appreciation which itself is very Blakean, as revealed in Blake's remark, in *The Marriage of Heaven and Hell*, that 'Opposition is true Friendship.' For while Yeats may have a predilection for one contrary over another – for subjectivity, for instance – it is clear that he does not think that, for those who live under the Tree of Life, under 'the boughs of love and hate', there can be any escape from contrariety. Of course, there are those who may wish to impose sameness on life. This is the case with St Patrick and Christianity in *The Wanderings of Oisin*, where Oisin, on his return to Ireland after years spent in the islands of the immortals, discovers that his homeland has been converted to Christianity in his absence, and that the Fenian heroes with whom he delighted in song and battle are long departed. Here, Christianity with its pacific morality and sense of duty represents another form of 'Grey Truth' and is made to adopt a role not unlike that of Urizen, who attempts to impose uniformity in *The [First] Book of Urizen*, unable to comprehend why the Eternals should want to live in 'perpetual burnings'.

A poet, such as Oisin, may well value imagination and songs of love and heroism. Furthermore, it is precisely those who value subjectivity, energy, imagination, over the Grey Truth of science or religion, who are likely to understand best the conflictual contrariety of existence. This is clear both early and late in Yeats's work. In 'Fergus and the Druid' (*YP*, 32–33), from *The Rose*, Fergus wishes to open the 'bag of dreams' carried by the Druid. The latter implicitly warns him that the knowledge this brings will destroy him. But

Fergus persists, and when he opens the bag he is able to enter into the secrets of transmigration, like the Druid himself:

> I have been many things –
> A green drop in the surge, a gleam of light
> Upon a sword, a fir-tree on a hill,
> An old slave grinding at a heavy quern,
> A king sitting upon a chair of gold –
> And all these things were wonderful and great;
> But now I have grown nothing, knowing all.
>
> (*YP*, 33)

To know everything in this way is to possess a general truth, rather than to enter wholeheartedly into life and the dreams which it generates spontaneously. Entering wholeheartedly into life means the acceptance of a real, individual, subjective existence, and that means coming into conflict with some other forms of existence. To realise this truth is to recognise the uselessness of general truth, of 'Grey Truth'. An epitome of this way of thinking is to be found in Yeats's later work, where, in *A Vision*, the word *antithetical* is used to denote the subjective temperament which reacts against the given, in conflict with it, transforming it. The *primary* in *A Vision* is, by contrast, that which accepts the given: it may analyse or seek to understand it, but not transform it.

That this way of thinking was already fundamental for Yeats is indicated by his occult Golden Dawn name, which was 'Demon est Deus Inversus' – '[a] Demon is [a] God Inverted'. (Yeats usually referred to this name by the initials DEDI.) Allen Grossman has noticed that he found the phrase in the first volume of Madame Blavatsky's *The Secret Doctrine*, and the words he cites offer strong corroboration of the idea that Yeats was indeed already thinking in terms of what he would later call 'the antithetical':

The ancients understood so well that their philosophers – now followed by the Kabbalists – defined evil as the lining of God or Good: *Demon est Deus Inversus* being a very old adage. Indeed evil is but an antagonizing blind force in nature; it is *reaction, opposition,* and *contrast*.[4]

As we have seen, 'reaction' might be against a position or statement of one's own. It is probably worth seeing Yeats's famous 'change of style' in the earlier years of the twentieth century in this light, especially as that change is itself bound up, in Yeats's thinking, with concepts derived from Blake.

To take first his way of thinking about his Nineties style, discussing the art of that period in terms of 'decadence' in 'The Autumn of the Body' (1898), he speaks of 'faint lights and faint colours and faint outlines and faint energies' (*EI*, 191). The words 'outlines' and 'energies', especially brought together like this, recall Blake, who espoused 'Energy' and clear outline. The fact that Yeats would think of his own early poetic style in terms of such 'decadence' is confirmed by the famous remarks he makes in favour of 'faint and nervous' rhythms (*EI*, 5) and about casting out 'energetic rhythms, as of a man running' (*EI*, 163). Indeed, given his knowledge of Blake, it looks as if Yeats consciously formed his early style as a partial 'reaction' against certain aspects of Blake's work.

In the early years of the twentieth century he reacts against that reaction. Writing to George Russell ('A.E.') in March 1903, Yeats declared his loss of sympathy with the vagueness, the flight from definite form, which had characterised the late nineteenth century, and which are praised in 'The Autumn of the Body'. Now, he says, 'I feel about me and in me an impulse to create form, to carry the realisation of beauty as far as possible' (*L*, 402). And in 1904 he tells the same correspondent that he has been 'fighting the prevailing decadence for years' and exclaims 'Let us have no emotions [...] in which there is not an athletic joy' (*L*, 434–35). So much for avoiding rhythms reminiscent of 'a man running'. Yeats now espouses Blake's twin insistence on Energy and the distinct outline of clear form.

This new clarity and energy is evident from the way in which the newly forceful persona of Yeats's poems now develops, and this development is itself bound up with that of the doctrine of the Mask. The idea, expounded in the occult speculation 'Anima Hominis' (from *Per Amica Silentia Lunae*), is that each person possesses a mask, the image of desirable characteristics which the self adopts to present itself to the world. Those characteristics are opposite to those of the given self – a notable piece of 'antithetical' thinking, which posits that a person is constituted by contrariety. Some of the sources of this way of thought lie in Yeats's involvement with the theatre. But others are to be found in occult speculations such as those deriving from séances in which he thought he had encountered his 'anti-self'. These ideas feed into the thinking of *A Vision*, but there are intriguing hints that Yeats was also capable of thinking in contradictory ways even about the 'antithetical' wisdom expounded there.

The wisdom contained in *A Vision*, which substantially derived from his wife's automatic writings at the instigation of the spirit world, could be seen as an expression of life. 'The Gift of Harun Al-Rashid', a poem originally published in the first version of *A Vision* (1925), reduces the abstract geometry of Yeats's theories to the expressions of his wife's living energies: 'all those gyres and cubes and midnight things / Are but a new expression of her body / Drunk with the bitter sweetness of her youth'. (*YP*, 450). Fittingly, the moon, emblem of woman and the goddess, is also the presiding emblem of *A Vision*. But where does this leave Yeats, the learned occult theorist? The original title of this poem was 'Desert Geometry', and the 'gyres and cubes' refer to the same idea: namely, that whatever the sources of this wisdom, its codification was, indeed, notably abstract and founded in what Yeats elsewhere calls 'measurement'. There is evidence that Yeats entertained mixed feelings about a poet's immersion in this kind of occult science. A piece of automatic writing produced by his acquaintance Lady Edith Lyttelton had warned that Yeats was 'a prince with an evil counsellor', and that he was to reflect upon the 'adverse principle' in relation to the myth of Phaeton.[5] Phaeton's chariot was pulled by a dark and a white horse, and this fact offers an analogy with Yeats's contrary principles of lunar and solar in *A Vision*. Lyttelton's script went on to assert, 'In the midst of death we are in life – the inversion is what I *mean*.'[6] The first phrase itself inverts the word-order of a familiar phrase from the Book of Common Prayer: the resulting suggestion is that Yeats is allowing the principle of death to predominate over that of life. One may relate this to the warning offered by his ghostly instructors that he was too keen to engage in the conscious ordering of the knowledge they imparted: 'the Guide emphasized that the System was "not from reading" but intuition: "dont deliberately read" [...]'.[7] A related point (in that it also refers to deliberation) is the idea of what the automatic script calls the 'Evil Persona', which refers to the willed assumption of the Mask: 'it is the conscious mind that makes the Ep [Evil Persona] in consciously seeking its opposite and then emulating it.'[8]

Of course, there is an irony attending these reflections: the terms in which Yeats understands the contrary principles between which he is torn are themselves capable of being related to the opposed 'tinctures' of the system whose very elaboration has provoked this tension in himself. There is an aspect of Yeats, revealed in a poem such as 'The Second Coming', which stands back from all historical phenomena, including his own turmoil, and offers an exceedingly long and detached view of history. But Blake has been there before him: it is scarcely original to note the trenchantly framed cyclical myth of his 'The Mental Traveller' – 'And he grows young as she grows old' – which mirrors the cyclical pattern of the gyres in *A Vision*.

On a superficial reading, Blake might seem an unlikely mentor for Auden. It is widely accepted that the latter is an 'Anti-Romantic Modern', and some critics still speak in terms that are guided by the assumptions encapsulated in John G. Blair's *The Poetic Art of W. H. Auden* (1965), from which that phrase is taken. Blair summarises the matter thus: 'Only Burns, Byron, and Blake does Auden recognize, and he chooses to imitate their satiric or light verse rather than their more serious poems.'[9] This does, indeed, isolate the Romantic-period poets Auden most admires; but it is a grave, tendentious and critically naïve over-simplification of the true state of affairs. The assumption that 'satiric' verse is less serious than other forms is untenable, especially as it appears to be invoked in relation to *Don Juan* (the style of which is an influence on *Letter to Lord Byron*) and *The Marriage of Heaven and Hell* (a masterpiece whose lasting impact on English literature would be hard to over-estimate). More generally, Auden was intellectually interested in the phenomenon of 'Romanticism', about which he entertained grave doubts, but which he came to see as an essential clue to the understanding of the modern world. This is clear from *The Enchafèd Flood, or the Romantic Iconography of the Sea* (1950), where the leading idea is of the individual confronted by modes of experience which are symbolised by the city on the one hand and the sea and desert on the other. The book uses Romantic iconography as a way of modelling modern experience, but builds into that experience the doubts one may have about the ultimate adequacy of Romantic conceptions, especially after the heyday of Nazism and fascism. But there is nothing scurrilous or disrespectful about the book, and Auden is concerned to give aspects of Romanticism their full due. Thus, in describing the Romantic reaction against Deism, he is naturally led to

Blake, in whom that reaction is most salient and self-conscious. The point at issue is the abstraction involved in the Deists' idea of a rational god, partly modelled on the Newtonian supreme being, versus the concreteness of the orthodox account of the incarnation. Blake has much of relevance to say about this, and Auden comments: 'With his usual unerring insight Blake saw that the crucial points at issue were the Incarnation of Christ and the Forgiveness of Sins. A supreme architect cannot incarnate as an individual, only as the whole building; and a pure Judge cannot forgive; he can only condemn or acquit.'[10] Of course, this is not the whole story for Auden. The Romantics, including Blake, err in the other direction: towards a conception of purely immanent divinity. But his sympathy, not just for Blake, but for the Romantic point of view, is evident from these passages. Thus, in developing the contrast between Deism and characteristically Romantic thought, he quotes with approval Blake's remark that 'Man is born a Spectre or Satan.'[11] Deism emerges as shallow by comparison with Blake's stern insistence on the need for individual redemption. This is hardly surprising in a poet for whom the work of Kierkegaard had been crucial in his re-conversion to Christianity.

However, *The Enchafèd Flood* is quite a late work with which to introduce the topic of Blake's influence. Blake had always been honoured in Auden's circle, as the famous story of Spender and the Oxford hearties might suggest; but Auden's knowledge and enthusiasm were so great that it is hardly surprising, once one reaches a true estimate of the matter, that James Fenton should have described one aspect of him as 'Blake Auden'.[12] (Apparently there is only one other aspect: 'James Auden'.) Fenton himself refers to the famous lines from poem XXXI in *Poems 1927–1931* about 'Lawrence, Blake and Homer Lane, once healers in our English land' (*TEA*, 49). Of course, the lines continue in a way which might be read as implying the irrelevance of Blake, and indeed of the other two: 'These are dead as iron for ever; these can never hold our hand. // Lawrence was brought down by smut-hounds, Blake went dotty as he sang, / Homer Lane was killed in action by the Twickenham Baptist gang.' Yet on the whole, these must be seen as rhetorical claims, partly intended to lead up to and bolster the sounding assertions with which the poem ends: 'If we really want to live, we'd better start at once to try; / If we don't it doesn't matter, but we'd better start to die.' You don't need

anybody to hold your hand because the responsibility of saving yourself is yours alone. In any case, it may not be such a bad thing to go
'dotty' or be 'killed in action': in one of his epigrams, Auden notes
that one is 'a long way off becoming a saint' as long as one suffers
'from any complaint'; but if you don't suffer in this way, 'The chances
are that you're not trying' (*TEA*, 50). It may be difficult for those who
befriend life to avoid going 'dotty'. As for intellectual opposition figured as military action, as in the words about Homer Lane, many of
Auden's early poems depend on that idea for their images of heroism.
For obvious reasons such as these, even the anti-Romantic Blair
concludes that the poetry of this first volume is clearly indebted to
Blake as well as to Lawrence.[13]

There are two aspects to this indebtedness: style and matter. As for the
first, even at the end of the Thirties, Auden was seen by a knowledgeable commentator as having a Blakean style among his accomplish-
ments. Michael Roberts, the editor of *The Faber Book of Modern Verse*,
reviewed *Another Time* in *The Spectator* in 1940 stating that it opened
with 'a very effective dedicatory poem in Mr. Auden's most characteristic Blake-ish manner'.[14] In this light, Fenton's concentration on the stylistic connection seems entirely orthodox: 'Blake sat at Auden's left
when he wrote, urging concision, definite views, plain language. He
was not the Blake of the long line, of the interminable prophetic books,
but the fiery Blake of *The Marriage of Heaven and Hell*, the Blake of the
notebooks.'[15] He cites, for instance, this kind of epigram from Auden:
' "The sword above the valley" / Said the Worm to the Penny' (*TEA*, 438).
These are early and uncollected lines (? May 1927), and they help to
establish the early influence of Blake. Fenton is right to quote also the
famous lines from the epigrams at XXXII in *Poems* about how 'Those
who will not reason / Perish in the act', while those who will not act
'Perish for that reason' (*TEA*, 50). But even here the indebtedness is very
much a matter of content as well, as the last line demonstrates.

A nice transition from the point about style to the one about content might be provided by the uncollected lines to Chester Kallman
written round about 1939: 'Every I must weep alone / Till I Will be
overthrown' (*TEA*, 456). Here the combination of form and thought
seem cogently Blakean. Blake, for instance, asserts in the Annotations
to Swedenborg's *Divine Love* that 'There can be no good Will. Will is
always Evil.' Auden makes a similar point about T. E. Lawrence: 'Only
the continuous annihilation of the self by the Identity, to use Blake's

terminology, will bring us the freedom we wish for, or in Lawrence's own phrase, "Happiness comes in absorption." '[16] The terminology is certainly Blakean, though whether the same is true of the conceptual framework into which it is inserted is another matter. Under the influence of Homer Lane, Auden believes that Blake's overturning, in *The Marriage of Heaven and Hell*, of the dualism of body and soul is proleptic of Freud's thought.[17] This sheds light on what the 'Identity' is for Auden: a unity in which 'Desire' (to use Blake's term in *The Marriage*) is unrepressed and unseparated from mental functions. But in being harnessed to Freudian conceptions Auden's Blake has to slough off much of his concern, however antinomian, with religious tradition and the radical re-thinking of Christianity.

Nevertheless, *The Marriage of Heaven and Hell* is a major influence on the early Auden, not least on *The Orators*. Reviewing this when it came out, William Plomer refers to the influence of Blake.[18] When Spender opines that *The Orators* recalls 'the satire of Blake' it is probably of *The Marriage* that he is thinking.[19] Richard Hoggart remarks on the indebtedness of *The Orators* to Blake's idea of 'the tension of contraries', expressed in *The Marriage*.[20] Perceptively, he sees this idea as influential on the complexity of Auden's thought at the point where it raises a doubt as to whether '(a) everything is a product of the enemy, or reaction; or (b) a relic of the obsolete past, perhaps once good but now to be deplored; or (c) an earnest of better things, a pioneer of the future'.[21] In broad terms, one can see a similar dubiety in Blake as to how to conceive of the role and image of Jesus: 'Miltons Messiah' is a dreary agent of repression, whereas the true Jesus is an energetic and provocative ethical revolutionary. Still, *The Marriage* offers some clear contrasts, such as that between Reason and Energy, and this is paralleled, as Auden was well aware, by the contrasting representations of Urizen and Orc elsewhere in Blake's work. The figure in *The Orators* who most recalls Blake is that of the Enemy, for this is deployed in a quasi-mythological representation of a fundamental antagonism in human experience and society. Like Blake's Urizen, the Enemy operates at both social and psychological levels. He orders attacks which have a social dimension; but he also disseminates insidious propaganda intended to undermine individual mental health: '*Unless* you do well you will *not* be loved' (*TEA*, 91, 90). This undermining extends to a malign influence on the unconscious, so that the Enemy is responsible for neurotic behaviour and psychosomatic symptoms: 'Three warnings of enemy attack – depression in the mornings – rheumatic twinges – blips on the face' (*TEA*, 82). This is the point at which the Enemy can be seen as a mythologisation of Freudian repression. But in view of his belief that Blake was a forerunner of Freud, one should also bear in mind a song from *Experience* such as 'The Sick Rose', where possessive love breeds disease, or a 'Proverb of Hell' such as 'He who desires but acts not breeds pestilence' (*E*, 35). The 'Proverbs of Hell', as Hoggart points out, show most forcibly what Blake gave to Auden.[22] In *The Orators* one can see this scattered throughout the book: 'Man miserable without diversion. But diversion is human activity. A man doing nothing is not a man' (*TEA*, 78).

Perhaps the most telling reminiscence of Blake, though, occurs at that point where the Enemy coalesces with the idea of God. By far the most obvious of these occurrences is to be found in the mock-hymn, 'Not, Father [...]' (*TEA*, 109–10) which is the sixth of the 'Six Odes' with which *The Orators* concludes. In context, the ode fits well into a book which begins with a parodic 'Address for a Prize-Day'. But the form of a parody of a hymn is reminiscent of some of Blake's *Songs*. A sinister air of humiliated submissiveness pervades the poem, from the first lines in which the 'Father' is entreated not to prolong any further 'Our necessary defeat'. There is no defence against his 'accusations'. He is like Blake's 'Accuser', who is 'The Prince of this World', but mistakenly called by the 'names divine' of 'Jesus and Jehovah'. The ambiguity of the word-order in the first line is deliberate: 'Not, Father, further do prolong / Our necessary defeat'. Clearly this is a slightly strained way of saying 'Do not'. But it is also capable of being read as referring to a 'Not Father': that is, to Blake's 'Nobodaddy'. In that case, it can also be read as asking the father actually to prolong the defeat, rather than curtailing it: a way of emphasising the air of defeat which pervades the poem. Of course, these two meanings are mutually exclusive, but the curious word-order is intended precisely to obtrude the ambiguity.

The Enemy as accusing Father shades into the 'supreme Antagonist' in 'Consider this and in our time' (No. XXX in *Poems 1927–1931*). The latter talks to his 'admirers' every day 'By silted harbours, derelict works, / In strangled orchards, and the silent comb / Where dogs have worried or a bird was shot' (*TEA*, 47). The landscape has been corrupted, and the word 'admirers', when read alongside the later injunction to summon those 'handsome and diseased youngsters', helps to evoke the image of the homosexual 'Uncle' (as in *The Orators*) perverting young men. Yet the Antagonist's encouragement of sexual and neurotic sickness, and his undermining of confidence in life, will destroy a society already dying. This poem, as much as any other of this period, reveals an even larger ambiguity in Auden's myth: the Enemy is aligned with the death instinct and brings neurotic sickness; this sickness will bring about the collapse of the repressive society by a kind of internal contradiction (the influence of Marx is to be seen here); therefore the Enemy's deadly attacks are, at least from this point of view, to be welcomed. In 'Consider', some of the more subtle ruses of the Antagonist sound like the way in which Auden liked to conceive, in this period, of the subversive potential of political art: the Antagonist will start 'a rumour' which is 'soft / But horrifying in its capacity to disgust'. This sounds very like the 'preliminary bombardment by obscene telephone messages' which will help to destroy morale in *The Orators* (*TEA*, 92). Looked at in the round, then, the idea of the Enemy is profoundly ambiguous in a way that was shrewdly summarised in Hoggart's remarks, quoted above, and which he related to Blake's contraries. Certainly, if one looks at the developing depiction of Orc in Blake's works, on the whole he comes across both as revolutionary and as a potentially destructive force, vitiated by the very corruptions he seeks to oppose.

The 'rumour', the 'obscene telephone message', may serve as a reminder that in the early Thirties Auden did indeed espouse a political art, albeit one that, like Yeats's nationalist poetry in 'To Ireland in the Coming Times', acted upon the associations and the unconscious of his readers. When Auden becomes disillusioned with his own part in the 'low dishonest decade', he turns his back on any idea of a political end and in the process is inclined to ever-estimate the extent to which he could ever have been merely epitomised as a political poet. This becomes very clear from the unpublished prose work, 'The Prolific and the Devourer' (1939), the title of which is derived from *The Marriage of Heaven and Hell*, as is much of the aphoristic manner.

Given the role that Blake played before this point, it is interesting to consider the role he now plays in Auden's change of heart. Fenton puts this change itself in terms of the relationship to Blake: 'Imagine someone who has grown up a great admirer of Blake'; but then the babysitter kills the baby; subsequently he picks up a copy of *The Marriage of Heaven and Hell* and reads: 'Sooner murder an infant in its cradle than nurse unacted desires.'[23] This is Auden at the end of the

Thirties. Nevertheless, as Fenton points out, 'of the old trinity [Lawrence, Blake and Homer Lane] it was Blake who lasted longest with Auden, and whose manner he was closely imitating in "The Prolific and the Devourer" '.[24] This is true, but it leaves unexplained the reasons why Blake can accompany Auden thus far into his new mental universe. In fact, Auden's view of Blake appears to have changed. He borrows Blake's terminology of the Prolific and Devourer in order to set up Blake as the artist opposed to the politician. 'The Prolific and the Devourer: the Artist and the Politician. Let them realise that they are enemies' (*TEA*, 404). This makes the politician parasitic on the fertile imagery of the artist. It is clear from the rest of the work that the true artist cannot be harnessed to single-minded and utilitarian programmes: 'The artist qua artist is no reformer. Slums, war, disease are part of his material, and as such he loves them' (*TEA*, 403). 'The voice of the Tempter: "Unless you take part in the class struggle, you cannot become a major writer" ' (*TEA*, 403). The politician is an Enemy of Promise.

There is one particularly revealing remark for an understanding of Blake's new role: 'The artist's maxim: "Whoso generalises is lost" ' (*TEA*, 404). This is clearly indebted to Blake's 'To generalise is to be an idiot', and one notes that Auden cites Blake's antipathy to generalisation as characteristically Romantic in *The Enchafèd Flood*.[25] In the context of that work, generalisation is associated with the Enlightenment, and Blake's view with the particularity of incarnation and human error. But this view of Blake is already present in *New Year Letter*, a poem completed in late 1939, so that it is nearly contemporaneous with 'The Prolific and the Devourer'. Here, he refers to 'Self-educated WILLIAM BLAKE / Who threw his spectre into the lake', broke off relations with Newton and 'Spoke to Isaiah in the Strand'.[26] Blake has become the religious poet who takes seriously the conflicted particularity of man's relationship with God and individual need for redemption. The Enlightenment, on the other hand, is the very precursor of the modern politician, certainly as technocrat, but even as communist and fascist.

Famously, in 1933 the young Dylan Thomas told Pamela Hansford Johnson, 'I am in the path of Blake, but so far behind him that only the wings on his heels are in sight', which suggests a kind of centrality not claimed for Blake by Yeats and Auden.[27] The influence is palpable, though not necessarily any more obvious than that which is to be discerned in the works of the older poets. But as with these two, the most obvious inheritance is that of the idea of contraries and the related ambiguities about what represents positive energy, and what negative. These ambiguities express themselves in the poetry in terms of the ambiguous idea of the sacred: is it the repressive and life-denying ideology of a tyrant god, such as one might learn in a sermon in chapel, or is it to be equated with the underlying creative power of the universe, such as one might discern in the rhythms of the Bible?

Thomas's so-called Poetic Manifesto, which appeared in the *Texas Quarterly* in 1961, was based on the replies he gave to a research student's questions in 1951.[28] It is thus a late production, but the questions are concerned as much as anything with the most important influences on his work. He makes it clear that Blake is central. In a discussion of Thomas's youthful reading, Blake appears on a fairly long list, including the Bible and Shakespeare and 'the Ballads', but of the other Romantic poets, only Keats.[29] But as he comes to reflect on the meaning of the list, Blake's centrality becomes more evident: he speaks of a reading that 'ranged from writers of school-boy adventure yarns to incomparable and inimitable masters like Blake' and goes on to summarise the whole question of what made him want to write in these terms:

> Let me say that the things that first made me love language and want to work *in* it and *for* it were nursery rhymes and folk tales, the Scottish Ballads, a few lines of hymns, the most famous Bible stories and the rhythms of the Bible, Blake's *Songs of Innocence*, and the quite incomprehensible magical majesty and nonsense of Shakespeare heard, read, and near-murdered in the first forms of my school.[30]

The interviewer, while recognising the fundamental importance of the Bible, is keen to introduce a modern note and asks if 'three of the dominant influences on my published prose and poetry are Joyce, the Bible, and Freud'. While Thomas claims that his remarks hitherto had been talking about his 'juvenilia', he disavows the influence both of Joyce and Freud and claims to have read very little of the latter.[31] Asked about whether or not he writes 'in the Surrealist way', he asserts that he disagrees 'profoundly' with their method, because they juxtapose words and images that have 'no rational relationship', whereas he believes that the images in a poem, wherever they come

from, 'must go through all the rational processes of the intellect'.[32]
The interview does not run on very far beyond this point, and one is
left with the impression that the early reading is indeed the most
important element, and that Blake is central to it.

Early Thomas, the Thomas of the earliest entries in the *Notebooks*,
is a very Blakean poet indeed. These occasionally reveal a direct
indebtedness to specific poems of Blake. These lines from the first
draft of 'The Force that Through the Green Fuse Drives the Flower'
make clear references to 'The Sick Rose':

> And I am dumb to tell the eaten rose
> How at my sheet goes the same crooked worm,
> And dumb to holla thunder to the skies
> How at my cloths flies the same central storm.

Citing this and other passages, Thomas's editor, Ralph Maud, claims
that 'It would not be far wrong to say that Blake's notions of 'Heaven
and Hell' and of 'Innocence and Experience' have acted as authority
for Thomas' dualistic view of the world and his antithetical mode of
expressing it'.[33] 'Antithetical', which implies the delineation of contrary principles, seems right. And Thomas aligns himself with life and
energy: like Blake he is not impartial. The point of view of the poems
merges with the persona of the man. As Don McKay says, 'Inspired
variously by the examples of Lawrence, Blake, and Joyce, he adopts,
in his letters of the period [1933–34], the role of the revolutionary
outsider.'[34] It may not clinch a connection with Blake to identify hyp-
ocritical religious would-be tyrants in his work, but it certainly
indicates a congruence of ideas, which, taken with other hints, sup-
ports the link. Gwilym, the young man studying to be a preacher in
Portrait of the Artist as a Young Dog, worships a Urizenic god:

> Thou canst see and spy and watch us all the time, in the little black
> corners, in the big cowboys' prairies, under the blankets when
> we're snoring fast, in the terrible shadows, pitch black, pitch black;
> Thou canst see everything we do, in the night and in the day.[35]

Like some of the characters in Joyce's *Portrait of the Artist*, he tries to
induce the narrator's youthful self to 'confess'. But he himself is torn
between God and sex. The narrator had found some poems in

Gwilym's bedroom, 'all written to girls', but subsequently he 'changed all the girls' names to God'. Furthermore, he 'goes with actresses'.[36]

Thomas's mature style may not bear the obvious sign of indebtedness, but a little analysis of its characteristic peculiarities often reveals a notably Blakean structure and imagery. 'There was a Saviour' (*CP*, 117–18), for instance, offers a Blakean tyrant-god who can only rule if his servants are mentally enslaved to him; but escape from his influence leads to a place of innocent sexual love. The saviour is 'crueller than truth'. His 'golden note' turns repetitiously 'in a groove'. The point about internalising his power is memorably made at the end of the first stanza: 'Prisoners of wishes locked their eyes / In the jails and studies of his keyless smiles'. One can only go metaphorically blind, through physical and mental limitation, if one is already the prisoner of unacted desires through the influence of the saviour's false, thin-lipped and unnervingly mysterious pretence of benevolence. But the saviour fades into the background as gradually the poem comes to concentrate on 'only yourself and myself', who are able to 'arouse' the 'Unclenched, armless, silk and rough love that breaks all rocks'. Among other things, this love successfully overcomes all barriers, especially those imposed by the saviour.

Yet as we noted earlier, in practice Thomas is just as liable as Blake occasionally to make his contrary principles seem to merge. The most memorable example of this is to be found in 'Fern Hill', where the dimly personified figure of 'Time' is responsible both for innocent joy and for death. In his youth, 'Time let [him] play and be', and 'it was all / Shining, it was Adam and maiden'. He had no thought for the coming loss of innocence: 'Nothing I cared in the lamb white days, that time would take me'. Yet in the end he would 'wake to the farm forever fled from the childless land'. The conclusion attempts to resolve the paradox: 'Time held me green and dying / Though I sang in my chains like the sea.' Time is the principle behind the singing and the principle of the ambiguous limitations which permit definite expression. Time is also the principle of death. More subtly, Thomas's work includes the notion of a force which may seem destructive and threatening to innocence but which is ultimately a principle of growth and escape from limitations. This force is given succinct expression in the figure of the Thief from 'In Country Sleep'. James J. Balakier describes the thief as stealing the child's 'old limited image of herself so that she can be liberated from captivity to dualities'.[37] John

Goodby understandably identifies this as 'a Blakeian figure paradoxically beneficial to the child'.[38]

For Yeats, Auden and Thomas Blake is a kind of sage who, more than his Romantic contemporaries, is able to speak essential truths to the modern world. Important for all of them are his suspicion of the Enlightenment and rationalism, his sense of the power of desire and of unconscious mental processes, and his attempts to overcome the dualism of body and mind. Blake's own conviction that such a point of view would need to contend rebelliously with the pretensions and power-lust of 'Reason' led him to conceive rebellion itself as a contrary principle and often to personify it. This is also an influential move, which finds its successors in the various 'antithetical' aspects of the work of these poets. But as with their master, 'oppositional' identity may merge easily with that which it opposes: the energy of the rebel may ultimately derive from the same source as that of the tyrant.

5

Blake and Joyce

So true is it that the nineteenth century is an age both of realism and romance – of realist novels and romantic poems, for instance – that sometimes moderns are inclined to forget the unstable effects this collocation could bring about: inclined to forget, also, that when moderns came to react against the nineteenth century, nevertheless both partners in this strange couple could continue to have effects. This is true, for instance, of Ezra Pound, whose hunt for accuracy and precision can be linked backwards to the realist tendency in nineteenth-century sensibility, but whose early immersion in medieval Provençal literature fostered a lifelong admiration for romance. This issued not only in such works as *The Spirit of Romance*, but also encouraged the persistence in his poetry of elements we would now call 'Romantic', or possibly 'late Romantic'. Thus, as late as the final *Cantos*, one may encounter a lyric plangency – and, indeed, a use of slightly archaic English – which makes one think back to the poetry Pound was reading in his formative years.

Similar considerations have to be borne in mind in the case of Joyce. Modern readers are more than ready to remember that the example of an 'epiphany' used by Stephen in the famous passage from *Stephen Hero* is the clock of the Ballast Office.[1] But the other side of this coin is to be found in the assertion that, by an epiphany, Stephen meant 'a hidden spiritual manifestation'. It is true that this might be found in 'vulgarity of speech or of gesture', but this and the Ballast Office are meant to suggest what is so often conceived as contrariety, but which in Joyce's estimation can be unified. The smell of 'horse piss and hotted straw' may contribute to an aesthetic effect, as we discover in the second section of *Portrait*. But it is equally instructive to recall the girl on the beach at the end of chapter 4: this 'mortal beauty' which makes Stephen self-contradictorily cry 'Heavenly God!' in 'an outburst of profane joy', this 'angel of mortal youth and beauty', constitutes a self-reflexive epiphany. For the epiphany itself is an angel of 'mortal beauty'. Such a conception may look forward to the more radical modernism of *Ulysses*, and it is probably also true that the aesthetic implications of *Ulysses* are subtly different: purged of this rarefied shadow of Romantic transcendentalism. Yet *Portrait* is radical enough, with its starkly juxtaposed episodes and chapters; and it cannot be dissociated from the aesthetic theories which are expounded by Stephen at the end. It is true that he does not mention epiphanies there. But it is surely unarguable that in fact *Portrait* is truer to the aesthetic of *The Book of Epiphanies* (which is excerpted in it) than is *Stephen Hero* itself. The formula for *claritas*, 'that supreme quality of beauty, the clear radiance of the esthetic image', is close enough to the formula for an epiphany.

And while the idea may look forward, it also looks back: in 'Drama and Life', the essay Joyce read in 1900 to the Literary and Historical Society at University College, we find a forecast of his future development framed in terms of an opposition between 'romance' and the 'commonplace'. He develops these ideas out of observations upon modern existence:

> Epic savagery is rendered impossible by vigilant policing, chivalry has been killed by the fashion oracles of the boulevards. There is no clank of mail, no halo of gallantry, no hat-sweeping, no roystering! The traditions of romance are upheld only in Bohemia. Still I think out of the dreary sameness of existence, a measure of dramatic life may be drawn. Even the most commonplace, the deadest among the living, may play a part in a great drama.[2]

They may play a part in a drama, and one may at least infer that they may supply the absence of romance, the term with which this train of thought begins, even if they cannot constitute it. The phrase, about the 'deadest among the living' reminds one of Ibsen and partly as a consequence makes one think also of 'The Dead'. But, of course, a story in *The Dubliners* ending with the disturbing but lyrically evocative image of the snow cannot be separated from the aesthetic of epiphany.

A similar structure is to be found in *Chamber Music*. In XII, the speaker asks what 'counsel' the moon has given his love. But he dismisses the moon as a 'sage that is but kith and kin / With the comedian Capuchin'. The moon, in its counsel, is a sort of jolly friar. But below this assertion lies the thought that it is even more empty than this. Instead, the speaker counsels his love:

> Believe me rather, that am wise
> In disregard of the divine,
> A glory kindles in those eyes
> Trembles to starlight[3]

The 'glory', a synonym for halo, represents not the divine, but at least a replacement for it.

None of this is to say that Joyce can be characterised by a taste for the transcendent dream. As Ellmann says, 'the daughters of memory, whom William Blake chased from his door, received regular employment from Joyce, although he speaks of them disrespectfully'.[4] Rather, the point is to advert to a certain tension in Joyce's aesthetic: a tension he sought to resolve, but which leaves its mark on his formulations and preoccupations. With this point in mind, one may interpret aright the celebrated remarks about 'the classical and romantic schools' with which the 1902 lecture on Mangan begins. It is true, of course, that Joyce says the highest praise must 'be withheld from the romantic school', though it is also true that he concedes that 'the most enlightened of Western poets' must 'thereby be passed over' (*OCPW*, 53) – and that this pre-eminent poet, according to Stanislaus, was Blake.[5]

More demonstrable from the lecture itself is a tentativeness and cautious even-handedness in the handling of these distinctions, a sense that they are complex phenomena, that they may understandably touch at the extremes, and that the classical, as well as the romantic, may be bedeviled by inherent dangers. Thus, each school may be 'advancing to the borders of the other'; and, while romanticism may fight 'to preserve coherence', classicism has to fight against 'the materialism which attends it' (*OCPW*, 53). Furthermore, in partial mitigation of the case against it, Joyce avers that 'the romantic school is often and grievously misinterpreted [...] for that impatient temper which, as it could see no fit abode here for its ideals, chose to behold them under insensible figures'. Joyce, then, proffers and solicits understanding of the 'impatient temper'. What he prefers, however, as nobody has failed to note, is a 'method which bends upon [...] present things and so works upon them and fashions them that the quick intelligence may go beyond them to their meaning, which is still unuttered'. To leave the meaning 'unuttered' in this way sounds like the aesthetic of epiphany: a radiant manifestation untrammeled by discursiveness. Furthermore, it is not, in Joyce's terminology, a 'materialist' method. Classical art has at least as much in common with romanticism, as with materialism: a desire to 'go beyond'.

This complex tension is the source of the overarching title of the 1912 Trieste lectures on Defoe and Blake, 'Realism and Idealism in English Literature' (*OCPW*, 163–82). The discussion of Defoe is well remembered by students both of Defoe and of Joyce, especially, perhaps, its concluding paragraph:

> Saint John the Evangelist saw on the island of Patmos the apocalyptic collapse of the universe and the raising up of the walls of the eternal city splendid with beryl and emerald, onyx and jasper, sapphires and rubies. Crusoe saw but one marvel in all the fertile creation that surrounded him, a naked footprint in the virgin sand: and who knows if the latter does not matter more than the former? (*OCPW*, 174–75)

While the point is posed in the interrogative, and it is clear that Joyce's mind constantly revolves this kind of alternative, it remains the fact that the startling observation embodied in Defoe's description of the footprint is indeed an inspiration to Joyce's writing and has nothing in common with Blake's most characteristic modes.

Yet there are some curious facts to remember, for the discussion of Defoe is not entirely conveyed in straightforward critical terms. There is a strong admixture of thinking about the contrasting possibilities of the Anglo-Saxon and the Celt. It is most memorably epitomised in a story Joyce recounts which in his handling becomes almost a racial allegory:

> This story, which must have been the result of a sojourn in Scottish Highlands or islands where, as is well-known, telepathy is

in the air, marks the limits of Defoe's method in these impersonal writings. Seated at the bedside of a boy visionary, gazing at his raised eyelids, listening to his breathing, examining the position of his head, noting his fresh complexion, Defoe is the realist in the presence of the unknown; it is the experience of the man who struggles and conquers in the presence of a dream which he fears may fool him; he is, finally, the Anglo-Saxon in the presence of the Celt. (*OCPW*, 171)

If Joyce is sufficiently convinced by these terms to use them in his argument, then he must also have been sufficiently convinced to think they might, in some fashion, apply to himself. In which case, as a Celt, he would appear to be a native dreamer. Certainly, the faculty of second sight, to which this passage alludes, was common to Gaelic Ireland as well as Scotland. One of the best-known literary representations of it is to be found in Synge's *Riders to the Sea*, which Joyce, while he professed objections to it on the grounds of its being insufficiently Aristotelian, knew well enough to have learnt some passages by heart as soon as he had read the manuscript.[6] But for Joyce, 'All the Anglo-Saxon soul is in Crusoe: virile independence, unthinking cruelty, persistence, slow yet effective intelligence, sexual apathy, practical and well-balanced religiosity, calculating dourness' (*OCPW*, 174).

These do not sound like entirely attractive traits. Indeed, they sound like some of the more lurid descriptions of the gloomy Saxon peasant to be found in Celtic nationalist propaganda, and they find more refined echoes in Arnold ('the prosaic practical Saxon') and in Yeats. On the other hand, Joyce assumes that in Defoe there is 'no lyricism, nor art for art's sake, nor social sentiment' (*OCPW*, 170). Granted that Joyce, in this period, is not strong in social sentiment, nevertheless, who would care to claim that there was 'no lyricism, nor art for art's sake' in his work? 'Art for art's sake' is not too rarefied a notion at least to associate with Stephen's aesthetic theories.

But if the attitude to Defoe is complex, so is that to Blake. In the first remaining paragraph of the incomplete manuscript one becomes convinced that these two writers are indeed to be seen as opposites. Where Defoe saw so clearly the irreducible and luminous facticity of the footprints on the beach, Blake's myriad visions' in the end 'blinded his vision'. A rather less negative judgement has it that Blake 'killed the dragon of natural experience and natural vision. By annihilating space and time and denying the existence of memory and the senses, he wanted to paint his work upon the void of the divine bosom' (*OCPW*, 181). Still, this would hardly be Joyce's prescription for the best art. However, Blake's propensity for going beyond the senses is qualified in a way that secures Joyce's admiration. Blake was unique among 'mystic' writers' because he combined 'intellectual sharpness with mystic sentiment' (*OCPW*, 180). St John of the Cross, by contrast, 'reveals neither an innate sense of form nor the coordinating force of intellect'. The implication is unavoidable that Blake possessed both. They are polarities which Joyce sees in classical art and wishes to foster in his own.

In relation to the point about form, it is significant that Joyce has Stephen, in the final chapters of *Portrait*, expounding his concept of *integritas* in unambiguously Blakean terms. The first phase of *integritas*, 'apprehension', is 'a bounding line drawn about the object to be apprehended'.[7] Blake had said 'the great and golden rule of art, as well as of life, is this: – that the more distinct, sharp, and wiry the bounding line, the more perfect the work of art' (*E*, 550). Gleckner claims that Stephen's development of the idea in terms of 'universal beauty' is 'quite foreign to Blake's aesthetics'.[8] This is an entirely unwarranted claim: Blake's later thought, to which the formulation of the 'bounding line' belongs, is steeped in the Platonic language of 'Forms Eternal'. Indeed, Joyce was well aware of this fact, as our account will suggest, and implicitly it is a factor in his developed rejection of Blake's 'idealism' in *Ulysses*.

There is a further point. The concluding pages of the manuscript of the 'Realism and Idealism' lecture are missing, but it ends with the words: 'And although [Blake] based his art upon such idealistic premises, in the conviction that eternity was in love with the products of time the sons of God of the Daughters of' (end of the manuscript). The point resides principally in that 'although': the concessive clause about Blake's thinking that eternity was in love with the products of time. The main clause would thus have admitted that Blake was able convincingly to register some aspect of 'the productivity of time', of nature.

Blake's 'idealist' temper aligns him with the Celtic, as Defoe's materialist one makes him Anglo-Saxon. This may seem unlikely, but one needs to hold firmly in one's mind the fact that Joyce's Blake is the

Blake to be found in Edwin J. Ellis's *The Real Blake*. We now know just how unreliable and adorned with the apocryphal this biography was. But Blake scholarship was in its infancy; and Ellis would have enjoyed the esteem of association with Yeats, with whom he collaborated in editing the great, three-volume *The Works of William Blake, Poetic, Symbolic, Critical* (1893). In any case, Robert F. Gleckner long ago proved beyond a doubt that Ellis's *Real Blake* was the source for many descriptions and formulations to be found in the Blake lecture.[9] In Ellis we discover that Blake's father was in reality a James O'Neil of Galway who had changed his name to Blake (itself, as a matter of fact, a common name in Galway) before coming to London. On these grounds Ellis informs us that 'Blake was, in blood and spirit, an Irish chieftain' whose Elizabethan ancestor was none other than the great 'John O'Neil'. Partial corroboration of this story, as it might seem to Joyce, was the inclusion of the Blakes alongside the Joyces in the list of the 14 tribes of Galway to which he refers in 'The City of the Tribes' (*OCPW*, 198 and endnote 10).

Thus it can be seen that, in his lectures on Defoe and Blake, Joyce is not setting up an opposition in which Defoe is the positive and Blake the negative. Rather, he is striving for a compromise which corresponds to his conception of classical art – a conception to which Defoe does not entirely belong, even though he undoubtedly approximates it. This compromise is a reconciliation of the best Anglo-Saxon and Celtic qualities, combining the descriptive cogency of the one and the intellectually coherent 'going beyond' of the other.

The high praise given to Blake in the critical works accords with what is reported of Joyce's preferences by those who knew him. Thus, C. P. Curran recalls that when he was a student, his interest lay in Yeats and Blake and in the French symbolists.[10] While Stanislaus Joyce reports that in his youth, Joyce's 'gods were Blake and Dante'.[11] There is some uncertainty as to the edition in which he encountered Blake. Curran asserts that Joyce read Blake's 'closely in the Ellis–Yeats edition' to which we have already referred; but Stanislaus refers singly to 'Yeats's edition of Blake's poems'.[12] This leaves it uncertain whether he is referring to the Ellis–Yeats or to Yeats's popular and well-known Muses' Library edition *The Poems of William Blake*, also of 1893. Gleckner is inclined to the latter and offers cogent textual evidence: in his Trieste lecture on Blake, Joyce quotes six lines from 'Auguries of Innocence' but identifies them as coming from the 'Proverbs of Hell'.

In his Muses' Library edition, Yeats prints the lines on 'To see a World in a Grain of Sand' under the title 'Auguries of Innocence', but the whole of the rest of the poem under the title 'Proverbs'.[13] Gleckner also notes that Joyce might well have read Yeats's early essays on Blake, 'William Blake and the Imagination' and 'William Blake and his Illustrations to the Divine Comedy', published in 1903 in *Ideas of Good and Evil*, and long known to later twentieth-century readers from the compilation *Essays and Introductions*. Joyce might well have read these in their original printing in *The Savoy* of July, August and September 1896. Gleckner points out that they contain, among other things, Blake's assertion in *A Vision of the Last Judgement* about poetry not admitting 'a letter that is insignificant', the proverbs about 'the road of excess' and bringing out 'number, weight and measure in a year of dearth', the passage from Milton about 'a pulsation of the artery' and the 'globule of man's blood', and the distinction between vision and imagination on the one hand and fable and allegory (which are formed by 'the daughters of memory') on the other.[14] As Gleckner reminds us, these are all materials that Joyce uses very early on in his career. Gleckner's discussion is systematic and careful, and perhaps for this very reason he does not mention the obvious possibility that Curran might be correct in reporting that Joyce read Blake 'closely in the Ellis–Yeats edition' even if the only one he possessed and made easy reference to was the cheaper *Blake* of Muses' Library. Joyce's knowledge of Blake's system was extremely good, and it would certainly have assisted him to have read the full and voluminously annotated Ellis–Yeats, even if some of its judgements are eccentric.

Gleckner goes on to draw some useful conclusions about early Joyce: that he had 'a particular interest in *The Marriage of Heaven and Hell*, especially the proverbs, and in two other Blakean ideas: (1) the poet's annihilation of time, and (2) the imaginative realities that are the "eternal attributes" of man and god, and that are perceivable only by the true poet'.[15] Gleckner's points out that 'both of these are supported by Joyce's adoption of Blake's distinction between imagination and fable or allegory, the former produced by the daughters of inspiration, the latter by the daughters of memory – Joyce adjusting the distinction to his own interest of opposing history and poetry'.[16] This seems to me to be an illuminating summary.

There are some other points to be made, though, and they are more in the nature of literary history. The conclusion that Joyce's Blake is mediated via Ellis and Yeats is uncontroversial. And in this pair, the most significant figure is Yeats himself. There are conclusions to be drawn from this. First, that a Yeatsian Blake vaguely, but unmistakably, reinforces the idea that Blake was Celtic in temperament. Second, it reminds us, yet again, that Blake was accepted into an environment where he was seen as congenial to a symbolist aesthetic: Joyce, we are told, read Yeats and the French symbolists; and the only reference to Blake in *Stephen Hero* refers to Stephen having read 'Blake and Rimbaud on the values of letters' (presumably a reference to the remark from *A Vision of Judgement*, already quoted). Third, we are reminded yet again of the importance of *The Marriage of Heaven and Hell* in the early modernist period. From one point of view, this accords with a certain symbolist immoralism, but from another point of view it predicts the iconoclasm and rebelliousness of the early twentieth century. Finally, looking beyond the case of Joyce alone, it is worth noticing how strongly the reception of Blake is associated with the mediation of Yeats. This is a point which bears special relevance to the case of Eliot.

The imprint of Blake on Joyce's major works is often signalled by fleeting phrases and can be hard to assess. It has been mediated through the consciousness and concerns of a writer with his own agenda. The idea of a rebellion against fraudulent authorities and powers is supported by Blake's *Marriage* and, as Ellmann suggests, is probably an influence on the early *Portrait* essay in its avowed ambition to 'recount the children of the spirit [...] against fraud and principality'.[17] Clearly, in this general sense, it is also an influence on *Stephen Hero* and *A Portrait*. It is hard to see much more than this in *Stephen Hero*. And when one turns to *A Portrait*, it is tempting to take things at face value and note that the more prominent Romantic poets in that work are Byron and Shelley. However, it is particularly important when noting this fact to pay heed to what Stanislaus Joyce says about how his brother passed in his youth from an admiration of Byron to Shelley and thence to Blake.[18] This means that we are entitled to regard the references to Byron and Shelley as securely in the range of things that characterise the artist as a young man whose ideas have not yet come to maturation. It is Blake's very status as the supreme Romantic poet which makes it undesirable for him to be mentioned in the company of the young Stephen's ideas. When one looks at the characteristics of *A Portrait* it is, as I have clearly suggested, at least possible to say that its aesthetic is comparable with Blake's, at least as Joyce conceived the matter. But it is possible to go further than that. The idea of depicting a 'young man' would evoke *Songs of Innocence* for a Blakean such as Joyce, especially when one bears in mind Blake's own propensity to let innocents speak in their own phrases, even to the extent of conveying a lisp: compare Blake's 'Chimney Sweeper' in *Experience*, unable to say 'sweep' but only 'weep' with Joyce's 'the green wothe botheth'. Second, the *Songs* offer a contrast of two opposing states of mind as conveyed in the moods and thoughts of the speakers, and there is some use of paradisal imagery in relation to Innocence, and infernal in relation to Experience (Heaven and Hell, again). The contrast between the more radiant epiphanies of *A Portrait* and some of its passages of fear and self-disgust (the sermon must be remembered in this context) is suggestive of a possible relationship. Finally in Blake's *Songs*, neither innocence nor experience has wisdom, but there is some reason to suppose that Blake was thinking of a 'progression' beyond these contraries (as he says in *The Marriage of Heaven and Hell*, 'without contraries is no progression'). The pattern of descent and ascent in *A Portrait* followed by a flight upwards into something which remains beyond the final page of the book is reminiscent of *Songs*.

Perhaps the chapter of *Ulysses* in which an idea of Blake is put to most extended work is *Proteus*. It will be recalled that this is the chapter in which there is an early reference to *Los Demiurgos*, Blake's invented character Los, who represents both Poetic inspiration and Time. Because of this dual aspect, his relationship with poetry comprises a sense of labour on definite poetic materials and not merely ineffable creativity. For the same reason, he is a *demiurge*, a creator active in the world of time, and not a transcendent figure.

The chapter begins with the famous line 'Ineluctable modality of the visible' but immediately continues into a phrase comprising an important indirect quotation from Blake: 'at least that if no more, thought through my eyes'.[19] This is a reference to Blake's celebrated couplet, 'We are led to believe a lie / When we see with not through the eye.' The first part of the sentence, then, refers to the fact that the visual world is always seen under modes: always constructed. The second part develops this idea in the direction of the subjective, an aspect of what Joyce called Blake's 'idealism'. We construct the world in accordance with subjective presuppositions. *Ulysses* will reveal that this is an inadequate formulation: the modalities under which the world appears in *Ulysses* are literary and cultural. To put it another way, we cannot see the world nor tell a story about it except through forms, which may include expressionist theatre, newspaper articles, romantic fiction or, indeed, moving-picture *actualités*. The modality is cultural and social: this is not a perception yet available to the still lost Stephen. Proteus revolves around the question of the relationship between an isolated subjectivity and the world.

At one point, Stephen closes his eyes and listens to his boots as he walks along Sandymount Strand. He conceptualises himself as walking through time and space, 'A very short space of time through very short times of space'. It is at this point that he evokes the name Los. In shutting his eyes, he might be said to approach more nearly Blake's concept of the Imagination – or whatever it is within the mind that makes seeing 'through' the eye better than merely seeing 'with' it. For this reason, it is important to remember that, although Los is a maker in time, his efforts should end by returning us to Eternity or Eden, not least because 'Eternity is in love with the productions of time', and his temporal labours are motivated by the vision of Eternity: as Blake says, he 'kept the divine vision in time of trouble'. But by shutting his eyes, Stephen toys with the idea that one can live in the eternal vision in this life without paying attention to its facticity: one can live as his Blake without having any of his Defoe. This is a possibility also alluded to by the phrase 'Put me on to Edenville.' But significantly, this phrase is prefaced by 'Gaze in your omphalos.' To return to Eden would be like a return to the time before birth; by the same token it would also be a self-enclosed and solipsistic experience. This is a possibility for any who take Blake's 'idealism' too far: to return to what Joyce said in the Trieste lecture, 'The myriad visions blinded his vision' (*OCPW*, 175).

The same train of thought is pursued through a different allusion in the opening paragraphs of 'Proteus', and it is worth examining because its source is so closely connected with Blake. The second sentence begins with 'Signatures of all things I am here to read', a reference to the *De signatura rerum* of Jakob Boehme, the mystical theologian and philosophical alchemist to whom Blake refers, approvingly, as 'Behmen' in *The Marriage of Heaven and Hell*: Joyce also refers to 'Behmen', in his Trieste lecture (*OCPW*, 180) as an influence on Blake. The signatures of all things are readable, of course, but for

Behmen what they reveal is the divine origin of things. As Enrico Terrinoni points out, this conception has to be understood in the light of Boehme's larger plan, which is strongly reminiscent of Blake's. Terrinoni refers to the title page of *De signatura rerum*, which asserts that the book shows how everything 'proceeds out of / Eternity into Time, and again out of Time into / Eternity'.[20] Whether with Blake or with Boehme in mind, Joyce is captivated by the ardour which would transform the given, but wants an art, as he implies at the end of the Trieste lecture, which is in love with the productions of time. He therefore wishes to stay firmly at one end of the Blakean and Behmenist cycle: to do otherwise is to be 'blinded'. In 'Proteus', while Stephen accepts that the visible is only apprehended under modalities, he has yet to learn that he must take a further step beyond Romantic idealism to an understanding that experience is shaped by social rather than individual forms. This is not only the meaning of the radical formal experiments of *Ullysses*, especially in its later pages, but is particularly implied in another large-scale allusion to Blake which is to be found in the 'Nighttown' episode.

The incident in which Stephen is assaulted by Private Carr is, as Morton Paley has shown, undoubtedly based on the one in Blake's life where he ejected a soldier from his garden in Felpham.[21] Carr is incensed when he thinks that Stephen has insulted his king; the soldier in Blake's garden claimed that Blake had insulted the king. However, the contrasts are as significant as the similarities. Blake succeeded in ejecting his soldier, but was ultimately put on trial for sedition. Stephen, however, was punched in the face and knocked down by Carr, only to be spirited away by Bloom, who adopts a paternal attitude to him, part of the motivation for which is underlined by the appearance of his dead son Rudy at the end of the Circe section. This is a crucial event in underlining the humane education that Stephen and Joyce's readers are being asked to undergo. (One should perhaps avoid the word humanist.) These implications of the event have little to do with Blake 'the idealist', then, and if anything tend in the opposite direction. Nevertheless, one should be wary of treating this episode, as Gleckner does, as if it is essentially an inversion of Blakean ideas. Stephen's attitude to Carr, his undoubtedly extremely witty ripostes, exhibit his superiority to his assailant, and his assailant merely underscores the point by attacking him. Such a victory is no more real than would have been the citizen's over

Bloom. Indeed, Stephen's true affinity is with a world far different from that of Nighttown. He slightly misquotes a couplet from Blake's 'Auguries of Innocence', substituting Ireland for England:

> The harlot's cry from street to street
> Shall weave old Ireland's winding street.

The sentiment confirms his superiority to mere 'corporeal' desire, to use a Blakean term, as his passivity in the face of Carr confirms his superiority to 'corporeal' warfare. 'But in here it is I must kill the priest and the king', he says, using the phrase Blake used for the malign powers of this world, and pointing to his forehead. The point is not so much anti-Blakean, then, as formed out of a dialogue with Blake: while Joyce has nothing to do in this episode with 'idealism', he replaces it not with what he calls 'materialism' but with the many-faceted competences and sensitivities of the humane mind inhabiting a material world.

It seems most tempting to find a strong parallel between Blake's prophetic books and Joyce's *Finnegans Wake*: an eccentrically innovative mythological work about the fall of a universal man, Blake's Albion, inhabitant of London, to be compared to Joyce's HCE, inhabitant of Dublin. And, indeed, it would seem perverse to suggest that Blake was not an influence on his conception, given the early influence on Joyce. The problems arise when one attempts to show how Blakean conceptions and symbols might be working in any detail in the work. Given the voluminousness of reference, as well as Joyce's reservations about Blake, as expressed in *Ulysses*, it seems, on the face of it, unlikely that *Finnegans Wake* could be Blakean in an extended and detailed fashion. Nor is it. Accounts of Blake's life and of his experiments with etching techniques are an influence on a depiction of Shem the Penman and of writing in general:

> He will be quite within the pale when with lordbeeron brow he vows him so tosset to be of the sir Blake tribes bleak while through life's unblest he rodes backs of bannars. Are you not somewhat bulgar with your bowels? Whatever do you mean with bleak? With pale blake I write tintingface. O, you do? And with steelwhite and blackmail I ha'scint for my sweet an anemone's letter with a gold of my bridest hair betied.[22]

Perhaps it is sufficient tribute to Blake to remark that it is hard to see how Joyce could have set off on the quest that led him to write *Finnegans Wake* without the early example of Blake. Joyce's indebtedness operates on more levels than that of most of Blake's disciples: symbolist suggestiveness; an interest in the constructedness of myth; a parallel interest in the deep roots of myth; and a sympathy with Blake's perceived oppositional stance.

6

'Deposits' and 'Rehearsals': Repetition and Redemption in *The Anathémata* of David Jones

A Comparison and Contrast with Blake

Blake and Repetition

Comparison is a dangerously seductive mode, and its seductions are perhaps most dangerous when they lead one to feel one is dealing with repetition. Yet, as with repetition, there has to be similitude as well as dissimilitude between the items compared for the word to mean anything in this fallen world. Blake has often, of course, been compared with Jones, who early became an admirer.[1] And there are sufficient similarities, at least when they are regarded in the light of my topic of repetition and redemption, for me to point to a useful contrast at the same time – one that I hope will make Jones's beliefs stand out more clearly. Most obviously, there is the topic of the fall and resurrection of Albion in Blake and the way in which 'All things Begin & End in Albions Ancient Druid Rocky Shore.' (*E*, 171) In other words, the large features of Blake's use of myth, and in particular his use of the Matter of Britain, yield a direct comparison with Jones: Jones's work privileges the Matter of Britain even more obviously, especially in its intersection with 'Romanitas'. For while it was providential that the witness of Christ could be spread through the medium of the Roman Empire, the Grail Legend (derived from the myth of the Cauldron of Plenty) fostered on its Celtic fringe is the nearest pagan approximation to the meaning of the Mass. Britain is thus the truest place of 'rehearsal', and in this belief lies a degree of similarity with Blake's myth of Albion.

But my only substantial ground of comparison here is the feature of repetition, since Blake is also one of the few poets to challenge comparison with Jones as a repeater, and since I believe that this particular topic is very illuminating for the understanding of the different attitudes to redemption of the two poets. Everyone is familiar with types of insistent verbal repetition in Blake's work, from 'Little Lamb who made thee / Dost thou know who made thee' (*E*, 8) to these lines from 'London' in *Songs of Experience*:

> In every cry of every Man,
> In every Infants cry of fear,
> In every voice: in every ban,
> The mind-forg'd manacles I hear.
>
> (*E*, 27)

There is also the biblical parallelism and repetition which Blake, like Smart, learnt to feel confident in valuing from reading Robert Lowth's *Lectures on the Sacred Poetry of the Hebrews*.[2]

There are larger effects of repetition, too. *Experience* is a kind of repetition of *Innocence*: the same phenomena seen through different eyes. (The smaller-scale repetitions within the two series of *Songs*, as in the lines quoted above, serve to tell us with great emphasis which state we are in.) And then there is Blake's practice as an engraver, which fed a fascination with the graphic possibilities of 'mechanical reproduction'.[3] There are many instances of the repetition of images in his art and of the issue of the same book in slightly different versions, with a different order of plates or different paint colour. There are also some interesting examples of the exploitation of the looking glass effect facilitated by the reversal of engraved images. To quote Walter Benjamin is not, I think, merely modish here. Benjamin's interest in the loss of aura in repetition does suggest a distant parallel with Blake's question whether repetition is dead (the re-cycling of past myths and influences) or can constitute the vision of 'Eternal' forms. But despite the historical anachronism (Benjamin was conscious of writing specifically about a later stage of capitalism) the parallel may not be quite as distant as it looks. His friendship with the Hebraist Gershom G. Scholem, author of *Major Trends in Jewish Mysticism*, is well documented and encouraged his interest in Kabbalah.[4] Benjamin's notion of the loss of aura is influenced by the

Lurianic Kabbalah.⁵ In this, the Tree of Life, with its seven manifest spheres (the Seven Days of the world of time) is deserted by the Godhead and left as mere external husk or bark. But this is also an idea which, from the same source, influenced Blake's conception of the Fall, especially in *The Marriage of Heaven and Hell*, where Reason is dismissed as 'the bound or outward circumference of Energy', and in *The Book of Urizen*, where the false god, Urizen, is separated from the other 'Eternals' and becomes a 'vacuum'.⁶

Blake's myths, as we have already hinted, are themselves self-conscious repetitions: the fears, for instance, of Urizen on hearing of the birth of the young revolutionary fire-principle, Orc, mirror those of Herod Antipas on hearing that the Messiah is to be born in Bethlehem, and those of Pharaoh confronted with Moses. But they also refer to Macbeth's desire to extinguish other claimants to the throne, and to the contention of Kronos and Zeus. Of course, it is easy to think one may assimilate such repetitions to a broad, Romantic, mythological syncretism which, while it may have a quasi-religious import, is not profoundly Christian: Nerval's *Chimères*, for instance, which conflates Old Testament figures with classical and Egyptian mythology – a self-conscious 'palimpsest' of myths, if ever there was one, to use a notion he himself invokes in *Angélique*.⁷ While one may nod to the Christian import of '*Christ aux Oliviers*', one may also ask whether Nerval is conscious enough of the Christian cost of redemption. One need not ask this in the case of Blake, who in his middle to late periods is a profoundly Christian thinker, albeit of an eccentric, and very definitely Protestant kind (and this point will be relevant to the later contrast with Jones). For Blake the crucial question concerns the unique moment of redemption and its character:

> Each Man is in his Spectre's power
> Until the arrival of that hour,
> When his Humanity awake
> And cast his Spectre into the Lake.
>
> (*E*, 184)

The Spectre is the unredeemed self: the Selfhood, as Blake often calls it. These words from *Jerusalem* (Plate 37) are printed in mirror-writing, suggesting both that Spectre and Humanity are opposites and that the Spectre cannot understand the gospel of redemption, partly because he repeats it the wrong way round, so to speak. We have to repeat, of course; this is something we cannot avoid in the world of time. For that reason both *Innocence* and *Experience* are repetitive. But we must learn living rather than dead repetition. 'Humanity', in Blake's little rhyme, has learnt precisely that: 'Humanity' is redeemed. Albion fallen and Albion risen, Job dejected and Job renewed, are Spectre and Humanity respectively. The point most pertinent to our theme here is the similarity in appearance of Job before and after his redemption, as they are depicted in Blake's *Illustrations of The Book of Job* (Plates I and XXI). The latter state looks almost like a repetition of the former. And here, along with Lorraine Clark in her *Blake, Kierkegaard, and the Spectre of Dialectic*, one may seek illumination from Kierkegaard: those who have cast off the Spectre of what Blake calls 'abstraction' are, in Kierkegaard's phrase, 'the same and yet not the same [...] the whole of existence begins afresh, not through an imminent continuity with the foregoing [...] but by a transcendent fact which separates the repetition from the first existence by such a cleft that it is only a figure of speech to say that the foregoing states are related to one another'.[8] The repetition that is redemption in Kierkegaard is a complete rupture: the appearance of being 'the same' may look 'uncanny', but only because the unredeemed self is a spectre, that is, a ghost.

Jones and Repetition

How different it is, in many ways, with David Jones. Where Kierkegaard says 'not through 'continuity', Jones speaks of 'continuings', and these 'continuings' are substantial and essentially connected. In the first instance, I shall merely rehearse the familiar. Jones's 'deposits' go all the way down through strata at the bottom of which is 'before all time', and in some sense the 'New Light' of Redemption beams for the existence of the 'fore-time':

> From before all time
>   the New Light beams for them
> and with eternal clarities
> *infulsit* and athwart
>
> the fore-times:
> era, period, epoch, hemera. Through all orogeny:
>   group, system, series, zone.

> Brighting at the five life-layers
>   species, sub-species, genera, families, order.
> [...]
>
> Lighting the Cretaceous and the Trias, for Tyrannosaurus must
> somehow lie down with herbivores, or, the poet lied, which is
> not allowed.[9]

Read in its entirety, this passage suggests that Isaiah's prophecy
(Isaiah 11:6) is not only a vision of the future but an insight into the
heart of all existence: the wolf has always dwelt with the lamb. In
itself, this makes for a contrast with Blake, who wants to emphasise,
not least in the *Songs*, with their opposed 'Lamb' and 'Tyger', that
they are often found apart: 'Opposition is True Friendship' *(The
Marriage of Heaven and Hell*, Plate 20, p. 42). If for Jones, as Saunders
Lewis says, 'The Mass concertinas all history', it does so by being
eager to embrace everything. And in *The Anathémata* it concertinas
prehistory, as well, not least human prehistory: 'Whose manhands
god-handled the Willendorf stone / before they unbound the last
glaciation' *(Ana*, 59).[10] These lines, on the prehistoric stone carving of
the Venus of Willendorf, are typically condensed in their resonances,
but their chief point is to symbolise an early 'rehearsal' of the Mass –
the god-handling of matter is itself a priestly task for a man, a man
who is already a type of Christ in the union of his man-hands and his
god-handling. Furthermore, the lines imply the identification of the
host with a goddess, making explicit Jones's sense of the complete
participation of the feminine in the divine, and this point at least
serves to emphasise Jones's inclusiveness. Now there are some
inhabitants of the past whose redemption has traditionally been
recognised: the Old Testament prophets and patriarchs. To say that
the Old Testament contains types of our redemption is in no way
whatsoever novel. But more to the point, the patriarchs and prophets
are traditionally not merely pre-figurings or pre-recognisers of
Christ's life and teaching but participate in his salvific mission and
thus are capable themselves of salvation. In *Inferno* IV, for instance,
Dante shows the Harrowing of Hell (a traditional belief which greatly
interested Jones). Christ comes to rescue from Limbo Abel, Noah,
Moses, David, Abraham, Israel and Rachel, *'e altri molti'* (line 61). But
the virtuous pagans have to remain where they are, for they were

unable to choose Christ even in the mediate form available to the patriarchs.

Leaving aside the question whether or not Dante's allegorical purpose may have been to show the limitations specifically of Humanism, it seems clear that the Upper Palaeolithic craftsman who formed the Venus of Willendorf could scarcely fare any better than Euclid in Dante's judgement. Jones's point, however, is to extend participation in Christ well beyond the charmed circle of the Old Testament. This is an important part of the implication of the following passage from 'An Introduction to *The Ancient Mariner*':

> By the time we come to the middle ages proper, the types and foreshadowings or however one cares to express it, were, at least for the great majority, drawn mainly from figures, signs, sacraments of the canonical books of the Old Testament [...] Yet we must not forget that not only did the stream of classical antiquity never dry up and that especially in the monastic houses the writings of the pre-Christian authors were conserved and transcribed.[11]

The point can be made even more clearly from the essay on 'The Dying Gaul'. This Gaul can be seen as prefiguring another dying Celt, King Arthur, who, like him, is expected to return. Another reawakening awaits Joyce's Finnegan, to whom Jones refers at the end of the essay by quoting the Dublin street-ballad from which Joyce took his title (*DG*, 58). But Jones, like Joyce, would have had in mind also the great Irish hero Finn Mac Cumhail, 'Finn Again', who returns through the agency of reincarnation.[12]

Significantly, for Jones the recuperative power of the Celts is entirely bound up with the sacramental office of art, which they embody, as he remarks, in the extraordinary institution of the bardic schools, thought to be a survival of Druidism, which staggered on even into the penal era in Ireland. As he says: 'Another essential institution that survived was that of the bardic academies whereby the collective memory of the community was safeguarded' (*DG*, 56). The 'extra-utile' – all making that is *poiesis*, that creatively adds spirit to matter – is sacramental and of our salvation, and thus, to cut a long story short, the story of the Gospels is apex and summary of all history, rather than a radical turning-point after which all has changed. Since it is in the nature of man to be craftsman and artist in the spirit of renewal, and thus to be a sacramental artist, the Mass is a repetition of that summary. And thus the story of Christ is written into the essential matter of all history and human prehistory.

For the sake of clarity, however, there seem to me two questions which need to be asked at this stage. One concerns the extra-utile and its precise character; the other is about the content Jones perceived in our redemption on Calvary.

The clearest exposition of the 'gratuitous' and the 'inutile' is to be found in the essay 'Use and Sign', where man is called 'not only the supreme utilist but the only extra-utilist or sacramentalist'. Immediate illustration is provided:

> The 'legion's ordered line', a thing of total practicality and devastating utility, ordained towards an end as obvious as are the tactics or any beast of prey, confronts us in history along with the ordered line of the hexameter, a thing wholly extra-utile and explicable only as a sign. (*DG*, 178)

Man is master of both utile and extra-utile, but the latter is the *differentia specifica*. And the extra-utile is a sign of something other: something that we add to the material world. In virtue of doing this, Jones would argue, we reveal that the transcendent is implied in man's creativity.

And now to my second question: what, in Jones's view, happened on Calvary? The question suggests itself because, if the Cross is seen as a summary of all history, rather than as a radical turning-point, we may hanker for more precise information about the nature of what did occur on it. And here Jones's answers do not seem to me to add much to what he asserts elsewhere about the sign. Thus in 'Art and Sacrament' we are told that Calvary itself, and not just the Last Supper, involves *poiesis*:

> For what was accomplished on the Tree of the Cross presupposes the sign-world and looks back to foreshadowing rites and arts of mediation and conjugation stretching back for tens of thousands of years in actual pre-history.[13]

But of sin and atonement nothing is said. Adam's sin appears (in the same paragraph) only as the 'truly necessary sin of Adam'. Subsequently, in the same essay, we are told (1) that the Last Supper was enacted in relationship to Calvary and (2) that the former must be 'repeated', as Jones puts it (*E&A*, 168). But we have already been told that Calvary, albeit in a qualified sense, is a repetition of earlier rites and foreshadowings. What we have, then, is the repetition of a sign of something other, while the doctrine of our redemption is evacuated of much of its orthodox content. So while there is no doubt but that Jones says that Calvary is the one event in history, we can interpret this, without violence to the language, as meaning that there are many repeated Calvaries and that other events are of little significance.

This analysis can be indirectly supported by a consideration of Jones's treatment of a powerful image of human redemption: Coleridge's *Rime of the Ancient Mariner.* The Mariner's blessing of the water snakes is a moment of radical redemption. Before he is able to do this he is sunk in hardness of heart.

Afterwards, he can at last pray, and the albatross falls from his neck in a powerful reminiscence of the burden falling from Christian's back in *The Pilgrim's Progress.* This is not redemption as 'continuing', but a Pauline and Protestant rupture with the past. When the Mariner later repeats his tale, he is not repeating his selfish past, but the story of his redemption from it: a story of radical change in the self. He is 'the same and yet not the same', like Blake's Job. Yet Jones, contrary to the Protestant spirit of Blake, chooses, in his illustrations to *The Ancient Marine,* not to represent the blessing of the water snakes.[14] Redemption as a radical break with the past does not commend itself to his imagination; and this fact is of a piece with his stress, elsewhere, on continuity. Blake's is a characteristically Protestant emphasis; Jones's, while it may not bear all the marks of Catholic orthodoxy, seems to me to be possible to maintain within the Catholic tradition in a way that it is not within the Protestant. Jones's, then, is a world of repetition of the same. 'Rehearsal' is both retrospective and proleptic, and that is the beauty of the word for him. 'The Wise Man said: "there is no new thing under the sun." ' (*E&A*, 99). It is in the light of this emphasis that one must read '*IT WAS A DARK AND STORMY NIGHT*' (*Ana*, 45). There is one tale and we always tell it and are always in it.

Jones and the New

So far, so relatively simple. Yet, as readers will have noticed, I quoted Jones out of context in referring to 'no new thing under the sun'. For he goes on to say, 'but the arts do at certain moments uncover relationships hidden since the foundation of the world' (*E&A*, 99). First, let us be clear what Jones is not saying. He is not saying that there *is* a new thing under the sun, but rather that *old* things – old 'relationships' – may be 'uncovered' by the artist for the first time. 'Relationships' is an important word here, for it seems to me to chime with the word 'juxtapositions' in an adjacent sentence: 'new juxtapositions of beauty' (*E&A*, 99). The artist's re-arrangements of material reveal previously unseen arrangements of events. This is repetition as 're-presenting' (*E&A*, 155). One may be reminded of Eliot's account of the genesis of new poetry in 'Tradition and the Individual Talent'; and there seems to me to be limited analogies with neo-classical theories of imitation and representation of the past within later artistic techniques.

It would perhaps be going too far to say that the adoption of modern forms seemed to Jones a sufficient condition for new perception, but I believe he thought it a necessary one: the 'breakdowns and fusions' which bring 'a new and unexpected life' are breakdowns and fusions of pre-existing artistic forms, brought thereby into new and previously unknown combinations, which themselves 'constitute a new sign' (*E&A*, 102). But 'breakdown' and 'fusion' are words that indicate resistance: the resistance of reality, which may submit to being seen in a new light, but never to being altered. So while on the one hand myth and legend may embody 'truths more real than historic facts' (as with Geoffrey of Monmouth), on the other hand Jones would have no truck with self-gratificatory fantasy. More important still, the material is resistant to facile synthesis. The very word 'anathémata' is glossed as 'The Profane things that somehow are redeemed' (*Ana*, 28–29). That 'somehow' contains the idea of difficulty. This is one reason for the prevalence of the *question* in *Anathemata*: it is not only, or even usually, a rhetorical question. On the contrary, it emanates from one profound dubiety: if we are to add our extra-utile signing to the otherness of the world, this will be a difficult labour not only for technique, but also for faith. Furthermore, in order to reveal the profanity which has to be redeemed, Jones's questions must express the incredulity not just of the doubter, but more particularly of the believer.

'Breakdowns' and 'fusions' go very deep in Jones's technique – as far as the handling of words, and even parts of words, in individual lines, where polyglossal juxtaposition and pointed etymology also constitute an incisive analysis and re-ordering. And 'incisive' seems an apt word: Jones's poetry is a sharp digging into layers of history, a sorting, and a re-assembling. If sacrifice there be in this, it is the artist's: it is the artist in humanity who both truly repeats and redeems. If Jones's concept of repetition makes him look like Eliot, his view of the artist is more akin to Blake's.

7
Blake, Postmodernity and Postmodernism

Romanticism and postmodernism

The question of Blake and postmodernism may usefully be considered as part of the broader question of Romanticism and postmodernism, which is beginning to become a subject of intellectual debate. A traditional model of the relationship between past and present might be used to support the claim that just as modernism was indebted to Romanticism, so postmodernism is indebted to such features as Romantic irony, the cult of the rootlessly self-fashioning hero and possibly a certain valuing of the incomplete and fragmentary. There are also some more particular questions: the continuing fascination of the Gothic and the theory of Lyotard that both modernism and postmodernism are inheritors of the concept of the sublime (specifically the Kantian sublime), an idea with strong romantic connections.[1] All of these possibilities are addressed in my edited volume, *Romanticism and Postmodernism* (1997), which includes essays touching on Wordsworth, Coleridge and Gothic fiction. It also includes a theoretical essay by Paul Hamilton which traces the ancestry of postmodernist 'indeterminacy' back to the concept of the sublime: associating the poetics of the sublime with the fashion for pantheism, Hamilton notes that 'the monism resulting from pantheism, in which, since you cannot find God "outside" you must find him everywhere, has all sorts of other implications. Fundamentally, it makes all critique immanent. It leads to the equality of particulars'.[2]

Lyotard's thesis includes the influential notion that the postmodern 'would be that which, in the modern, puts forward the unpresentable in presentation itself; that which denies itself the solace of good forms'.[3] The idea of the 'unpresentable' is developed out of his discussion of the sublime, which, according to Lyotard, 'takes place [...] when the imagination fails to present an object which might, if only in principle, come to match a concept'.[4] The idea of the unpresentable clearly has the potential for flexible adaptation to all kinds of artistic experiment, though Lyotard makes the important qualification that modern and postmodern aesthetics take different approaches to it: modern aesthetics, unlike postmodern, remain 'nostalgic', longing for what is 'missing'.[5] What is missing is some totalising framework which traditionally would have been conceived in terms of what Lyotard calls a 'grand narrative'. For our purposes it is interesting to note that William H. Galperin, in *The Return of the Visible in British Romanticism* (1993), asserts the 'postmodernism' of Byron's *Childe Harold* in a manner which is indebted to Lyotard. Specifically, he finds Cantos I and II to be characterised by postmodernism because they show the visible world without assimilating it to an overarching narrative, even as they gesture towards narratives of various kinds.[6] In Canto IV, the narrator is seen as renouncing his appropriation of the visible at points where he is represented as feminised, and this too is seen by Galperin in terms of the category of postmodernism.[7]

Some (though not all) of these topics are of obvious potential relevance to Blake. For instance, it could be said that Blake's irony is far more destabilising than would be allowed by an interpretation that showed it as undermining false prospectuses of one kind or another. Thus, one may concede that there is undoubtedly a strategy in *Songs of Innocence and Experience* which leads us towards mutual ironising as constitutive of the relationship between the two 'contrary states': the reader perceives the limitations of each state and is led to ask how the qualities of each might be enhanced, and the limitations overcome, by their integration. But it is possible to suggest that this strategy is itself undermined by a combination of factors. The subtlety and far-reachingness of the irony, combined with the absence of a clear way out of the impasse of innocence and experience, and the way in which each contrary term actually contains hints of its supposed opposite could be claimed to demonstrate that this binary was in fact a way of representing an unstable politics of power in the self and in society: one that was too unstable, indeed, to be explained in terms of a political ideology. As we shall see, precisely this kind of point is made by Nicholas Williams, in his *Ideology and Utopia in the Poetry of William Blake* (1998), though he uses the example of *The Marriage of Heaven and Hell*.[8] It is worth noting that he also links the ideological indeterminacy of *The Marriage* to Lyotard's concept of the 'unpresentable'.[9]

But to return to Romanticism in general, it must always be remembered that we ourselves are to a significant degree constructing the 'Romanticism' to which we are supposedly to some degree indebted. This is a process which has been going on since the word 'Romanticism' was adapted in the 1840s to define a supposed movement, after most of those we now think of as the canonical Romantic poets were dead. In the so-called Romantic period it was Walter Scott, Samuel Rogers and Thomas Moore who dominated the poetic scene, as Byron recorded in his journals.[10] These writers were gradually replaced over the nineteenth century by the canon we have come to know in the twentieth century, a process involving, among other things, the further promotion of Wordsworth and Coleridge and the addition of Blake. When one analyses this in more detail, it appears that the canonisation of this group is in fact part of a wider tendency towards Modernism. Indeed, their canonisation is only part of the story, for there is also selection within their works, in such a way that the lyrical and the intense is valued over the discursive. Thus Frank Kermode, in his classic work *Romantic Image* (1957), can isolate a tradition of concentration on the image, of allowing its radiance or eloquence to do the work of the discursive. This clearly looks like a process which leads up to Modernism. Arguably, however, the thesis, though valid, is made to look more straightforward than it really is by an unwillingness to confront the complexity of the literary history of the large period it surveys. In this connection it seems worth noting that, in the contemporary, Blake has become one of the most approved artists from the past, and this too is something the postmodern appears to share with the modern. Blake was admired by Wilde, Yeats, Shaw, Auden and Huxley. He went on to be admired also by Dylan Thomas, Ginsberg, Ted Hughes, Geoffrey Hill and Angela Carter. One of the interesting questions about Blake and the canon is why he appears to be important to the process by which the modernists defined themselves and why, in the postmodern, he continues to be important, becoming one of the few sages to be largely immune from postmodernist habits of cynicism and debunking.

The postmodern also brings to the past a self-consciousness about reading and interpretation, about the inescapability of sign and convention, and about the inaccessibility of any truth beyond such signs, for which arguably there is no strong precedent in the Romantic period. However, the point about the inaccessibility of truth is that it bears on questions of historical truth, and this complicates the idea of constructing the past. For some postmodern thinkers, there is no truth or historical reality to construct, for the fact that one cannot get beyond the interpretative sign means that one cancels out the idea of objective truth in the equation: it simply has no function. A radical expression of this view is to be found in Ira Livingston's *Arrow of Chaos: Romanticism and Postmodernity* (1997), in which he characterises changes in historical views and historiography in relation to the image of a snake which represents the whole of history. In such changes, 'history *really* moves across its whole length at once or doesn't move at all', and he goes on, correctly, to point out that 'This is very different from weaker assertions that our perspective on the past and future change, or that we "reinterpret" events as we will come to be reinterpreted. These assertions are simply damage-control maneuvers to preserve the notion of an objective reality.'[11] Livingston's book is a significant contribution to the question of Romanticism and Postmodernity, but it has added relevance for our discussion since he attempts, as we shall see, to promote his thesis with some interesting discussions of Blake. As far as the general question about Romanticism and postmodernism is concerned, not surprisingly we find the whole snake (or perhaps just the snake from the Romantic period onwards) moving in a very postmodern kind of way. The cancelling out of objective reality is important, but even more significant is the accompanying assumption that chaos theory furnishes the postmodern with its chief intellectual paradigm. Fractal patterns iterate all the way down the snake of history. For that matter, the word 'pattern' is too univocal: we should think of 'patterns, tricks, episteme engines, ideologemes, programs, protocols, genes, dynamos, mantras, paradigms, metaphors, metonyms, symbols' and so on, and they are to be understood as shallow rather than 'deep' structures.[12] These 'tricks' or 'patterns' are structured around similarity and difference: 'things are always falling apart and together in the drift of the Arrow of Chaos'.[13] This, then, is the process that iterates all the way up and down history, and from the smallest to the largest cultural phenomena.

Blake and the postmodern: an early theory

An early attempt to relate Blake and 'the postmodern' was that of
Hazard Adams in 1969, in Alvin H. Rosenfeld's collection, *Essays for
S. Foster Damon*. He notes, though without offering many examples,
that 'postmodernism' in literary theory encourages a dialectical criticism 'of a Blakean sort', but is also influenced by Husserl's phenomenology and by existentialism.[14] The reference to dialectic evokes the
period of the rise of the New Left and the revival of Marxist criticism
in the English-speaking world. Adams also reminds his readers that
languages 'build actuality' in Blake, who is inimical to the idea of
'unmediated experience'.[15] This was an emphasis promoted at roughly
the same time by another respected Blakean (to whom Adams refers) –
Northrop Frye, in his collection of essays, *The Stubborn Structure*
(1970). Frye's insistence on the inseparability of literature, education
and knowledge from structures, forms and conventions was congenial in a period when structuralism had joined Marxism as a fashionable intellectual current.[16] This insistence, as is well known, had
grown out of his study of Blake in *Fearful Symmetry* (1947), which pre-
dated and prepared the ground for his great theoretical work, *The
Anatomy of Criticism* (1957).

There is yet more to be learned from Adams's essay: references on
the one hand to phenomenology and on the other to the linguisti-
cally constructed world again make it very much of its time, a period
when English-speaking readers are aware of the phenomenologist
Merleau-Ponty's essays in *Signs* (1960, trans. 1964) as well as of the
early work of Barthes. Merleau-Ponty's essays mark the point at
which a Husserlian concern with intentionality, perception and living
experience enters into negotiation with structuralism, including
structural linguistics.[17] It is worth remembering that this is the area of
negotiation in which Derrida began to evolve his characteristic concepts, even though his conclusions are not sympathetic to Merleau-
Ponty's. The key concept of *différance* was developed, in *Speech and
Phenomena* (1967, trans. 1973), as a central part of the critique of
Husserl's notion of self-present signification. Arguably, there is thus a
broad connection between the ideas discussed in Adams's essay and
later postmodernist developments. This is also suggested by his characterisation of postmodernism as involving plurality and difference
in the construction of reality: he notes with approbation that Ernst

Cassirer 'refused to limit ways of knowing to the understanding and proposed the existence of additional ways of "constituting" reality.'[18]

It would be unfortunate, though, if one were merely to see the importance of Adams's essay through the lens of our own fashionable perspective. Contemporary readers may have something to learn, and to apply to Blake, by re-examining the phenomenological idea of the bodily situatedness of the subject. But the still noticeable distance of Adams's essay from the dominant theoretical trends of today may also serve to remind us that in the late sixties 'postmodernism' was a term used without its current implication of a profoundly ironic, and possibly alienated, world view. In those days, it seemed to refer either to further developments of modernism or simply to the world after modernism without any confident sense of what that world was like. For this reason, I prefer to use the word 'postmodernity' or 'the post-modern' as a term to cover the whole period from the mid-twentieth century onwards, and 'postmodernism' for the radically ironic tendencies in some art from the eighties onwards. In what follows, 'postmodernism' is subsumed into a discussion of Blake in postmodernity.

Blake in postmodernity

It is something of a truism of literary history that the Forties, under the pressure of war and social crisis, see a reassertion of the Romantic tradition in a manner which is congenial to the idea of the artist's privileged and therapeutic vision of ancient and possibly sacred truths. Perhaps one of the most Blakean literary works in English literature is Joyce Cary's *The Horse's Mouth* (1944), whose artist narrator's every perception is buttressed by a quotation from the master. Gulley Jimson is known to be based on the painter Stanley Spencer, who was indeed influenced by Blake. The novel's date offers a plausible point of entry into the postmodern. Set in London just before the outbreak of the Second World War, it nevertheless seems a characteristic work of Forties Britain in its valuing of the visionary and forthrightly anti-bourgeois artistic genius, selflessly dedicated to his work in a world of unpredictable chaos. Its outrageously bohemian ambience of drunken pub-going painters and self-taught intellectuals also seems very much of its time. Blake's works, which are quoted with genuine knowledge and understanding, are enlisted in the service of the idea of artistic genius, and Jimson also pays Blake the tribute of putting a high valuation on the ideal in art. Thus he labours for many pages over a painting of 'The Fall'. Nevertheless, one of the delights of this appropriately energetic and witty book resides in its memorable, if painterly, evocations of the sensuous and concrete: indeed, the painterliness is really as significant as the sensuousness, for it implies that Jimson is far more indebted to impressionism, in the broadest sense of the term, than his Blakean utterances would suggest. Indeed, as Annette S. Levitt points out, Jimson's thoughts about his own career focus on Turner, Manet and Cézanne.[19] This hardly seems surprising, since it offers the artistic correlative of his bitter-sweet infatuation with the chaotic experience in which he is immersed.

The book offers an allegorical counterpart of this oblique relationship to Blake in its presentation of the hero's lovers. The eleventh to thirteenth chapters show Jimson reciting much of 'The Mental Traveller' to himself and relating it to his experience. In particular, the female principle of the poem – the 'woman old', the 'maiden' – is identified with the women in his life: 'Till he, that is Gulley Jimson, became a bleeding youth. And she, that is Sara, becomes a virgin bright'.[20] Indeed, some of his most significant paintings have been depictions of these women, particularly of the Sara referred to here: some of the paintings – the 'bath' paintings, for instance – sound as if they are influenced by impressionism, since they obviously recall the work of Pierre Bonnard. But Blake's female is not to be closely related to individual women, being a symbolic representation of what he calls 'Nature'. Jimson is certainly aware of other connotations of the female in Blake's work – among other things, he equates the male–female relationship in 'The Mental Traveller' with the artist's imaginative mastery of experience. But an important element in the book resides in the appreciation of women's beauty and in the love (however flawed) of women as individuals. Such love, it becomes clear, has been at the centre of Jimson's life, and the book contains many poignant passages where the old man reflects on this fact. Blake seems to operate in this novel as a symbol, for one who is far more submissive to 'Nature' than Blake, of a desirable pursuit of the ideal in art. Appropriately enough, though, the reader is well aware that the 'historical Blake soon disappears from Gulley's commentary.'[21]

There are grounds for thinking of this problematic relationship between chaotic experience and a sage who represents an ideal as characteristically postmodern. The work of Cary's friend Iris Murdoch offers a case in point.[22] She is frequently discussed as a postmodern artist these days: even as a postmodernist. Yet her life-long meditation on Plato, and her commitment to the search for truth and goodness, can make her look an unlikely candidate for such descriptions. But it is the search that is important to her: the idea of a secure possession of these things is a dangerous illusion. As Peter Conradi puts it, 'There are short glimpses of clarity and insight, but the single Big Truth is always illusory.'[23] Furthermore, Murdoch makes it difficult for the reader of her works to arrive at a Big Truth about her fictional meanings, through her manipulation of point of view and the unreliable narrator. In the case of Cary, the gap between the long, italicised quotations from Blake and the experience and practice of the artist is patent, sometimes painfully so. This type of gap is different in kind from that which we perceive between myth and reality in modernist works such as Eliot's *Waste Land* or even Joyce's *Ulysses*. Both of these use the mock-heroic device of contrasting the unheroic present with the aura of the past, and one may discern a parallel between that aura and the authority invested by Cary and Murdoch in Blake or Plato. Nevertheless, Eliot's use of myth seeks to tell a central truth about all human experience, past or present, and Joyce's references to the *Odyssey*, while they ironically underscore his valuing of the facticity of modern life, also imply a humanist reading of the Greek epic. Things are not so secure with Cary, and his obtrusive foregrounding of the gap between experience and interpretation makes him a remote forebear of postmodernist writers such as Pynchon or Iain Sinclair. Interestingly, Oedipa Maas, the heroine of Pynchon's *The Crying of Lot 49*, regards Blake, along with Berkeley, as one of her most important points of reference, although there is undoubtedly an uncertain hint of irony in this fact: a suggestion of a mental imposition on experience, in line with her famous question, 'Shall I project a world?' This, however, is precisely illustrative of the general point.

In this neo-Romantic period of the Forties, Blake is also important to the work of Dylan Thomas and Kathleen Raine. Thomas's work is indebted to Blake, to the Wordsworth of 'Intimations of Immortality', and of course to Yeats, for images of innocence and experience, of a redeemed and miraculous nature, and of the poet as visionary. Indebtedness of this kind is obvious in, for instance, 'Fern Hill'. Dylan Thomas's admiration for Blake is well-attested and is a determinant in the development of a symbolism of contraries which operates at several levels: there is an opposition between what is creative and what deadening. But there may also be a very Blakean opposition between the contrasting manifestations of what is sacred or creative, which may seem cruel and violent as well as kind. There is a corresponding contrast in the attitudes of the speaker, which may be rebellious or tender. As a critic, Kathleen Raine reads Blake as a visionary re-interpreter of an ancient mystical tradition incorporating the truths of neo-Platonism, the Kabbalah and philosophical alchemy. While her own poetry is gentler and less assertive than that of Blake, it is clear that she sees herself as being in the same tradition. The postmodern is a period of increasing uncertainty and moral relativism, and it is striking to see the way in which Blake appears at this stage already to be accounted a sage in possession of insights which are still relevant. At the same time, Blake is often associated with, or at least conscripted in support of, bohemian wildness, in a late-Romantic fashion which does not accord with current scholarly interpretations. These, on the whole, are more aware of Blake's seriousness about the political.

Although an account which includes the word 'bohemian' might also be offered of Blake's role in the work of Robert Duncan and Allen Ginsberg, it would be qualified by the word 'Beat'. They share with Dylan Thomas a confidence about harnessing Blake's influence to a late Romantic agenda of their own, but unlike Thomas, they can also be seen as late Modernists, responding to (among other things) the influence of Pound and Williams on the poetic line. They are avantgarde poets, believers in the unsullied freshness of their vision, and cannot be assimilated to that category of postmodernism which embodies irony about form and convention, or anxiety about the role of their many mentors. Not surprisingly, Blake's influence has to compromise with elements of an American modernist inspiration. In Duncan's work, as befits one who was associated with Black Mountain and was an avowed admirer of Charles Olson, there is a palpable emphasis on experience and process. As Robert J. Betholf puts it, 'while Blake evolves a complicated system with a cast of characters, divisions of those characters, a symbolic landscape, and a host of derived associations which define, in mythological form, his vision of mythological reality, Duncan evolves a poetry of process in which the drive of the imagination to propose approximations of eternal images takes precedence over the approximations which illustrate that process'.[24] The general tenor of Duncan's poetry is consonant with Olson's idea of 'Projective Verse' which comprises an emphasis on the poet's direct transfer of energy onto the page. Accordingly, Duncan can refer to 'The design of a poem' as 'constantly under reconstruction', something where 'thot shows its pattern', 'a proposition / in movement'.[25] We discover in the same place that this process is embodied in 'alternations of sound, sensations', and the reference to sensations seems appropriate to the model of experience implied elsewhere by Duncan. Thus, in 'Variations on Two Dicta of William Blake', when he meditates upon the assertion that 'Mental things alone are real' and invokes Olson as an example of a poet whose work illustrates the truth of that assertion, he introduces him in relation to the 'change in pulse' which occurs when the heart receives an 'answer' and goes on to describe how words can 'awaken / sensory chains between being and being'. He also recalls that 'like stellar bees my senses swarmed'.[26] This emphasis on the senses within the general depiction of experience as process is not notably Blakean, and in fact Duncan explicitly revises Blake's dictum about 'Mental things' by adding his own qualification that 'There is no mental thing unrealized'. This reformulation, while its precise philosophical bearings might be inexplicit, certainly shifts the terrain from the mental to a channel of transformation issuing in something relatively concrete and embodied, while at the same time taking Blake's more idealist formulation as its starting-point.[27] The simile of the stellar bees implies a parallel notion: the bees are the senses, and the idea of their swarming vividly evokes their activity; but their 'stellar' quality connotes the mental in the form of the ideal and is a gesture towards Blake.

Anyone who knows anything about Allen Ginsberg knows that his sense of poetic vocation is founded on the relationship with Blake, in the sense that it was given decisive impetus by a visionary encounter which issued in a dedication of the self. In 1948, living in East Harlem while a student at Columbia, he heard 'the voice of Blake himself' while he was masturbating and reading 'Ah! Sun-Flower': Ginsberg realised that he himself was the sunflower, and this realisation issued in a sense of the profound significance of his momentary existence as part of the 'spirit of the universe'.[28] As a result, Ginsberg believed that 'from now on I'm chosen, blessed, sacred poet'.[29] Appropriately enough, his works are full of references to Blake, and a number of them catch something of the Blakean prophetic note.

Chief among these are 'Howl' and its brief sequel, 'Footnote to Howl', which was written contemporaneously. This contains the line 'Everything is holy! everybody's holy! everywhere is holy! everyday is an eternity! Everyman's an angel!' The reference to *The Marriage of Heaven and Hell* and the idea of the immanence of eternity are sure pointers to the influence of Blake. Most of the expansive lines in the 'Footnote' begin with the word 'Holy', and parallelism of this kind, combined with a long and relatively loose line, is reminiscent of Blake and of the prophetic poetry of the Bible which both Blake and Ginsberg are imitating. But this fact should serve to remind us that this stylistic influence is also transmitted to the twentieth century via Whitman. Indeed, it is significant that in *Howl and Other Poems* a tribute to Whitman ('A Supermarket in California') follows immediately after the 'Footnote', beginning with the famous words, 'What thoughts I have of you tonight Walt Whitman'.[30] The statement in 'Footnote' that 'The bum's as holy as the seraphim!', while not itself notably Whitmanesque in style, is more akin to Whitman than to Blake in its trenchant assertion of the democratic. Furthermore, apart from Biblical parallelism there is another feature of Ginsberg's style which is reminiscent of Whitman, namely the accretion of details, sometimes approximating lists. A useful example can be found in Ginsberg's Moloch, whom Ostriker describes as 'a broadly Urizenic figure'.[31] This is apt, and there are similarities even in the lists of Moloch's attributes and connections provided by Ginsberg:

> Moloch whose mind is pure machinery! Moloch whose blood is running money! Moloch whose fingers are ten armies! Moloch whose breast is a cannibal dynamo! Moloch whose ear is a smoking tomb! [...]
> Moloch whose love is endless oil and stone! Moloch whose soul is electricity and banks! Moloch whose poverty is the specter of genius! Moloch whose fate is a cloud of sexless hydrogen! Moloch whose name is the Mind! (*HOP*, 21–22)

Just as in Blake, there are plenty of contemporary phenomena which count as Urizenic. If we know the Bible, we know that Moloch 'is the Canaanite god of fire to whom children were offered in sacrifice', and we may infer that for Ginsberg, as for Blake, Moloch 'represents the obsessive human sacrifice of war'.[32] But unlike in Blake there is little attempt to specify the characteristics of Moloch as a personification, and there is no Fall narrative. In sum, this quality of the accretion of lists contrasts with Blake's structured allegorical landscape, which, as in Duncan, is absent.

There are other stylistic features which contrast with Blake, and these might be pointedly illustrated by some lines which actually refer to him: near the beginning of 'Howl' Ginsberg is qualifying 'the best minds of [his] generation', the 'angelheaded hipsters burning for the ancient heavenly connection to the starry dynamo', and notes that (among many other things) they 'passed through universities with radiant cool eyes hallucinating Arkansas and Blake-light tragedy among the scholars of war, / who were expelled from the academies for crazy & publishing obscene odes on the windows of the skull' (*HOP*, 9). This is very characteristic of Ginsberg: it offers Burroughs-like kennings with narcotic connotations, but is also slightly reminiscent of symbolism in its deliberately surprising suggestiveness – what is it to 'hallucinate Arkansas'? Perhaps a memory of a rustic home. What is 'Blake-light tragedy'? This seems slightly harder to identify. None of these stylistic features is especially reminiscent of Blake, but they do suggest that counter-cultural area where Modernism, surrealism, symbolism and the influence of popular culture join to promote a demotic version of the drug-inspired bohemian late-Romantic sage.

Somewhat unexpectedly, perhaps, given the genuineness of his indebtedness to D. H. Lawrence, and the seriousness of his interest in the visionary powers of the imagination, there is a strong case for seeing Ted Hughes's *Crow* (first edition 1970), as a significantly post-modern response to Blake. In the quasi-mythological and decidedly unmelodious 'songs' in *Crow*, in which there is an element of the parody of Genesis, it is possible to discern a similarity with another such parody, Blake's *The Book of Urizen* (1794). Furthermore, the famous dust jacket illustration by Leonard Baskin is arguably intended to function as a kind of 'illumination.' As David Trotter notes, *Crow* 'might almost be part of the 'Bible of Hell' announced by Blake in *The Marriage of Heaven and Hell*: a counter-myth, Creation and Fall seen from a different point of view'.[33] This is by no means a far-fetched suggestion. Hughes's interest in mythology and in philo-sophical alchemy (alchemy interpreted as spiritual symbolism), although it owes something to his reading of Jung, makes Blake a sympathetic forebear. Such a suggestion would be supported by works such as *Cave Birds: An Alchemical Cave Drama* (1978), which presents the reconciliation of the sexual contraries by reference to the idea of an alchemical marriage: that is, to the many symbols of the marriage of opposites which are to be found in the alchemical tradition, a tradition upon which Blake was drawing in *The Marriage of Heaven and Hell*. This book also intersperses the text with illustrations by Baskin.

The postmodernity of Hughes's *Crow* would reside in the combination of two factors which Trotter discusses in terms of a quality he calls 'anti-pathos': first, and more simply, there is the shocking squalour of what Hughes offers as a creation myth; second, as Trotter nicely puts it, Hughes's aim is 'to put about as many stories as possible, or as many versions of one story, rather than to describe a first-coming creator and so nurture the pathos of origins'.[34] This aim seems postmodern and might be seen in the light of concepts such as Lyotard's idea of the death of grand narratives. And arguably the connection to Blake is one which makes us aware of the postmodernism in Blake: it is notoriously difficult to isolate an original structure for Blake's myth. Here we have one of those indications as to why Blake remains such a congenial figure in the postmodern.

Later references to Blake seem increasingly dark, harnessing Gothic elements in his work to our own postmodern Gothic. The occasional references to Blake in the gloomier sort of graphic novels offer a handy example. Thomas Harris's *Red Dragon* (1981) includes the incident where a killer called Dolarhyde, who thinks that he is possessed by Blake's image of the Red Dragon from Revelation (*The Great Red Dragon and the Woman Clothed with the Sun*), devours the original watercolour. In another best-selling novel, Michael Dibdin's clever Gothic-influenced thriller, *Dark Spectre* (1995), Sam, a disturbed Vietnam veteran, founds a society of drifters called The Sons of Los and teaches them to murder at random, on the theory (which he thinks Blakean) that those they happen to choose are damned. Both these novels are arguably offering slightly more than a superficial reference to something almost Manichean in Blake's vision. Furthermore, as Shirley Dent and Jason Whittaker remark, Blake has 'come to signify in the popular imagination a shorthand for a particular type of evil: a demented, perverse but highly intelligent, even empathetic, evil associated particularly with psychopaths and serial killers'.[35] This, of course, is only one of the things that Blake can mean today, but the fact that there is some truth in the remark demands understanding. It looks as if, in a society which is increasingly paranoid about the extent to which it is influenced by dark forces of multinational capital, or the extent to which it is coming adrift from any centre of value, or simply about the persistence of evil and suffering in a society of plenty, Blake is seen as offering appropriate imagery – even if, as with Dibdin, the implied view of him is not unambiguously complimentary. It should, of course, be remembered that Dibdin's title refers ironically to his hero, who is alienated from the feminine; and given his war experiences it is clear that an accusatory finger is being pointed at society and the state. But the title also refers critically to the dark unconscious of the Sixties: the reference to Manson is no less obvious for being inexplicit. The implication is that Blake's antinomianism is too easy for us to appropriate, and that this may have its dangers. Blake, it is suggested, offers a well-intentioned analysis of evil and one where postmodernity finds his mistrust of authority congenial; but his liberating message may lead to a malleable ethics and offer a hidden opportunity for unhinged malevolence.

Red Dragon raises similar questions, in so far as the ingestion of a Blake painting can figure the incorporation of authority. But it also offers a reflection on the status of works of art, since the authority of a Blake painting derives from its high-art status and is inseparable from its aura. The novel self-consciously obtrudes these concerns by exploiting the implications of Dolarhyde's profession as film developer. He chooses his victims from home-movies he has developed and subsequently splices in footage of their slaughter and also of himself with a copy of Blake's *Red Dragon*. Furthermore, he is described as hoping that 'he could maintain some aesthetic distance, even in the most intimate moments'. As Nicholas Williams points out, this episode 'forms part of a reflection on the competing claims of high art and mass reproduction'.[36] Indeed, it could be said that Dolarhyde performatively undermines the claims of high art for autonomy even as he paradoxically submits to them, while at the same time he demonstrates that the kinetic affect of popular art (he masturbates while watching his film) is deferred and complicated by the demands of the aesthetic. As Williams puts it, this indicates a double failure: Dolarhyde can neither maintain 'aesthetic distance' nor 'intimacy', a fact which is predicated on a view which shows 'high' and 'low' art approximating each other, not least in the problems of representation which confront both.

Williams also notes that the eating of a Blake figures the consumption of art. He brings to bear two complementary frameworks of interpretation, that of Bourdieu, who links the consumption of high art to the class-based prestige it confers on the consumer, and that of Michel de Certeau, who, by contrast, emphasises the active role of appropriation.[37] Williams does not privilege one view over the other, drawing illumination from Derrida's discussion of the way the eater both incorporates and learns from the other that is eaten. He notes that both views involve sacrifice, either by the 'propitiation of the faceless god of necessary social structures (Bourdieu)', or by the destruction of 'the oppressive high art text (Certeau)'.[38] In this perspective, the undoubted 'superficiality' of Harris's references to Blake are not only understandable, but necessary, since notwithstanding the broad outlines of Gothic imagery the most important thing is the art-work's symbolic status in these transactions.[39] Nevertheless, Blake turns out to be a very fitting object of consumption in the light of his own incorporation of Milton via his foot, which permits him both to expand his own 'productive poetic vision' and to prepare for the self-annihilation which will unite him with Milton.[40]

Blake has made his way into non-Anglophone cultures, also, sometimes as part of the wider phenomenon of what I term 'postcolonial romanticisms'.[41] As part of this voyage he has been adopted by the oriental culture which, more than most, may lay claim to having entered the postmodern: that of Japan. He has long enjoyed popularity there, partly because of his supposed mysticism, which strikes a chord in a nation imbued with Buddhism. He makes a strange, poignantly discordant appearance in a work which bears the imprint of postmodernity, not least because of the way that it handles what it presents as Blake's 'wisdom'. Kenzaburo Oe's *Rouse Up O Young Men of the New Age* (1983; trans. 2002) offers the first-person narrative of a novelist who has a mentally and physically disabled son. The painful, moving and awkward episodes he has to recount are interwoven with his earnest reading of Blake, which is clearly motivated by a desire to learn, but also comprises a stranger element, whereby some hidden sympathy is suggested between the events which currently preoccupy him and the particular lines of Blake he is studying. This is another example, then, of the postmodern adoption of Blake as sage, but it also raises characteristically postmodern questions about the grounding of interpretation, and in a characteristically postmodern way: the question is raised whether the narrator is imposing a subjective interpretation, and the sublimity of some of Blake's lines contrasts piquantly with the pathos and ordinariness of the lives depicted. Yet the book also raises political and moral questions about the post-war development of Japanese society: how can a society which has been steeped in militarism, and which is strongly influenced by a traditional male warrior-code, come to accept the humanity of his touchingly comical, lugubrious and tender son, whom for most of the book he calls 'Eeyore'? Who, then, are 'the young men of the new age', and in what manner will they 'rouse up'?

The Gothic strain is also present in Iain Sinclair's books, *Lud Heat* (1975) and *Suicide Bridge* (1979), but arguably they conform more truly to the narrow definition of postmodernism proposed above, in embodying postmodernist blends of Burroughs-like prose and post-Olsonian poetry, which make extensive and significant use of Blake. Hand and Hyle, for instance, re-appear as sinister agents of late capitalism. There is a significant thread of parody in these books, for instance of the popular occult, which helps to validate the description 'postmodernist'. Thus it is maintained in *Lud Heat* that the Hawksmoor churches in London are linked by sinister lines of force and that this sinister character can be gauged in part from the Egyptian motifs to be found in them. (Blake's negative symbolism of Egypt is cited in evidence.) Apart from referring to these connections in his text, Sinclair provides a useful map.[42] Dent and Whittaker put it well when they say that Sinclair overlays 'a hieratic chart across London and thus uses Blake's systems of configuration of Albion, such as Los's naming of cities and attributing parts of the body and country to points of the compass, in an attempt to extrapolate a mysterious code'.[43] The dark London of Sinclair's work is a place of mysterious evil forces which have found a new and congenial home in the postmodern, but which Blake understood in a way which is still relevant. On the other hand, the bizarre pseudo-scientific and occult connotations of Sinclair's map suggest a contrast with Blake: as if, where Blake offers the truth of vision, Sinclair is parodying the work of those who actually believe in the objective truth of occult forces such as he describes. But because of the eccentricity of such a view, the result is to make his map seem like a subjective imposition, on the lines of Slothrop's map of London in Pynchon's *Gravity's Rainbow*, which in any case is probably an influence. Pynchon and Sinclair are in the same postmodernist universe, where the map becomes a figure for paranoid interpretation. On the other hand, the fact that Blake's own mapping activities can be an influence on Sinclair's in itself suggests that they look sufficiently arbitrary and subjective themselves to be a congenial source for this kind of postmodernist topos. Jim Jarnusch's film *Dead Man* (1996) provides a close analogy in its playing with arbitrary-seeming interpretation. It offers another version of Blake as sage in a chaotic world; this time associating him with shamanic wisdom. But reality is mysterious, and the chief protagonist in a sense becomes Blake, the poet and painter, because his own name happens to be William Blake.

Blake and theory

Whether motivated by an interest in Lyotard on the sublime, or deconstruction, or chaos theory, or the work of Walter Benjamin, contemporary theoretical treatments of Blake have stressed the plurality of meanings and the effects of difference in his work. As for deconstruction, while it is something of a solecism to equate post-structuralist theory with postmodernism, there is a cogent argument that the work of Derrida, in particular, has been a major instigating factor in the development of the late twentieth-century/early twenty-first-century postmodernist sensibility and a major influence on the criticism which appreciates and promotes postmodernism in art. While not definitively deconstructionist, Nelson Hilton's *Literal Imagination* (1983) is congenial to that trend in the importance it accords to polysemy. Peter Otto's *Constructive Vision and Visionary Deconstruction* (1991) points to Blake's deconstruction of tyrannous unities, but believes that ultimately an important difference between Blake and Derrida resides in the former's unironic rousing of the faculties to act. My own *William Blake* (1985) brings together deconstruction and Marxist criticism in a manner broadly analogous to the contemporaneous 'deconstructive materialism' of Marjorie Levinson in her work on Wordsworth and Keats.[44] I note the way in which Blake's works make reference to a number of discourses which are to some extent incommensurate with each other: antinomian

Protestantism, mainstream dissenting Protestantism, Enlightenment liberalism, Romantic aesthetics (for example, of the sublime). One may offer a description of this confluence in terms of ideology and note the likely connections of Blake's family with radical Protestant traditions. At the same time, however, the result of this uneasy confluence is undecidability, for instance in the interpretation of 'London'.[45] This situation is later addressed by Livingston, when he says (referring to the use of the words 'mark' and 'marks') that for Blake's narrator 'the marking isn't so simple. It marks victims, but everyone is a victim (and an oppressor)'.[46] In my own account, such undecidability can be described in terms of deferral and *différance* and leads to formal effects whereby 'the clash of styles foregrounds style itself'.[47] This last remark is indebted not just to the author's development of thoughts about difference, but also to his use of an unjustly neglected essay which reads Blake in terms of Bakhtin and Russian Formalism: Graham Pechey's '1789 and After: Mutations of "Romantic" Discourse'.[48] My own book asserts that Blake apprehends not only undecidability, but also the multiple indebtedness which gives rise to it, within his own texts. This apprehension, it is claimed, is the source of ambivalence about the 'bound' and the 'bounded', which can represent form (understood as created by some tradition) either as expressive or as limiting.[49]

Nicholas Williams offers an original development of some of these topics in the conclusion to his *Ideology and Utopia in the Poetry of William Blake* (1998). In my book, I had observed that the phrase 'we impose on one another' from *The Marriage*, addressed to the Angel, could be taken to imply that imposition 'is a feature of all discourse including Blake's'.[50] 'Imposition' can thus be related to 'difference', inasmuch as it seems to deny objective grounding to propositions. Williams conducts the thought-experiment of interpreting Blakean 'imposition' not in terms of the aggressivity of opposing 'stances' or 'world-views', but of Lyotard's aesthetics of unpresentability. As world views, even discourses of utopia degenerate into narrow 'ideological programs'.[51] But 'if opposed in a mutually defining, though not mutually imposing, aesthetics of unpresentability, they [...] revive the utopian dynamics at the heart of even our most resistant present moment'.[52] This formulation seeks to encompass a sense of the way in which Blake encourages a productive openness, an avoidance of foreclosure. It suggests a parallel with Livingston's approach to Blake: applying the analogy of chaos theory, he asserts that 'The force of Blake's often-repeated instructions on how to "see the World in a Grain of Sand" [...] is again to resist the reduction of the universe to individual particles or discrete singular units [....] Blake proposes a 'scaling' and plural universe of worlds within worlds'.[53] The perception of such a universe may open 'a liberatory path [...] that performs difference on what was otherwise the same.'[54]

There is another aspect of Blake's work which can be aligned with difference, namely his printing method. Stephen Leo Carr has argued strongly for the significance of the facts of variation in different printings, in terms both of different ordering of the plates and different approaches to colouring.[55] He has connected this variability to Derrida's concept of *différance*, especially in point of the way that notion comprises the concept of 'iterability': the capacity for a use of words or signs to be repeated, which entails that it can never be exhaustively explained by reference to an original context.[56] Robert Essick and Joseph Viscomi have both disagreed with this analysis, not on theoretical grounds, but on the evidence of Blake's actual production and its context. Essick suggests that the variability is not as significant as the continuity and refers to remarks such as 'My Designs unchangd remain' (*Notebook*, 87).[57] Both Essick and Viscomi cite the frequency of variation in eighteenth-century prints, though Essick concedes that the 'degree of variation' is greater in Blake.[58] This seems to me to be an important concession. Furthermore, one might ask if prints, rather than books, are the closest analogy with Blake's works of composite art. If one is prepared to concede significant variability in Blake, then it becomes interesting to ponder Stephen Leo Carr's suggestion that Walter Benjamin's essay, 'The Work of Art in an Age of Mechanical Reproduction', is illuminating.[59] (Naturally, Carr is not claiming a literal or historical relationship to Benjamin's study, with its references to photography and cinema.) In my essay, 'Spectral Imposition and Visionary Imposition' (1999), I suggest that variability in Blake is an attempt to overcome 'the loss of aura in repetition' associated with 'mechanical reproduction'.[60] Here, perhaps, is another example of Blake's attempt to overcome the effects of 'commerce'. Since those days, his works have joined the ranks of the most auratic in our culture, as Nicholas Williams notes.[61] Indeed, that is part of the point of eating a Blake in Harris's *Red Dragon*. The irony is that Blake's works may be co-opted for an exclusive and disempowering view of art, when he himself was trying to 'open up the scope of artistic production in his time, to retain the right of production for a broad variety of people and approaches'.[62] At the same time, it is to be hoped that one of the chief points to be gathered from a study such as this is the way in which Blake is indeed apprehended as attempting what Williams describes.

8
Joyce Cary: Getting it from the Horse's Mouth

It is well known that Joyce Cary's *The Horse's Mouth* is possibly the most Blakean literary work in the language, at least on a straightforward definition, outside those of Blake himself. In any case, that is one way of describing a novel in which most of the thoughts of the central character – Gulley Jimson, a painter – are buttressed by quotations from the master, many of them of some length. It is not surprising to find that Blake was a formative influence, read, studied and admired long before Cary had meditated the composition of this novel or indeed had written any published novels. As he said, later in life, in a letter to the Blake Society when sickness prevented his attending one of their meetings, 'I still possess the two volumes of the Ellis edition which I used at College, heavily annotated. He is for me the only philosopher, the only great poet, who had a real understanding of the nature of the world as seen by an artist.'[1] It is interesting to note that he refers to the 'two volumes of the Ellis edition', for this must mean the three-volume edition by Edwin Ellis and Cary's fellow Anglo-Irishman, W. B. Yeats. This means that Cary was familiar with a reading of Blake informed by esoteric traditions such as were bread and butter to these editors, fellow members of the Golden Dawn. And this was not even the only edition which Cary annotated: he did the same thing to Max Plowman's Everyman edition of 1927.[2] It is also significant that he refers to Blake as a philosopher: the comparison and contrast of Blake with academic philosophy was an abiding preoccupation. This comes across very strongly in *The Horse's Mouth* and is confirmed in a manuscript memoir on 'My own religious history' quoted by Alan Bishop in his biography. He contrasts Blake with the philosophers he read at Oxford and remarks that 'Blake, whom I read and studied at the time, had more effect on my idea of the world, for he introduced me into a highly complex universe where what is called the material is entirely dissolved into imaginative construction and states of feeling, where matter, mind and emotion, become simply different aspects of the one reality.'[3] Obviously, this contrast bears on the conception of the artist in *The Horse's Mouth* and is also quite precisely evoked in passages such as the one where Spinoza is unfavourably compared to Blake.

But before we turn to the implications of this contrast, there is another point to be made about Cary's understanding of Blake's ideas and intellectual provenance. For he is one of those commentators on Blake (Shaw, as we have seen, is another) who, in a period when a somewhat ahistorical, esoteric version of Blake was prevalent, and which often valued Blake in those terms, nevertheless was strongly aware of the dissenting Protestant context of Blake's thought.

Plantie, one of the eccentric autodidact intellectuals of the 'Greenbank' area of London, is a cobbler by trade, and a part-time preacher. The combination of humble craftsman, dissenting Protestant and self-taught intellectual is itself redolent of Blake's own ambience. It is Plantie who pays part of Gulley's subscription to the Blake Society.[4] Establishing the context in which Plantie moves, Cary notes that 'There's a lot of religion about Greenbank; I mean real old English religion', and goes on to claim that, if you hear hymns, 'it may be Bunyan's great-great-great-grand-daughter teaching a class of young walruses to sing the International or a dustman starting a revival among the Unitarian Prebaptists branch of the Rechabite nudists' (*HM*, 46). As he moves his narration towards Plantie's part-payment of the Blake Society subscription, Cary describes how 'All the London prophets have strong followings round Greenbank; that is Bunyan, Wesley, Richard Owen, Proudhon, Herbert Spencer, W. G. Grace, W. E. Gladstone, Marx and Ruskin' (*HM*, 46). Although the intellectual bearings of such a diverse group of thinkers range far more widely than what could be learnt from Blake – not to mention the fact that most of them lived after him – the working-class, Protestant affiliation of their Greenbank enthusiasts situate Blake within a continuing tradition of dissent. Combining this sense with a knowledge of Blake's esoteric sources, Cary is effectively as knowledgeable about Blake as any commentator in the period.

Not all Protestant dissent is equally laudable in Cary's eyes, however. It could be said that, in his opinion, Blake transcends the limitations of the tradition from which his thought is admittedly inextricable. Nevertheless, Cary's own contradictions make him tolerant.[5] In *To Be A Pilgrim* we have a novel whose title is derived from Bunyan's well-known hymn from *Pilgrim's Progress*, a reference which is ironic enough as applied to its timorous and conservative protagonist, Tom Wilcher, but which also alludes to a serious belief of Cary's about the English Protestant tradition: namely, that an 'evangelical strain opposed and intensified by native conservatism' is the explanation for the particular form of Liberalism that had come to dominate English society.[6] In Wilcher we see all the conservatism, but we are constantly reminded of the evangelical tradition, and Cary takes trouble to embody the virulence of its pure form in the character of Lucy. In *The Captive and the Free* (1959), Cary's last, unfinished novel, he explores what may be valuable in such virulence, even as he characteristically incorporates all the reasons for doubt into his handling of the topic. The preacher and faith-healer Preedy, may seem to be a charlatan, and some of his actions appear to support that view. Yet Cary will not allow us to dismiss the unyielding faith and the sense of saving power and grace which guide him.

The nature of the value Gulley places on Blake is in part deducible from his contrast of Blake and academic philosophy, summed up in the contrast of Blake and Spinoza. It involves a loosely existentialist point of view which goes some way to explaining the important point that Cary saw Blake as a kind of philosopher himself, as well as a visionary artist. The crucial passage is this, from chapter 17:

> Contemplation, in fact, is ON THE OUTSIDE. It's not on the spot. And the truth is that Spinoza was always on the outside. He didn't understand freedom, and so he didn't understand anything. Because after all, I said to myself, with some excitement, for I saw where all this was leading to. Freedom, to be plain, is nothing but THE INSIDE OF THE OUTSIDE. And even a philosopher like old Ben can't judge the XXX by eating pint pots. It's the wrong approach.
>
> Whereas Old Bill, that damned Englishman, didn't understand anything else but freedom, and so all his nonsense is full of truth; and even though he may be a bit of an outsider, HIS OUTSIDE IS ON THE INSIDE; and if you want to catch the old mole where he digs, you have to start at the bottom. (*HM*, 103)

To live by a philosophical system is to live on the outside of life, the real thing. It is like trying to get at beer by eating the pot. Alan Bishop thinks that Cary began to study Existentialist thought in the early 1940s and quotes a later remark that 'Kierkegaard states the uniqueness of the individual and I stand by that'.[7] Indeed, Gulley's critique of Spinoza is similar to Kierkegaard's of Hegel. But even without this knowledge, one can see how the characterisation 'existentialist' is rendered more than merely facile by the word 'freedom'. Cary's characters inhabit a world of moral value, like that which existentialism describes. Furthermore, the universe they inhabit is an absurd one, akin to that described by Sartre or Camus.[8] We cannot know if there is another world after this one: probably there is not. The rewards of this life are haphazard and irrationally distributed. Even if, like Gulley, one has the passionate perceptiveness to see the Inside and attempt to live there, and then produce an authentic art, the world may not be ready. And it is certainly not ready for Gulley, any more than it was for Blake. Finally, Gulley esteems most highly the capacity to embody the truth of life – the kind of truth we have been sketching – in art: a value-judgement shared by Nietzsche, Sartre and Camus.

Yet the freedom of an absurd universe is balanced by an opposing trend for which Cary also finds sanction in Blake. For like his friend and compatriot Iris Murdoch, Cary is torn between existentialist and Platonist tendencies, though where Murdoch would offer a reasoned account of her dissatisfaction with either pole, Cary's position emerges from his fiction.

A crucial passage is that in which Gulley recounts that having had an argument with an adherent of Spinoza, he becomes interested in Blake, and 'Blake led me back to Plato, because he didn't like him, and the pair of them took me forward to black and white drawing and formal composition' (*HM*, 86–87). This paradoxical-seeming passage is in fact very Blakean, as Cary is of course well aware. To be led back to Plato because Blake did not like him is to defer to Blake's nostrum that 'Opposition is true friendship'. It is also to recognise that such opposition in Blake is productive, and the proof is not far to seek in the later Blake's Neoplatonic terminology of 'Forms Eternal' and 'Generation'.

Appropriately enough, Gulley's conception of art instantiates precisely such a contradiction. His instructions to Cokey on how to look at a picture begin with a very painterly discourse on abstract qualities

and relationships of form and colour. 'Feel it with your eye [...] feel
the shapes in the flat – the patterns, like a carpet [....] And then you
feel it in the round [....] Not as if it were a picture of anyone, But a
coloured and raised map. You feel all the rounds, the smooths, the
sharp edges, the flats and the hollows, the lights and shades, the
cools and warms. The colours and textures. There's hundreds of little
differences all fitting in together' (*HM*, 100). The remark, 'Not as if it
were a picture of anyone' is especially telling. Yet gradually the dis-
quisition moves in a different direction. At first it begins to apprehend
the objects and people for what they are in fact, in a conception
which is closely akin to Stephen Dedalus's exposition of *quidditas*:
'then you feel the bath, the chair, the towel, the carpet, the bed, the
jug, the window, the fields and the woman as themselves' (*HM*, 100).
The painting has become representational, but it is still capable of
being associated with major tendencies in Modernism. But finally,
the woman's legs are described as 'divine legs [...] ideal legs' (*HM*,
100). At this point, one is bound to be reminded of Blake and of those
aspects of Blake which seem less concerned with 'minute particulars'
and more with 'Forms Eternal'. And while Gulley clearly does wish to
incorporate a sense of abstract beauty into his account of painting –
and remember that Clive Bell was able to see even Blake in terms of
significant form – it is clear that this sense of the ideal, the eternal,
has to be present.

This is the point upon which Cary's use of Blake really bears. It is
difficult to maintain, at length and in detail, the idea that Blake's
technique, whether in poetry or graphic art, is especially concerned
with the realism of appearances: he always expressly disavowed any
intention to imitate 'Nature'. Blake's Neoplatonist formulations
about Eternal Forms – and his advocacy of an art based on their
depiction – are late developments. The results are perhaps best
gauged from his various prospectuses of the engraving of Chaucers's
Canterbury Pilgrims. The pilgrims represent a kind of test case, as it
were, for Blake's sense of his own artistic vocation, for they might
seem to offer the kind of particularity which would be inimical to
Eternal Forms. But Blake avers,

The Characters of Chaucers Pilgrims are the Characters that compose
all Ages & Nations, as one Age falls another rises. different to Mortal
Sight, but to Immortals only the same, for we see the same Characters

repeated again & again in Animals in Vegetables in Minerals & in Men.
Nothing new occurs in Identical Existence. Accident ever varies
Substance can never change nor decay. (*E*, 569)

This is the kind of thinking of which Cary makes use in his overt
handling of Blake. It also has implications for other aspects of this
novel.

As for the overt handling, this is dominated by an extended dis-
quisition from chapter 11 to chapter 14 (inclusive), on Blake's 'The
Mental Traveller' and its relevance to the course of artistic imagination
in general, and to Gulley's development as an artist in particular,
although, as with Blake, that development is inseparable from wider
human questions. Blake's cyclical poem traces the fate of the male
child: the 'babe' who is 'born a boy', who represents imagination. The
power of this faculty is chiefly conveyed in terms of the dynamics of
its relationship with the female, who represents Nature, the given,
the material moulded by the imagination. At first, the female is 'a
woman old' who 'nails him down upon a rock': Nature, the given,
dominates imagination, the power of which is all the less for that. As
he grows older, she grows younger: weaker – and more alluring, 'a
Virgin bright', until at last 'he rends up his manacles / And binds her
down for his delight'. As a result, she 'becomes his dwelling-place /
And garden fruitful seventy fold'.

This part of the Blake poem is handled by Cary from two related
points of view: the discovery of vision ('Yes, I found out how to get
Sara on the canvas') and his mastery of Sara as his spouse and lover.
She had at first been constantly putting him 'to bed' (*HM*, 51). But in
the end he hits her. He sums up the relationship in a way that comprises both the psycho-sexual and the imaginative elements of the
allegory: 'Materiality, that is, Sara, the old female nature, having
attempted to button up the prophetic spirit, that is to say, Gulley
Jimson, in her placket-hole, got a bonk on the conk, and was reduced
to her proper status, as spiritual fodder' (*HM*, 52).

The rest of Blake's poem details how the male spirit grows old, and
finds a little 'Female Babe' on the hearth. Ultimately, she 'comes to
the Man she loves', and the now aged man is driven away, until he
can find another 'Maiden'. Her charms and beauty beguile him to
infancy, and he grows younger and younger as she grows older. This
is the period of the domination of Nature, a malign notion in Blake,

and correspondingly, the imagery is sinister in Blakean terms: thus, 'The Senses roll themselves in fear / And the flat Earth becomes a Ball' are lines that refer to modern science and the philosophy of materialism. Gulley maps onto these lines his increasingly difficult struggle (as he feels it) to find an appropriate form for his vision. Tracing his various flirtations with different schools of painting, he implies that he is dissatisfied with all (*HM*, 61–65). Though Cézanne might be an original genius, there is a sense that one cannot repeat his originality, that there are too many cubists (representing the next generation, who developed his ideas). Furthermore, Cubism appears to have an unedifying social correlative: 'Cubism. On the gravel. All services. Modern democracy. Organized comforts. The Socialist state. Bureaucratic liberalism. Scientific management' (*HM*, 65). But soon the aged man has become a 'frowning Babe' again: the male principle of imagination will be strong once more. And Gulley remarks, 'And I was thinking of Artist Hitler' (*HM*, 71). The topic of Hitler had been introduced by a smart person called Mr Moseley, whom Gulley mistrusts, and it is tempting to associate him with the leader of the British Union of Fascists. But Moseley does not appear to be wholly, if at all, in sympathy with Hitler: it is rather that his name is a way of opening up, in an unstable fashion, the whole question of the rise of fascism and how to regard its historical significance. That Hitler should, even tentatively, be identified with the 'frowning Babe' who ushers in a new era is no more to be accounted praise than Yeats's 'The Second Coming' constitutes praise of the 'rough beast'. Cary sees a new dispensation emerging from the deadliness of socialist bureaucracy and scientific management, but there is no suggestion that he approves of the way in which it is coming into being.

However, the link with Yeats is both real and instructive. Yeats's cyclical system in *A Vision*, as Cary would have been very well aware, was in part modelled upon 'The Mental Traveller'. In this perspective, Cary's imagination can be seen as characteristically Anglo-Irish in the way that his conservatism gives sharp relief to a specific kind of internal contradiction: valuing the world of contingency, of the eccentric, of characters, and likewise valuing the untrammelled and untidy energy of the artist, at the same time it links that world to a strongly conceived realm of eternal and endlessly repeated values which must be respected and nurtured. Of course, an even wider perspective would show that we have here another example of the modern tension

between the need to depict contingency and the insecure require-
ment for an explanatory myth or grand narrative. But the Anglo-Irish
connection bestows upon this tension its particular form, just as the
existentialist bearings of Cary's novel give it a notably mid-century
caste, one that is in some ways comparable to that which can be
found in the work of another Anglo-Irish writer, his friend Iris
Murdoch.

9

Two American Disciples of Blake: Robert Duncan and Allen Ginsberg

Robert Duncan

Burton Hatlen, in a chapter on 'Robert Duncan's Marriage of Heaven and Hell', claims that the poet is a true heir of the Judeo-Christian tradition because his work incorporates the 'magic' which had been discarded by fundamentalists and demythologisers alike.[1] Hatlen makes the word magic do a lot of work, for he moves swiftly from the topic of lost wonder to the traditional structure of magical belief, as if the wonder were always a by-product of such belief. It matters little, though, that the ruse seems to beg so many questions, since Duncan would doubtless agree with Hatlen, and in particular would agree that magical currents in Judeo-Christian tradition 'tend to conceive of the world in terms of opposing powers: the male sulfur and the female mercury in alchemy; *Din* and *Hesed* in Lurianic Kabbhalah'.[2] He goes on to point out that all forms of magic seek to 'join these opposites and thereby uncover a 'lost state of perfection', a 'golden world' or Eden.[3] These claims provide a way into Duncan's philosophy of contraries which, while it defers to Blake's influence, emphasises in particular that of the Kabbalah – the major symbol of which, The Tree of Life, is alluded to in the title of the volume Hatlen examines: *Roots and Branches* (1970). Hatlen claims that Duncan's treatment of a major pair of contraries – good and evil – is 'radical in the same way that Blake's was radical. Both Blake and Duncan seek a reconciliation of good and evil, and this aspiration places them in opposition to all orthodox religion'.[4] Whether or not Blake actually seeks a 'reconciliation' of good and evil – or any of his other contraries, for that matter – might at least be a hard-pressed question of definition. While 'marriage' is the alchemical word in the title of one of his best-known works, this is the book that contains the statement 'Opposition is True Friendship'. But, as we shall see, Duncan's interest in Kabbalah does lead to a toning down of the oppositional dynamic of Blake's contraries. Even so, the imprint of Blake is present in the rebellious radicalism Hatlen identifies and in the interest in depicting both benign and malign versions of Jehovah and the archetypal Father.

Roots and Branches is, indeed, both more Kabbalistic and more Blakean than Duncan's other volumes, because of the insistence with which the theme of contraries is invoked in relation to both influences. This is the volume that contains the important sequence, 'Variations on Two Dicta of William Blake'. Near the beginning of the volume, in 'What Do I Know of the Old Love', Duncan speaks of 'that Tree of Trees', the Tree of Life, which contains 'shared loves and curses interwoven and fair and unfair establisht in one'.[5] Guided by such knowledge, but drawing on Blake, Duncan can announce, in 'Osiris and Set', that 'Now it is time for Hell / to nurse at the teats of Heaven' (*RB*, 69). And in 'Adam's Way', Erda informs us, speaking of 'Adam', that 'His name is Hell and Heaven too' (*RB*, 142). The 'radicalism' to which Hatlen refers has fed into this concept, however, for in 'Cover Images' Duncan informs us that 'Strands / of Belsen and Buchenwald / issue from Eden' (*RB*, 53). The reference to the Holocaust is rendered all the more shocking in context, given the overt references earlier in the volume to the Jewish character of the Kabbalah. It also points to a specific and unprecedented challenge posed to the post-war writer inclined to admire Blake's Satanic vision. In England, both Ted Hughes and Geoffrey Hill have risen to this challenge. At a more banal level, it is interesting to note that in an interview with Robert Peters and Paul Trachtenberg, Duncan gets involved in a discussion of sadomasochism, in the midst of which Trachtenberg observes that 'Anger, it seems, must be played out for sanity.'[6] This is a point which Duncan himself makes in 'Structure of Rime XV': 'The lioness made demure from cruelty/ cast down her eyes / before our frightened eyes' (*RB*, 64). This is an example of his frequent Blake-like use of the image of lion or tiger to represent wrath or dangerous energies often categorised as evil. Characteristically, it contains a clearer sense of reconciliation than is to be found in Blake's *Marriage*. This comes across in the interview, as well, where Duncan, having conceded that his 'enemy is somebody who is antithetic', goes on to explain that 'if I killed the person I'd never be able to change the idea of him. You've got to keep your enemy alive':[7] without wishing to kill his enemy, and while conceding that the Prolific and the Devourer are necessary to each other, Blake says that '[they] should be enemies'.

One example of a difficult productive conflict in Duncan's own life is provided by his relationship with his mother. In 'A Lammas Tiding', Duncan had explained that the composition of his poem 'My Mother Would be a Falconess' was precipitated by the line 'with what sense is it that the chicken shuns the ravenous hawk' from *Visions of the Daughters of Albion*[8] (*BB*, 51). The poem powerfully evokes the speaker's sense of being subject to a limiting control. 'Yet it would have been beautiful, if she would have carried me,/ always, in a little hood with the bells ringing' (*BB*, 53). But the speaker tears at her wrist and manages to get 'beyond the curb of her will'. And yet, even so, and even though she is not dead, he still treads her wrist, is still hooded, 'talking to [him]self' and would still draw blood (*BB*, 54). The implication is that his poetry arises out of the painful tension between the cruel energy his mother has bequeathed him and the need to fly beyond her influence. Then it is there, under the hood, he is 'talking to [him]self'. Indeed, Duncan is precisely explicit about the emergence of poetry from conflict. In 'A Set of Romantic Hymns', developing the idea that the strings of the lyre lay in 'the curve between two horns', he switches to the image of the piano, implying that the '*Ivory and Ebony*' of the keys are an apt symbol of the contrariety out of which poetry and song are formed.

Duncan's response to the challenge of evil is markedly Blakean, though this does not mean, I would claim, that it is definitely non-Kabbalistic. The figure with whom the speaker is in implicit or explicit conflict is the malign Father, mythologised as a tyrannical Jehovah who is clearly modelled on Blake's Urizen. This connection is clearest in the poems originally published in small volumes such as *Of the War* (Oyez: Berkeley, 1966), and collected in *Bending the Bow* (1971), which register Duncan's interpretation of the Vietnam war and the Civil Rights struggle. The 'absolute authority' who is, as in Blake, 'the great dragon' (*BB*, 70) is also explicitly identified with Blake's Nobodaddy (*BB*, 71). In 'Passage 26: The Soldiers' he is Ahriman: he contains 'the inner need for the salesman's pitch'

(*BB*, 115), is 'Grand Profiteer', and his capitalist dreams are related to 'the snaking field, the B-52, flying so high' (*BB*, 116). 'Up Rising: Passage 25' places the Vietnam war within the context of a mythological history which begins with Blake's vision of America 'in figures of fire and blood raging' (*BB*, 81) and unexpectedly links this to the modern, destructive form of the 'secret entity of America's hatred of Europe, of Africa, of Asia', positing a dark inflection to Blake's continental myth, whereby the once-positive spirit of rebellious America has degenerated into a new tyrant. This in itself, of course, is a characteristically Blakean progression. Then it is true that the new Jehovah appears, identified with Satan, and looking through the eyes of President Johnson:

> and the very glint of Satan's eyes from the pit of hell
>> America's unacknowledged, unrepented crimes that I saw in
>> Goldwater's eyes
> now shines from the eyes of the President
>> in the swollen head of the nation.
>
> (*BB*, 83)

The union of the supposedly liberal Johnson with the right-wing ideology of Barry Goldwater represents another form of the large-scale degeneration.

But there is no point in a complete rejection of the evil Jehovah. In psychological terms, this would be the denial of the 'jealousy or wrath' (both Urizenic words) which exist in us all. As Duncan puts it in the interview quoted earlier, 'most anti-christians want to demolish Yahweh – [...] I'm not against my own jealousy and wrath, for these forces are the beginning of creativity seeking to transform the flawed state'.[9] This is another form of Duncan's forgiving interpretation of 'Opposition is true Friendship'. The end of such a process will be the rediscovery of the father as love, the return of the Urizenic Priest to his original status as bard. This is the 'Father' who is addressed in 'A Sequence of Poems for H.D.'s Birthday' and is enjoined, 'Father who has sent a message with blessing, / stand against Jehovah who is jealous in Thy place' (*RB*, 12). This Jehovah is a perversion; but, as in Blake, perversions, being visions, have extraordinary power. Duncan lays out his thinking on these matters with the greatest daring in *The*

Truth & Life of Myth (1968):

> [Christians] where their humanitarian ideals were strong, came to
> apostasy when faced with the immoveable reality of Jehovah who
> declares Himself a God of Jealousy, Vengeance and Wrath. Reason
> falters, but our mythic, our deepest poetic sense, recognizes and
> greets as truth the proclamation that the Son brings that just this
> Wrathful Father is the First Person of Love.[10]

The Son who redeems the Father is symbolised by Jesus, of course; but
in a reversal which is also essentially Blakean, and very reminiscent of
The Marriage, he is just as likely to be Lucifer. In 'The Law', the poet
awaits 'the orders of the Lord of Love' and expands on this by
exclaiming 'Let me await thee, Prince of the Morning' (*RB*, 43).
Duncan can also identify with Lucifer himself, in lines which
consciously evoke the idea of the homosexual love-object as eroticised
father and which are described as 'Lucifer's Song in Love of His
Lord'.[11]

The Law, while it certainly carries wide-ranging connotations, is
partially conceived in terms of the organising principle of art. When
freed from the role of coercion, this principle can be seen in the image
of the Father as 'Architect Divine', building a 'Temple' (*RB*, 34, 43).
Duncan is trying for an ideal balance for which many have
striven since the Romantic period: that whereby form is both
self-generating and organised, while at the same time being neither
anarchic nor coercive. This problem breeds anxiety in Blake, an anxiety which is indeed registered in the contrary depictions of the
Father as tyrant or bard. Duncan describes the tyrannical conception
of form in words which recall two of the sources of Urizen's name,
'reason' and 'horizon':

> Form, to the mind possessed by convention, is significant in so far
> as it shows control. What has nor rime nor reason is a bogie that
> must be dismissed from the horizons of mind. It is a matter of rules
> and conformities, taste, rationalizations and sense.[12]

In contrast, Duncan, as Robert J. Bertholf points out, thinks of poetic
form as arising out of 'process'.[13] This is a conception which bears the
imprint of the poetics of his associate, Charles Olson. 'Poetic Process',

for Duncan as for Olson, is a matter of 'moving weights and duration of syllables' and is formed from 'the language of our human experience'.[14] An apt image of poetic form is dance: *'The numbers have enterd your feet'*.[15] Olson's general concept of 'open field' composition hovers in the background, not least in the title of Duncan's *The Opening of the Field* (1969). In this work, a Blakean 'Lion' asks questions about human limitations which are clearly modelled on those at the end of *The Book of Thel*: *'The Messenger in guise of a Lion roared: Why does man retract his song from the impoverished air? He brings his young to the opening of the field. Does he so fear beautiful compulsion?'*[16] 'Beautiful compulsion' is the ideal balance of organisation and freedom, here conceived in relation to an 'open field'. As Bertholf points out, though, the results in Duncan are both like and unlike Blake: 'Blake evolves a complicated system, a symbolic landscape [...] Duncan evolves a poetry of process in which the drive of the imagination to propose approximations of eternal images takes precedence over the approximations which illustrate that process.'[17] In his earlier work this sense of approximation and process was capable, under the influence of Gertrude Stein, of expressing itself in an uncompromisingly radical fashion: 'Beginning to write. Continuing finally to write. Writing finally to continue beginning.'[18]

An agonistic form of this process is 'struggle', and the struggle is cast in notably Blakean terms. As he says, 'recently I have come to think of poetry more and more as a wrestling with Form to liberate Form. The figure of Jacob returns again and again to my thought'.[19] 'Wrestling with Form to liberate Form' sounds like an interpretation of 'Striving with Systems to deliver individuals from those systems' and 'I must create a system or be enslaved by another man's.' Such struggle can be quite straightforwardly identified with the process of poetry; as in the significantly entitled 'The Law I Love is a Major Mover':

> Look! The Angel that made a man of Jacob
>   made Israël in His embrace
>
> was the Law, was Syntax[20]

'Syntax', indeed, is another formula for the dance or process which Duncan prefers when he wishes to comprise in his account of creativity the notion of a resistant medium: 'It has seemed to me that I wrestle with the syntax of the world of my experience to bring forward into the Day the twisted syntax of my human language that will be changed in that contest ever with what I dread there.'[21]

Behind all of this struggle with the bad Father who must be redeemed one may, as we have seen, discover the features of the terrible Jehovah. But in line with the ambiguity we have been sketching, even that very terror may be invested with Romantic sublimity. It is true, of course, that that sublimity itself can seem freighted with a sense of evil:

> My Father flies upon the air,
> shakes down black night around me,
> for where I think of him
> his wings are there, his
> crownd eye, his horny beak,
>   his lingering air. (*RB*, 109)

But even the creative God is characterised by 'terror', as Duncan makes clear in *As Testimony* (1964), quoting Charles Williams.[22] Something of this sense of creative terror is conveyed in other terms when Duncan, in 'Of Blasphemy', equates Satan with Pluto: 'Satan that was once great Pluto underground!'[23] This underground is fertile, in the way we might expect of the realm once visited by Persephone. Yet Duncan insists on his interweaving of Satan and Classical imagery:

> Again and again return underground
> To the dark fires, the Satanic thriving.
> The First Prince is of Light ignorant.
>   Toward *scientia* he strives.[24]

This 'Prince', like Blake's Orc, is a figure of creative burning. Interestingly, he is here on the way to becoming Lucifer, rather than already there. This is quite a good example of the improvisational quality of Duncan's myth-making, since one could not reconstruct one immutable version of his myth of Satan from this example. Here, then, we have an example of the way in which, in the post-modern, Blake has the capacity to become the patron of improvised myth-making. Equally important, we also have an example of the continued vitality of myth in the postmodern; a vitality which sets itself apart from a certain strain of late modernist objectivism. In this connection, it is interesting to note that Duncan's involvement in meditations on mythology, and his references to traditional 'wisdom', became something of a bone of contention between himself and Olson, although, as Bertholf points out, Duncan was pleased to be able to regard this contention as an example of creative contrariety.[25] Duncan cannot dispense with myth: for him it is the story of the self; for 'there is a Self that belongs to a Story that determines the sense of truth and life in my own daily living'.[26] This is the essential context for Duncan's belief that 'the literal' is not 'a matter of mere fact' since the world is imbued with 'the inner Fiction of Consciousness'.[27] For Duncan, Blake's importance is related to precisely this point: namely, that rather than invoking myth as structure, he writes out of a world experienced as myth at every level:

> With Blake, the poet's sense of his primordial inspiration, his coexistence in the original time of spiritual beings and the very presence of powers, appears in his actual life itself. He does not write poems as ways into the mythological; he writes poems *from* the realm of that reality.[28]

Allen Ginsberg

Ginsberg believed that, practically, Blake had initiated his maturity and power as a poet when he was young. Other teachers followed, but Blake was the first and the most important. The relationship was very similar to that Blake thought obtained between himself and Milton, as described in Blake's *Milton*, especially in that moment where Milton descends into Blake's garden in Felpham and enters his left foot, after which they are joined in inspiration. As Ginsberg says, 'I heard the voice of Blake in a vision, and repeat that voice' ('Kral Majales').[29] He told an interviewer in 1956 that Blake's voice 'is the voice I have now'.[30] There was, in fact, a series of three visions all of which happened in 1948 while Ginsberg was a student at Columbia University, living in Harlem and melancholy because of the break-up of his affair with Neal Cassady. He had been reading *Songs of Innocence and of Experience*, but only the first vision involved an auditory hallucination and was closely linked to the *Songs*. Ginsberg thought that he heard Blake's voice reciting 'Ah! Sunflower' and 'The Sick Rose', and then experienced a sense of God's omnipresence. Ginsberg, there and then made a vow that he 'never forget, never renege, never deny' the experience, and the dedication was accompanied by a sense of vocation; 'from now I'm chosen, blessed, sacred poet'.[31]

The other two experiences were less radiant, but arguably just as important for Ginsberg's later work. In the first, he was in the Columbia University bookshop, flicking through a copy of Blake. As he did so, he felt that he was 'in the eternal place once more'. But the vision was rather different: he felt as if the other people in the shop were like strange animals. But then he perceived that, nevertheless, under this appearance they were enlightened beings. He interpreted this duality in terms of a dual aspect to humans: everyone underwent 'a hardening, a shutting off of the perception of desire and tenderness', but those qualities remained within. What was experienced was a reaffirmation of these qualities and the communication of the realisation that they existed under the hardening.[32] The final vision was that of God turned into a devil, which he thought of in terms of Blake's phrase 'the gates of wrath'. Ginsberg found this experience terrifying and hard to assimilate.[33]

Both the hardening vision, and the God-devil one, find echoes in Ginsberg's work. In general terms, a deep ambivalence structures his approach, especially to one of his subjects, America itself. The New York through which 'the best minds wander in 'Howl', 'hallucinating Arkansas and Blake-light tragedy' is darkly sublime, chillingly attractive. It is the terrain of much of Ginsberg's poetry. Even at its darkest, when described as the land of Moloch, who is like Ginsberg's own Urizen, it is still the only America Ginsberg knows: 'Moloch whose factories dream and croak in the fog! Moloch whose smokestacks and antennae crown the cities!'. It is not at all surprising, then, to find that Moloch may also be associated with holiness – 'holy the Angel in Moloch!' – especially as Ginsberg also intones 'holy the solitudes of skyscrapers and pavements!' ('Footnote to Howl', *CP*, 134) Ginsberg reveals the holiness in what he also describes as repellent. As for the God-turned-devil, Moloch himself is the most obvious version of that, but there are others, as we shall see.

The moment of inspiration in Harlem is itself a recurrent theme of Ginsberg's poetry. Apart from the examples we have already mentioned, there is the experience of the 'Ignu' in the poem of that name (*CP*, 203–05): an 'ignu' is an undeveloped Ginsberg *alter ego*, ignorant of the ways of the world, naked (or nude) within it, a lover of poetry, gentle, a good lover. He 'hears Blake's disembodied voice recite the Sunflower, in a room in Harlem'. And in 'Psalm IV' (*CP*, 238) we have a relatively detailed account of the whole episode, from initial masturbation, to looking at the design of the sunflower, to hearing Blake's voice recite the poem. But in this version, Blake's voice gives way to some concluding apostrophes:

> Love! thou patient presence & bone of the body! Father! thy careful
>   watching and waiting over my soul!
> My son! My son! the endless ages have remembered me!
>   My son! My son! Time howled in anguish in my ear!
> My son! My son! my father wept and held me in his dead arms.

The phrase 'My son! My son!' recalls one of the engraved emblems from Blake's *The Gates of Paradise*, in which a naked youth (the son) threatens with a spear a weary, bearded old man, seated on a throne. The echoes of David and Absalom are less important for Blake, or Ginsberg, than the sense of conflict between son and father. But in Ginsberg's poem this is only hinted at and is followed by another reference to a Blake design of slightly different purport: that in *Milton* where a slumped, dejected father holds a radiant young Christ in his arms. Ginsberg's Blake is his own: the lines convey the reconciliation of God as father and Ginsberg, even as they suggest a parallel reconciliation with his actual dead father.

The sunflower is subject to a different development. In 'Sunflower Sutra' (*CP*, 138–39), Jack Kerouac shows Ginsberg a dirty grey sunflower, the first the latter had seen; he is reminded of his Harlem experience. But this sunflower is not quite the Blakean one: it is 'grey' and 'dusty with the smut and smog and smoke of olden locomotives in its eye – / corolla of bleary spikes pushed down and broken like a battered crown'. The connotations of the crucified Christ are undeniable: the mode of crucifixion is the existence of the principle of beauty in the damaged, industrial world. Here we have, from one point of view, another example of the ambivalence discussed above: the flower is damaged by the world, but in an important sense it is also the flower of this world. This interpretation is made clearer if one turns to an earlyer, very fine lyric, 'In back of the real' (*CP*, 113), from *The Green Automobile*. The poem does not refer to the Harlem incident, and it is not about the sunflower, but 'the dread hay flower', which is lying on the asphalt highway in the back of the railroad yard in San Jose. It has a 'corolla of yellowish dirty / spikes like Jesus' inch-long / crown'. It suffers, thus, in the world, like the sunflower. We are told that it is 'the flower of industry', that it is 'ugly', but that it has 'the form of the great yellow / Rose in [its] brain!' And Ginsberg concludes that it is 'the flower of the world'. The reminiscence of Yeats is telling and to the point. Yeats's Rose is the principle of Eternal beauty as found in this world, not in the other. So while it remembers the eternal, it is only to be found in this world, a world of contrariety and struggle: this last fact means that Yeats finds it appropriate to compose a poem 'To the Rose upon the Rood of Time' – that is, to the Rose crucified on the world of time. The Yeatsian reference here is reasonably precise, but that does not put it at odds with Blake, or at least the later Blake, who spoke of how 'eternity is in love with the productions of time'. On the other hand, contrary to what Ginsberg seems to think, Blake's 'The Sun-flower' does not conceptualise the relations of Time and Eternity in quite the same way. One of the *Songs of Experience*, it offers an emblem of declining energy: the sunflower is 'weary of time', tired of life, wishing for sleep and death. Ultimately the weariness can be linked to the fear and envy of youthful energy to be found in *The Experience* version of 'Nurse's Song'.

'In back of the real' shows the same ambivalence, specifically about the industrial world, that can be found in 'Sunflower Sutra'. But more than perhaps any other poem of Ginsberg's, perhaps because of its intense lyric organisation, it reveals the sources of his poetic style in that ambivalence. For 'In back of the real' displays a tough, 'spiky' (to use an adjective applied to the flower) musicality which is a strong form of the style Ginsberg characteristically employs. Just to take the first stanza, with its lead-in title:

In Back of the Real

railroad yard in San Jose
I wandered desolate
in front of a tank factory
and sat on a bench
near the switchman's shack.

The syllable [ak] is present here in 'back', 'factory' and 'shack', and approximated in 'tank'. Various alliterations help to pull the stanza even closer together, but it is particularly the strong, if irregular, rhythm heightened by the [ak] sound which makes one think of a jazz whose rhythm remembers the railroad. Thus it is that this is quintessentially a 'Beat' poem. That does not sound especially Blakean; but it is worth remembering that the style is indeed in part bound up with ideas nurtured on a particular reading of Blake – of later Blake, as much as early, given the importance of the relationship of Time and Eternity.

The emphasis on the 'real' in that relationship is an early one. Thus, another poem that seems to remember Yeats (and through Yeats, Mallarmé), 'The Trembling of the Veil' (*CP*, 14), while its title intimates the pressure of the ideal on the sacred, consists almost entirely of exact descriptions of some trees ('I saw the scarlet and pink shoot-tips') – except for the statement that they 'seemed like live / organisms on the moon'. This initial perception imparts just sufficient strangeness to the picture to link up with the idea of the trembling of the veil and suggest that something more than mere facticity is being registered. Yet in the end, like so many twentieth-century poems, this one merely ends up by registering the strangeness of the real itself: which is to say, its strangely compelling beauty. The underlying point is succinctly made in 'Metaphysics', where it is asserted that 'This is the one and only / firmament'; that 'There is no other world' and that the author is therefore 'living in Eternity' (*CP*, 33). A better-known (and better) statement of the literary corollary of such a belief is to be found in the short poem 'On Burroughs' Mask', from which the later title *Reality Sandwiches* derives:

> The method must be purest meat
> and no symbolic dressing,
> actual visions & actual prisons
> as seen there and now. (*CP*, 114)

But the phrase 'actual visions' intimates the ambiguity which hovers around this conception. And unlikely as this might seem, a claim can be made that neither this nor 'Metaphysics' is actually anti-Blakean. Blake's early insistence in *The Marriage of Heaven and Hell* that 'Man has no Body distinct from his Soul', if combined with the associated assertion that 'Energy is the only life, and is from the Body', would seem to Ginsberg like an affirmation of a particularly sensuous kind of natural supernaturalism. In no way was he 'reneging' on the vow he made in Harlem after experiencing a hallucination, which, after all, followed closely on a bout of masturbation.

But speaking of style, there is one respect in which there is a clear link between Blake and Whitman, and that is their use of a Biblical-sounding long line characterised by parallelism and repetition. Indeed, it is surely significant that the fullest poetic account of the Harlem experience should be called 'Psalm IV'. A connected point: Ginsberg shares with both Blake and Whitman the attribute of writing a kind of prophecy, in which, true to much Biblical prophecy, the spiritual state of the nation is a central topic. It is entirely evident that prophetic wrath is prominent in Ginsberg's response to contemporary America. This fact in itself becomes part of his subject-matter, and is handled in a recognisably Blakean way in 'The Lion for Real' (*CP*, 174–75). The speaker, clearly a Ginsberg *alter ego*, finds a lion in his living room. That this lion is a transfiguration of Blake's 'Tyger' is confirmed by yet another reference to the vision in Harlem; for the poem is dated 'March 1958', and Ginsberg writes of 'Lion that eats my mind now for a decade knowing only your hunger'; that is, since 1948, the time of the original vision(s). Indeed, this lion is located in Harlem. Furthermore, he exclaims, 'how am I chosen'. The lion is associated with untrammelled desire, as is confirmed by the fact that he visits his friend and Joey and listens for lions in his 'poetries'. All he hears, however, are 'Elephant Tiglon Hippogriff Unicorn Ants,' but figures 'he really understood me when we made it in Ignaz Wisdom's bathroom'. The lion appears to be both insatiable and starving, but refuses to eat the speaker: a symbol of the way in which the speaker himself is gnawed by a hunger and an anger which have no natural conclusion, and which are identical with his continuing poetic vocation.

While the 'Moloch' section of *Howl* might seem like the most obvious candidate for Ginsberg's *Book of Urizen*, there is another: one which is at least as profound, and is strangely marked by the influence of Biblical parallelism, namely 'Hymnn' (*CP*, 225–27), one of the poems ('Kaddish' is another) in which he seeks to come to terms with the troubled life of his mother, who ended up incarcerated in a mental hospital. God – or a God – is central to this poem, and he seems to be a source of ill as much as of good. We begin with an ecstatic devotional cry, 'In the world which He has created according to his will Blessed Praised / Magnified Lauded Exalted the Name of the Holy One Blessed is He!' But the world which he has created includes 'the madhouse', in which his mother languished and raved ('In the madhouse Blessed is He!'), and it is not entirely clear whether madness is inspiration or suffering, especially as we are told 'Blessed be He in homosexuality' alongside both 'Blessed be He in Paranoia' and 'Blessed be He in the book!' The desolate evocation of his mother's eyes in Part IV is followed by an antiphonal evocation of Godhead, apostrophes to the Lord interwoven with the cawing of crows, recalling the crows 'shriek[ing]' over his mother's 'grave stones in Long Island'. The alternation ends up producing a partial equivalence, as if God were both the Lord and a crow. In the process, neither crows nor Lord remain unaffected by each other: the Lord is a 'great Eye' that moves 'in a black cloud', while the caw of the crows is 'the call of Time'. This is the most desolate expression of Ginsberg's ambivalent vision, and it bears a general resemblance to Blake's own conflation of Fall and Genesis.

This touches again on the idea of a potentially malevolent Deity, like Blake's Urizen or Nobodaddy. And indeed, Nobodaddy himself appears in 'Yiddishe Kopf', equated with the God of the Jews, 'Blake sd "6000 years of sleep" since antique Nobodaddy Adonai's mind trap'.[34] But Ginsberg proceeds, again with characteristic ambivalence, to undercut, to some degree, the negative implications of Blake's concept by immediately exclaiming, 'Oy! Such Meshuggeneh absolutes'. 'Sleep' is too absolute an idea to cover the influence of Adonai. And when one looks back on the poem, one can see that there is good and bad in being Jewish, and in having a Jewish God. Ginsberg, we are told, is 'Jewish because Buddhist, my anger's transparent hot air, I shrug my shoulders'. This equates Jewishness with the tolerant qualities of Buddhism, a non-theist religion. But in the very next line we are told that he is 'Jewish because monotheist Jews Catholics Moslems 're intolerable intolerant –'. This is the line which precedes the one about 'Nobodaddy Adonai'. The net effect is to imply that there is nothing absolutely negative about Nobodaddy Adonai: all depends on how he is interpreted by society and, by the same token, by individuals. Ginsberg's ambivalent Buddhist Jewishness leads to a tolerant rage for Justice: a tolerant intolerance of evil. But Jewish (and

Muslim) monotheism may equally become the pretext for endless territorial disputes, racial hatred and war, as in 'Jaweh and Allah Battle' (*CP*, 614–16): 'Jaweh with Atom Bomb / Allah cuts throat of Infidels / Jaweh's armies beat down neighbouring tribes / Will Red Sea waters close & drown the armies of Allah?' Such religion leads to exclamations like these: 'We shall triumph over the enemy! / Maintain our Separate Identity! Proud / History evermore!' These gods represent the principle behind the popular paranoia lampooned in 'America': 'America it's them bad Russians; / Them Russians them Russians and them Chinamen.'

It appears that Ginsberg's ambivalence about the idea of God was paralleled by an ambivalence about Blake's very influence. As he said in 'The Change', in 1962,

> There was a cycle that began with the Blake vision which ended on the train in Kyoto when I realized that to attain the depth of consciousness that I was seeking when I was talking about the Blake vision, [...] I had to renounce it [...] give up this continual churning thought process of yearning back to a visionary state.[35]

But as Alicia Ostriker points out, 'renunciation does not prevent him subsequently from recording his own settings of *Songs of Innocence and of Experience*, staging them at poetry readings, referring to Blake as a major influence in interviews, and employing Blake as a gloss to explain other artists'.[36] Influence is as likely to involve oedipal ambivalence as is the reaction to a patriarchal father god. The evidence that Blake ceases to be important in Ginsberg's work after 1963 is simply not there. Indeed, the next year, when he writes 'Today' (*CP*, 345–47), a somewhat Frank O'Hara-ish poem in which he records the events and thoughts of an ordinary day, we are told that he 'thought a few minutes of Blake', and in 1965, having been expelled from Czechoslovakia, on the plane to Britain in 'Kral Majales' (*CP*, 353–54) he yet again assigns his prophetic role to the fact that he 'heard the voice of Blake in a vision'. He promises himself that he will visit 'Bunhill Fields' (where Blake is buried) once he has landed at 'Albion's airfield', as if to reaffirm the root of the inspiration that had landed him in trouble. A similar connection to prophetic roots is effected in 'Wales Visitation' (*CP*, 480–82). A visit to Tintern Abbey, which might make one think only of Wordsworthian

Romanticism, and a progress to Capel-Y-Ffin, once home of Landor, nevertheless make Ginsberg think principally of Blake. The 'Bardic' is glimpsed in' a vale of Albion', the lambs are 'heard in Blake's old ear', and beyond Capel-Y-Ffin, at Lord Hereford's Knob, he had a vision of 'all Albion one'.

Of course, it is true, as Ostriker says, that some of the references to Blake are 'space-filling throwaways'.[37] But on the whole, meaningful references to Blake are regular, though not all-pervasive, and, as we have seen, Ginsberg's method and preoccupations are to be seen in relation to Blake. Thus, when he records a kind of re-dedication to the Blakean vision, in 'Contest of Bards' (*CP*, 665–79), this should not be seen as a sudden return, but rather as a deepening of the relationship.

The poem is preceded by an 'ARGUMENT', the context for what follows. The Blakean connection is established by reference to 'prophetic dreams' and 'the old Bard', and this makes it clear that the Argument is a reference to a couple of similar Blakean narrative structures: the introductory lines to *Europe* (Plate iii; *E*, 60), which is formally set off from what follows; and the Bard's Song from *Milton* (2:25–13:44; *E*, 96–107). In *Europe*, the opening lines acquaint us with a 'Fairy' who dictates all that follows; in *Milton* the Bard's Song recounts another version of the fall, the situation from which the remainder of the poem must wrest the clues to salvation. In Ginsberg's 'Argument', a young poet arrives naked and announces 'his own prophetic dreams to replace the cold Bard's boring verities'. The young poet has seen in vision 'an Eternal Rune cut in stone at the hearth-front under porphyry bard-throne'. The 'Rune' is printed next to the poem (*CP*, 669). Its grammar is elliptical, but it places confidence in the idea that a realm of 'Beauty' lies beyond death – 'the Rune' is very conscious of ageing and death. In the next section of 'The Contest' the old 'bard' is enjoined, as another 'Argument' explains (*CP*, 670), to 'seek the ancient unearthly Beauty the riddle indicates'. The ensuing lines reveal that the boy is more enamoured of transcendent than earthly beauty. The bard, without conceding the totality of this point, appears to accept that there must be an ideal that goes beyond the corporeal. He recalls that he himself had once known the rune, and 'For thirty years enriched with witty penury I gathered Amber from the generous laurel' – Thirty years: back to 1947, since the poem dates from 1997, but near enough to 1948, when the original Blake visions occurred.

Conclusion

There are similarities between the reactions to Blake respectively of Duncan and Ginsberg. Both are gay poets who regard Blake as an ally in the reaction against orthodox heterosexuality; both see him as a kind of father; both see in Blake's work images of the bad father who rejects them; both, as Blake did, see the possibility that the bad father is within themselves; both are capable of equating the bad father with political reaction in the United States, and both employ this interpretation in their critique of the Vietnam entanglement. These particular cases are, furthermore, illuminating about Blake's persistence in the postmodern. For Blake is seen by so many both as an ally and as one who dramatises the tangled politics of alliance and enmity.

10
Postmodern Myths and Lies: Iain Sinclair and Angela Carter

Iain Sinclair

In discussion of 'small-press' or alternative poetry in Britain from the Sixties onwards there is one adjective which occurs very frequently – and with justice: American. In looking for models which transcended what were seen as the limitations of the Movement and post-Movement poetry which constituted the British 'establishment', America seemed to offer not only a view of human nature which transcended the 'gentility' of which Alvarez complained in *The New Poetry* and elsewhere. It also offered the innovativeness which seemed to permit the exploration of a wider range of experience and states of mind. Within the metropolitan establishment, Alvarez's espousal of the 'confessional' mode encouraged the expression of the mind *in extremis*. Yet in the poetry of Lowell or Plath it might plausibly be claimed, without necessarily impugning their work, that the picture of this mind was not radically different from that which appeared to be posited by a poem of Thom Gunn or Donald Davie. Indeed, a curious and little-remarked feature of Alvarez's anthology is the extent to which even in its second edition, with its suggestive division between British and American poetry, it remained the best readily-available selection of Movement poetry. The other traditions represented by the American Beats and the poets associated with Black Mountain College found little favour in mainstream British publishing, although the Sixties saw a temporary shift in this direction in the activities of Cape Goliard and Fulcrum Press. The presiding notion for many poets who looked to America was that the work of Charles Olson and other Black Mountain poets, such as Denise Levertov, Robert Creeley, Robert Duncan and Ed Dorn, offered innovative ways of building upon what were seen as the poetic advances of Ezra Pound and William Carlos Williams. But some took their bearings both from these poets and from the Beats.

One such is Iain Sinclair, a writer now well known as a London 'psychogeographer' from novels such as *White Chappell: Scarlet Tracings*, which won the Guardian Fiction Prize in 1987, or *Lights Out for the Territory* (1997), the record of a perambulation around the streets of the city. Sinclair figures in the Carcanet anthology of poets originally published in small presses from the 1960s onwards, *A Various Art* (1987). The editors, Andrew Crozier and Tim Longville, refer to the context of 'English interest in the 1960s in American music, painting, and writing' and the tradition of 'Pound and Williams' ('not that of Pound and Eliot').[1] Sinclair was not the only American-influenced, small-press poet to be engaging in large-scale topographical poetry about London in the Seventies: Peter Barry points out that Allen Fisher was writing *Place* (1974–77) contemporaneously with Sinclair's *Lud Heat* (1975).[2] Sinclair's early work makes allusions to Ginsberg (an admirer of Blake, like Sinclair himself); but, with its pared-down, free verse lines, compact with taut energy, it looks indebted to the school of Olson as well.

The work of Olson provides one point of entry for Sinclair's 'psychogeography' – his exploration, elaboration and mythologising of the chains of association emanating from place. In *The Maximus Poems*, Olson offers the history and geography of Gloucester, Massachusetts, as the relevant context for Maximus: that is to say, an individual's relationship to the history and geography of one particular place, as opposed to, let us say, the history of American capitalism or the American middle-class education. A succinct sign for the reader is provided by the map of Gloucester harbour which used to adorn a widely distributed edition of *The Maximus Poems* published in 1960.[3] The nature of the relationship Olson has in mind can be further specified by reference to his *A Bibliography on America for Ed Dorn*. Here Olson advises Dorn that the 'Best thing to do is to dig *one thing or place or man* until you yourself know more abt that than is possible to any other man. It doesn't matter whether it's Barbed Wire or Pemmican or Paterson or Iowa, But *exhaust* it. Saturate it. Beat it. And then u KNOW everything else very fast: one saturation job (it might take 14 years).'[4] The presence in this list of the town which was the subject of Carlos Williams's *Paterson* is significant. 'Place' was Olson's preferred object, and Carlos Williams's poem was a model for a poet's historical geography: an 'Objectist' (to use his word) exploration of the relationship of place with man 'as a creature of nature', without 'the lyrical interference of the individual as ego, of the "subject" and his soul'.[5]

Olson's work is familiar to Sinclair.[6] But another Black Mountaineer, Ed Dorn, best known for his long poem *Slinger* (1975) – for a while called *Gunslinger* – appears to be the more influential figure. The four constituent books of *Slinger* appeared individually between 1968 and 1972. Dorn is referred to in *Lud Heat* (*LH*, 41; *LHSB*, 56); in *Suicide Bridge* Dorn's use of Howard Hughes plays an important part in a discussion of Hughes's significance (*LHSB*, 230–38); and *Lights Out for the Territory* (1997) reveals a knowledge of Dorn's family and connections.[7] Dorn's own reaction to Olson is illuminating about Sinclair's psychogeography. Dorn had begun by following in the master's footsteps. Indeed, an early poem, 'From Gloucester Out' (1964), is an exorbitant eulogy of Olson as a great man, and one that explicitly identifies the greatness with his idea of geography: it ends with lines about how Olson 'sees all things and to him / are presented at night / the whispers of the most flung shores / from Gloucester out'.[8] This is another way of putting Olson's concept of deriving everything from one place. The following year, Dorn's *Geography* was published in London by Fulcrum Press, and in 1967 the same press published his *The North Atlantic Turbine*, which comprises several explanations of historical facts in terms of the influence of geography: the North Atlantic Turbine – the Gulf Stream system – draws together the countries 'along the North Atlantic perimeter'.[9] In 'Oxford', from the same volume, there is a detailed consciousness not only of the provenance of the stones that built the city, but also of the geological formations from which they derived, and their place in the geography of England.[10]

Yet Dorn's geography mutates into something far more fantastic than Olson would encourage. While *Slinger* is clearly meant to be a poem specifically associated with the American West, it is also a surreal fantasy involving figures deliberately fashioned to resemble those from comic-books, like the Gunslinger himself, or Lévi-Strauss, the talking horse. The surrealism is openly referred to the influence of drugs. Richard Brautigan, in a blurb for the 1975 edition, puts the relationship between landscape and consciousness in a usefully succinct form: 'It was a fine trip with some splendid scenery.' Perhaps Dorn had always felt too impure for Olson's 'Objectism'. In 'From Gloucester Out' he refers, thinking of the master, to 'the guilt / that kills me / My adulterated presence'.[11] Dorn, hailing from the West, was not conscious of the same historical rootedness he felt in Olson. Yet perhaps this is what liberated him sufficiently to say that 'the art of poetry is not the same thing as the art of perception'.[12]

There is probably more than one way of taking this remark, but it seems that, among other things, Dorn was implying that the idea of perception as providing an objective view was flawed. As he suggests in *Slinger*, 'The inside real / and the outsidereal form a continuum.'[13] The punning play on 'sidereal' evokes a cosmos which generates and does not suppress imagination. This is the foundation for Dorn's imaginative geography, and it offers a partial parallel with the use of mapping in another of Iain Sinclair's favourite authors, Thomas Pynchon. In *Gravity's Rainbow*, the targets of rocket attacks in London, late in the war, can be shown on a map to coincide with the locations of Lieutenant Slothrop's love-trysts. This leads Pynchon to ask, 'Could Outside and Inside be part of the same field?'[14] The idea of coincidences that can be mapped is central to Sinclair's work, but so is the connection of the science of coincidence to a critique of the 'objective'. As he says in *Lud Heat*,

> *the objective* is nonsense
> & *the scientific approach* a bitter farce
> unless it is shot through with high occulting
> fear & need & awe of mysteries. (*LH*, 89; *LHSB*, 113)

Blake is the 'godfather of all psychogeographers' because he provides not just a map of London, but also a goodly measure of 'high occulting / fear & need & awe of mysteries'. The map is a way of referring to Blake's location of his myth within a symbolic arrangement of places in London. For instance, Sinclair quotes the line about Albion from *Jerusalem* 28: 'At length he sat on London Stone, & heard Jerusalems voice' (see *LH*, 15; *LHSB*, 26). The Blakean symbolism provides an important aspect of Sinclair's own symbolism. One of his central notions is that the Hawksmoor churches in London are 'Temples' and 'cult-centres' (*LH*, 17; *LHSB*, 28). The cult is Egyptian, as proved in part by the fact that Hawksmoor was 'obsessed / possessed by pyramids' (*LH*, 20; *LHSB*, 32). The overtones of the cult are sinister and deathly, involving an impersonal type of human sacrifice motivated by 'the unacknowledged magnetism & central power, built-in code force, of the places' (*LH*, 11; *LHSB*, 21), which gives rise to appalling murders, including the Ripper murders. This is the line of thought which is developed in *White Chappell: Scarlet Tracings*, specifically in relation to the Ripper murders, though developed more towards an atmospheric portrait of Victorian London and away from the plotting of occult lines of force. Even so, the idea of the occult map remains suggestively present. At one point Eves deals out some cards with the names of the Ripper's victims, 'a kind of tarot'.[15] We are still in the realm of occult interpretation. Taking the cards back, he presses his thumb against a desktop magnifying glass and announces, 'This is the true spiral [...] the first map of the labyrinth.'[16] Immediately the last stanza of Blake's 'London', which refers to the 'harlot', and is thus linked to the idea of the Ripper's victims, is slightly misquoted. But this is also a poem which opens with a complex reference to the idea of mapping London ('charter'd streets').

This cruel Egyptian cult is illuminated by Blake's references to Egypt. For him it is a place of evil, an identification established by the venerable symbolism whereby Moses in Egypt represented the soul in captivity to the fallen world. But Blake, as usual, bends traditional symbolism to his own uses and adds his own favoured associations. Thus, Sinclair himself cites the association of Blake's Urizen with geometry, and in particular with the pyramid (*LH*, 23; *LHSB*, 36). This is Blake's way of linking the ideas of the fall and the limitations of reason and 'Mathematic Form'. Like Urizen's attempt at rational and 'geometric' control, Hawksmoor's cult is oppressive and murderous. It is also doomed to failure, as Simon Perrill points out.[17] This is also the case with Reason's attempt to control Energy in Blake; and indeed, as Perrill points out, the 'Heat' of Sinclair's title is indebted to Blake's fiery and Satanic concept of 'Energy' in *The Marriage of Heaven and Hell* (see *LH*, 15; *LHSB*, 26). Of course, Blake's concept is quite ambivalent, and soon after the composition of *The Marriage of Heaven and Hell*, one encounters notions of Energy as blind violence, as, for instance, in the famous 1795 Colour Print, *The Good and Evil Angels*

Struggling For Possession of a Child (Tate Gallery). Certainly, if Blake can be associated with 'Heat', then he is also associated with blood, one of the suggestions of the word 'Lud', which ostensibly is merely the name of the Celtic god after whom London is reputedly named. In *White Chappell*, also, after the quotation from 'London' to which we referred above, Sinclair speaks of 'Drumming Blake, Blake drumming like a madness, one of those sugar-hook addictions that get into your head, a spasm, won't be shifted'.[18] There is a sense of menacing irrationality about this description.

The sinister interdependence and similarity of good and evil in *Lud Heat* is summarised in somewhat paradoxical fashion by Peter Barry: 'This is a very polarised "Jansenist" universe and the same being can simultaneously embody both forces.[19] This point is the subject of a very thoughtful and perceptive letter from Douglas Oliver to Sinclair which obviously impressed the latter sufficiently for him to reproduce all five printed pages of it in *White Chappell*. Oliver puts Blake's morality at the top of his list:

> And first, we find of course a Blakeian stance towards good and evil: very much a Marriage but not of the Christian-like entities: more the creativities of the new sciences giving birth to phantoms more fit for our times.[20]

It is doubtful that Blake is really quite such an obvious advocate of 'Marriage' as this and later remarks of Oliver imply. Blake's statement that 'Opposition is true friendship' could be assimilated to some such view; but it is relevant to point out how scathing he is about 'Angels' and 'Reason'. Nevertheless, he does demonstrate the interdependence of good and evil, even if he is not impartial, so, thus qualified, Oliver's point can stand. Oliver proceeds to address at some length the question of whether Sinclair is, in effect, toying with evil in a sensationalist manner. While conceding that Sinclair's phantom world, 'with its pairings and opposites', is real, he wishes to insist that evil is not sublime, glamorous, 'it is small and limiting':[21]

> In act, [evil] is the implosion into nothing whereas good is the simultaneous fructification of nothing. They are utterly interdependent dynamically and yet good is the sovereign just as 'all we have' is sovereign over 'all that we shall not have.' Unless there is

the gradient of value – unless the very coincidence of contraries in the Blakeian sense has this gradient, as I think Blake say – I can explain neither our actions nor our words.[22]

In fact, Blake, Sinclair and Oliver all adopt different positions. Most to our purpose here is the contrast between the gloomy, postmodern sublimity of Sinclair's sensibility and Blake's Romantic construction. Sinclair discovers a profound similarity between good and evil, or what has been publicly represented as good and evil; Blake, on the other hand, espouses a liberating form of 'Poetic Genius' which stands over against the limitations of 'Reason'. He concedes that 'Reason' and 'Poetic Genius' are interdependent, but only in a hierarchised way, with Reason as subordinate. As for Oliver, his formulations are impressively subtle, but belong more to the realm of philosophical ethics, with their reference to Iris Murdoch's ethical writings, than those of either Blake or Sinclair. The ethical is a category of acknowledged centrality in Oliver's work.[23]

Possibly because he was dissatisfied with the apparent moral neutrality of *Lud Heat*, Sinclair's next book, *Suicide Bridge* (1978), is less impartial. It even begins with a dedication ('offered to THE ENEMY'; *LHSB*, 145) which makes an avowal of antagonism – as well as sounding like what James Fenton calls 'Blake Auden'. Antagonism is a fitting note to strike, for the chief conceit of *Suicide Bridge* is to make use of some of Blake's 12 sons of Albion – fallen beings indeed – many of whom were associated with Blake's trial for sedition, including 'Skofeld' (Private Scholfield, whom Blake ejected from his garden, and who fomented the charge) and 'Kox' (Private Cock), who supported Scholfield. Important also are 'Hand' and 'Hyle', the latter being a disguise for Blake's patron, William Hayley, whom Blake at one point suspected of hiring Scholfield to get him executed because he had failed to seduce Mrs Blake.

Sinclair converts these figures into sons of contemporary Albion and associates them with the ill-gotten gains of a corrupt capitalism: the ambience of one of the sons, Kotope, is 'the City, wealth / a casting of high diseases', where 'defiant ghost pornographies / accosted his office-hour meditation' (*LHSB*, 175). But when first mentioned he is only a 'humble clerk, with savage ambitions, / odeon land-dreams'. He becomes involved in what appears to be a cult combining Cathar and Egyptian associations, but only to gain wealth and power: 'what

you need you get; / for Kotope, the Way' (*LHSB*, 178). We already
know that he 'waits for the weekly envelope // "on the payroll" '
(*LHSB*, 177). There is a curious but symbolically compelling sense of
gangster occultism, so to speak. But Kotope, as can occur with satanic
pacts, takes on more than he can handle. Soon we see him 'in fear,
plung[ing] through ancient systems, his Rolls Royce Corniche cruises
the eastern city' (*LHSB*, 180). Although he 'arranges for a small
assassination' (*LHSB*, 182), it is he himself who is assassinated (*LHSB*,
184–85).

Suicide Bridge draws on a similar eclectic amalgam of occult sources
to what we find in *Lud Heat*, but it is not so systematic in organising
them: its main organsing principle is that of the Sons of Albion, and
two of these, Hand and Hyle, bear the weight of cosmological myth-
making. In a postmodern version of *The Book of Urizen*, Hand and
Hyle, who represent evil, are born at the edge of a Black Hole: 'singu-
larities occur along the edge / the birth, the notice, of Hand & Hyle'
(*LHSB*, 156). However, this emphasis on Hand and Hyle in particular
is also true to Blake, in whose work they are often mentioned
together, joined by a lust for revenge (*Jerusalem* 15:1) and by hatred of
the Saviour (*Jerusalem* 18:36).

Modern London, then, is an 'island city' of 'corruption' (*LHSB*,
159), and Sinclair's psychogeography appears less politically impartial than in *Lud Heat*. But some doubt is cast upon this by the essay
with which the book begins, 'Intimate Associations: Myth and Place'
(*LHSB*, 147–54). Sinclair opens by baldly stating that 'Myths are lies'.
Continuing by way of Blake's mythology of place ('PEACHEY HAD
NORTH WALES', *LHSB*, 150), and thence to prehistoric figures carved
in the chalk downs of England ('Cerne Abbas & the White Horse of
Uffington are data'; *LHSB*, 152), Sinclair comes round, towards the
end of his argument, to an apparently paradoxical development of
his initial equation of myths and lies. 'Myth is what place says. And
it does lie. It spreads a seductive field of pits & snares. You go mad if
you try to pursue place through myth: your path will disappear over
the nearest cliff. Place is fed by a sacrifice of the unwary – though the
truly innocent, those born to innocence, according to myth, survive'
(*LHSB*, 153). The problem appears to be what one might call 'myth-
power', one version of which Sinclair has already postulated in *Lud
Heat*. The trick would appear to be not to become trapped in fixity, to
recognise that 'Myth is the living breath of place' (*LHSB*, 149), but

not to turn it into 'a weapon' (*LHSB*, 148). This, however, has the disadvantage, for the mythological poet, that the myth may seem to advance no truth-claims: that it is, precisely, an ungrounded piece of arbitrary postmodernist pattern-formation, laced with ill-focused postmodernist paranoia.

This is a possibility alluded to in *Downriver* (1991), a suitably meandering novel, which nevertheless, as Dent and Whitaker point out, 'uses Blake in particular to orient [the] depiction of London'.[24] A self-mocking summary of Sinclair's quest for myth in place concludes with the words, 'We have cruised the South Downs on Blakean away-days, and crawled on our hands and knees over the sharpened limestone combs of Gower. The routine never changes.'[25] Dent and Whittaker comment that 'One suspects that for Sinclair all significances are ultimately arbitrary, and the Blakean allusion is suitably ironic.'[26] Of course, the sublime darkness of Sinclair's London might lead one to suppose otherwise, if only that the oppressiveness seems too weighty not to be significant. But despite this, the chart upon which this structure of feeling is erected does flaunt its imaginative arbitrariness. This aspect of Sinclair becomes very evident in a surreal fantasy in *Lud Heat*, 'A Theory of Hay Fevers', which develops the idea that hay-fever sufferers are a priestly caste. Aspects of the disease may be signs of this: 'Red eye, streaming nose, skin irritation: are caste badges' (*LH*, 51; *LHSB*, 66). The privations imposed by the affliction actually function as cult prohibitions: 'These summer days in length of riot and grass orgy are forbidden to the sufferer/adepts' (Ibid.). But as a high caste, they gain power through their sacrifice: 'Darkness is the price of their power. Power is the measure of their failing, as natural men' (Ibid.). As if to clinch the interpretation, the ancient cycle of fertility festivals is brought in evidence:

They may not celebrate the season of fertility in the land. The May Day dances seal their door. The Green Man is a tree of blades they may not embrace. The July oak-sacrifice is their order of release [...]. Their time of action is the autumnal equinox. (*LH*, 52; *LHSB*, 68).

This aligns the hay-fever sufferer with the controlling caste we have already encountered. And sure enough, in the lines that follow we are reminded, apropos of the autumnal equinox, not only that 'The Irish

ritualised the date of the beheading of John the Baptist as August 29',
but also that 'Jack the Ripper took his first victim, Mary Ann Nicholls,
on August 31.' We are provocatively informed that 'These are
rhythms to recognise, to accept or to oppose.' Which is presumably
what we assumed in any case. But the remark self-consciously draws
attention to the implausibility of the rhythms.

However, for those to whom such postmodernist playfulness is
unsatisfying, there are compensations to be drawn from the side of
Sinclair's work which simply lets the world speak for itself, in all its
sometimes ludicrous and sometimes radiant unknowability. In *Lud
Heat* this is partly conveyed by the black and white photographs with
which the first edition is regaled. At one level, they signify in yet
another way that this is indeed a work about a specific place. At
another level, the level at which one is attempting to pull the threads
of the book together, their blankness contrasts oddly with the torrid
'heat' of the book's dark, symbol-strewn matter. At any rate, three of
the photographs (*LH*, 30, 33, 92) appear simply to record moments in
Sinclair's then career as a municipal assistant gardener. They also
point a contrast with some works one is bound to compare them
with, given the context: Blake's illuminated Prophetic Books. For the
first edition of *Lud Heat* contains not only photographs, but also
drawings by Brian Catling, and eighteenth- and nineteenth-century
engravings. Unlike in the Prophetic Books, there is no attempt to
unify text and design compositionally. And the photographs and
engravings give the impression of hard data, so that Sinclair's psychogeography, wherever it may end up, sets out from a fairly sharp
separation between 'objective' and 'subjective'. The effect, in fact, is
rather like that in some of W. G. Sebald's work.

This separation even affects the way the writer's own experience is
presented in *Lud Heat*. Parts of the text consist of journal entries
describing the humble and squalid events of the municipal gardener's
life. Rather more of the book is taken up with poems which embody
a more lyrical take on the same matter, as in 'The Wheel of his Days'
(*LH*, 33–39; *LHSB*, 46–53). There is little enough in either kind of text
to remind one of the occult systems and theories which pervade so
much of the rest of the book, though they are gestured at. Thus, we
are informed in a journal entry that 'Foreman 4th Class P. Hartley is
a hay fever victim. His sufferings, an early warning' (*LH*, 28;
LHSB, 40). In the last poem in 'The Wheel of his Days' we are told

that '16 / EYE // is the glyph / that indicates the secret gateway to Victoria Park', which hints both at the Egyptian and at an occult reading of London space. Nevertheless, on the whole there is a relatively clear divorce between the parts of the book which reflect experience and those which elaborate the psychogeography and its symbolic fabric.

The 'EYE', however, is deliberately placed so that it precedes a section called 'Rites of Autopsy' – the word 'autopsy' being immediately glossed in terms of a literal translation of its Greek roots: 'The Act of Seeing With One's Own Eyes' (*LH*, 40; *LHSB*, 54). And, in effect, what *Lud Heat* does is to offer two related, autonomous but overlapping versions of 'seeing with one's own eyes'. The psychogeographical sections present themselves as evidence: this must be seen with one's eyes, but, accordant with the more common meaning of the word 'autopsy', it may require a series of incisions – in this case through time and mystification – in order to see the evidence out of which the pattern emerges, or seems to emerge. This aspect of 'autopsy' links up with the detective aspect of Sinclair's imagination, which is very active in relation to theories about Jack the Ripper in *White Chappell*. The other aspect of 'autopsy' is 'seeing with one's own eyes' in the most straightforward sense and finds frequent expression, especially in the poems about the gardener's experience, in the recording of some notably fine images: 'the sunset is sand on the floor of the lightbulb' (*LH*, 33; *LHSB*, 46); 'the pain is in the northern sky / fish fires light the low horizon' (*LH*, 38; *LHSB*, 51). Rather than postmodernist in the sense that has now gained currency, these lyrics are late Modernist, of a post-Poundian variety. As Simon Perrill astutely observes, Sinclair is indebted to the Poundian idea of the 'Luminous Detail', though he means this observation to apply to both of the aspects of Sinclair that we have been proposing: the 'Luminous Detail' is also another version of 'heat'.[27]

These facts suggest an intriguing twist in the lineage for Sinclair's work. Clearly he is indebted to a certain kind of mythologising and essentialising Modernist mythological poem: Pound's *Cantos*, Eliot's *Waste Land*, David Jones's *Anathémata*, HD's *Trilogy*. The difference is that the 'mythic method' in Sinclair's hands turns into the sceptical, ironic proposal of shifting patterns we have been analysing. At the same time, much of the small-scale poetic method of his work remains formally late-Modernist and presupposes an isolated consciousness yearning for meaning. Arguably, such a conjunction is very much of our time and very instructive about its character.

Angela Carter

That Blake is one of the most important influences on Angela Carter is a fact acknowledged by all commentators on her who possess the breadth of reading to go beyond the 'specialism' of late twentieth-century literature. Lorna Sage, for instance, puts Blake, as well as Swift and Lewis Carroll, at the top of her list of influences.[28] Elsewhere, she notes that 'Blake, along with de Sade (both great guerillas of the Age of Enlightenment) was a favourite source, because of his radical irony and the parodic authority of his devil's aphorisms.'[29] Blake is, indeed, a frequent point of reference for Carter, often invoked in discussions or episodes of central significance in her work. She herself approvingly places the 'Surrealists' in the same company as Blake, and Lewis Carroll, and Bishop Berkeley.[30] This is quite close to one of Sage's lists of primary influences on Carter. In fact, the influence of Blake can be examined under three headings: the unconscious; terror as contrary; and myth as construct. Naturally enough, the subject-matters under these headings overlap.

To take first the idea of the unconscious: the above remarks about Blake and the Surrealists, especially because they put him next to Carroll and Berkeley, emphasise the way in which Blake can be conceived as revealing the hidden truth about the human psyche. In a 1978 article in *New Society*, 'Little Lamb Get Lost', Carter discusses Blake's 'tygers' both as they appear in the famous proverb, 'The tygers of wrath are wiser than the horses of instruction', and in 'The Tyger', from *Songs of Experience*. Carter notes that the illumination depicting the 'Tyger' looks rather tame: like a 'frubsy beast' who 'should have a zipper down his back and a pair of pyjamas inside him'. He does not look like the 'unpleasant familiar of Nobodaddy' who appears in the poem itself.[31] In a curious twist to this argument, Carter assigns this discordance to the symbolic nature of the beast:

> But of course, he is not talking about tigers at all. He is talking about something blind, furious, instinctual, intuitive, savage and *right* [... .] representative of the unrepressed subconsious, even the id, possibly the mob storming the Bastille.[32]

It is worth noting several things about this, not because they are intellectually obscure, but because they enter into dialogue with other concepts to which Carter has resort, also influenced by Blake, and which tend in a different direction. First, the concept of the 'subconscious' is aligned with instinct, and not with the kind of Lacanian psychoanalysis where the unconscious is 'structured like a language'. Second, the reference to 'the mob storming the Bastille' shows an understanding of the way Blake does indeed equate psychological and social processes, not least those which can be epitomised as 'rebellion'. This points to one reason for her admiration of him. Finally, the description of the Tyger as a 'familiar' of Nobodaddy reveals an understanding of the way in which authority and rebellion are mutually dependent in Blake, Nobodaddy being the tyrant father-god against whom the Tyger rebels. But in all of this the main emphasis is on psychological process. Guido Almarsi notes, as regards the short story, 'Lizzie and the Tiger' (from *American Ghosts and Old-World Wonders* (1993)), Carter's misquotation of Blake, 'The eye sees what the heart knows', and he concludes that for both Carter and Blake this means that 'The heart already knows the tiger before the eye tells it.'[33] This conclusion is identical with the statement that the unconscious mental processes insistently express themselves in the conscious world. Such assumptions lead to Carter's conclusion that 'all myths are products of the human mind.'[34]

The aspect to which I have referred as 'terror as contrary' refers to terror as one of a pair of contraries, the opposite of which is innocence, in a couple which is modelled on Blake's own contraries in *The Marriage of Heaven and Hell*. This aspect is closely related to the discussion so far. 'The tygers of wrath' appear in *The Marriage* representing the sublime wrath and terror which Blake praises and associates with the conventional representation of hell. This sublime conception can be equally well epitomised in other proverbs from 'Proverbs of Hell': 'The wrath of the lion is the wisdom of God' or 'The roaring of lions, the howling of wolves, the raging of the stormy sea, and the destructive sword, are portions of eternity too great for the eye of man'. Carter believes in what she calls 'the subconscious', but most of all she believes that the subconscious is the site of terrifying, violent, but potentially liberating energies such as can be symbolised by Blake's wild beasts. It is for this reason that the tiger represents the subconscious for her, and for this reason that she is the author of stories such as 'The Courtship of Mr Lyon', 'The Tiger's Bride' and 'The Company of Wolves'. This is the aspect of Carter where Blake is the natural companion of de Sade. But it is also true that she adopts the idea of contraries: the tiger brings with it the lamb. In practice, this means the innocence of characters who discover the terrible sublime and their own fascination with it, erotic or otherwise. In this light, Blake is a major influence on that fundamental structure of otherness and difference which critics have noticed as characterising all of Carter's work. Furthermore, other symbolic structures apart from the obviously Blakeian run closely parallel with his symbolism and are, in fact, probably to be accounted for by his influence as well. The most relevant example is that of alchemy. The title of the Blake work which was most important to Carter, *The Marriage of Heaven and Hell*, refers to the idea of an alchemical 'marriage': that is, to the union of contrary principles such as Blake refers to within the work itself. One of these references, early on in the text, is of especial significance: 'Without contraries is no progression.' The alchemical idea that the philosopher's stone might be discovered by bringing together the supposedly opposed chemicals, mercury and sulphur, lies behind this. For the philosophical alchemists, those who were interested in alchemy mainly for its spiritual symbolism, the discovery of the philosopher's stone represented spiritual rebirth. Jakob Boehme was Blake's source for this idea, and he refers to him in *The Marriage of Heaven and Hell* as Behmen.[35] Carter's knowledge of alchemy, including philosophical alchemy, was quite learned. Thus, she refers in *The Passion of New Eve* to 'the six volumes of Manget's *Bibliotheca Chemica Curiosa*, the *Splendor Solis* of Salomon Tirsmosia, and Michael Maier's wonderfully illustrated *Atalanta Fugiens*.'[36] And the idea of alchemical transformation via the opposition and marriage of contraries is clearly central to the symbolism of *The Passion of New Eve*. But this example is especially telling: for the idea of alchemical contraries is given a strongly Blakean inflection by means of her celebrated re-use of Blake's conception of 'Beulah' to represent the theatre of operations, so to speak, of Mother, the 'Grand Emasculator'. 'There is a place where contrarieties are equally true. This place is called Beulah' Carter quotes (*PNE*, 48) from Blake's *Milton* (30:1). That she is not using the concept quite as Blake intended is not to our purpose here, though it will certainly be worth investigating at a later point. In any case, the alchemical influence, to which Blake contributed so strongly, is not confined to *The Passion*, being obviously important also to *Nights at the Circus*.

The idea of contraries leaves its most palpable mark on Carter's critical writing in *The Sadeian Woman*. This is not only because, as Lorna Sage points out, she imitates the 'mockery of authority' to be found in the very style of Blake's *The Marriage of Heaven and Hell*.[37] The title itself is a marriage of Heaven and Hell, at least as far as social prejudice is concerned – and that is what matters most to her. Women, the 'charming sex', as de Sade calls them, in a remark quoted by Carter, are, it is implied, capable of responding with vivacity to some of the practices he describes, even if not in quite the same spirit as he. De Sade claimed 'rights of free sexuality for women, and instilled women as beings of power in his imaginary worlds'.[38] Carter's positive revaluation of de Sade includes some Blakean moments. For instance, he is said to be 'capable of believing [...] that it is possible to radically transform human society and, with it, human nature, so that the Old Adam exemplified in God, the King and the Law, the trifold masculine symbolism of authority, will take his final departure from amongst us'.[39] De Sade also reveals the weakness of pornography, that its heartlessness is insatiable, but this realisation too can be related to Carter's reading of Blake, for she emphasises de Sade's identification of the end of pornography as hell. In the light of Blake's idea of contraries, one can see that Carter is proposing that women enter that hell as part of a 'progression' to a free sexuality.

The third Carter concept influenced by Blake is 'myth as construct'. By far the most succinct statement relevant to this idea, and to Blake's part in forming it, is to be found in her article 'Notes from the Front Line'. It is here that she states that her concern is the 'investigation of the social fictions that regulate our lives – what Blake called the "mind-forg'd manacles" '; and the main way in which she qualifies the slightly ambiguous phrase 'social fictions' is by identifying them with 'myths'.[40] She moves freely between the idea of myth as symbolic narrative and myth as ideological false consciousness: thus, not only does she trace her concern to 'an absolute and *committed materialism*', but she also asserts that myths '*are* extraordinary lies designed to make people unfree'. It is for this reason that she asserts 'I'm in the demythologising business'. One does not have to look far for the likely source of an amused, appreciative but ultimately mistrustful ideological analysis of myth which blurs the boundaries (as Carter does) between popular culture, especially film, and what myth has classically meant. Roland Barthes is known to be a favourite of hers.[41] In his *Mythologies* he engages in a structuralist and semiological analysis of such topics as 'The Face of Garbo' in pursuit of such conclusions as 'Myth is depoliticized speech'.[42] The inspiration of this source give a particular inflection, then, to Carter's admiration for what she calls 'the Blake of the self-crafted mythology of the Prophetic Books'.[43] The word 'self-crafted' suggests both constructedness and a re-making of myth: a re-making in which the transformation itself enacts a critique of previous myths and the social prejudices they enshrine.

Carter's fictions offer pervasive evidence of being representations of a fantasy life that is often repressed – though it may be hard to find confirmation of this amidst so many other emphases which tend more in the direction of the social constructedness of mental life and its imaginings. Perhaps the most telling confirmation of the way in which sexuality, in particular, is supposed to be 'instinctual' (to use the adjective Carter applies to Blake's 'The Tyger') is simply the way in which she never forgets to include this aspect, even when describing imagery and role-play. For instance, when referring to Leilah's elaborate preparations for love-making, which include a highly-charged use of cosmetics as well as erotic clothing, Carter explains that 'she sprayed herself with dark perfumes that enhanced rather than concealed the lingering odour of sexuality that was her own perfume' (*PNE*, 29). The point is a precisely Baudelairean one: Carter was to put into the mouth of the husband in 'The Bloody Chamber' translated words from Baudelaire's 'Les Bijoux': 'Of her apparel she retains / Only her sonorous jewellery.[44] The first words, however, are 'La très-chère était nue' ('The beloved was naked') and we later learn that her eyes are fixed on her lover 'comme un tigre dompté' ('like a tame tiger'). The poem seeks to define the point at which artifice enhances sexual arousal. But the last thing it intends is to dissolve sexual energy into pure artifice: the desired point is a collaboration between Art and Nature. And this is the point Carter defines in terms of a perfume which enhances rather than conceals the odour of sexuality. A similar interpretation can be placed on Fevvers's 'highly personal aroma, "essence of Fevvers" ' in *Nights at the Circus*.[45] This should be seen in relation to one aspect of Fevvers's contrary nature: 'she was a big girl' (*NC*, 7). Her size and weight are further emphasised by her initial difficulty in flying (*NC*, 30). This aspect of Fevvers, then, is woman's powerful physicality, just as the other is her transforming imagination. And this is the meaning of the pun of contrariety in her name: the *fevers* of physicality, and the *feathers* of imaginative flight,

As for the contrary of terror, in *The Bloody Chamber* this is conceived as a feature of experience to be discovered by innocents. Beauty, in 'The Courtship of Mr Lyon', the father's 'pet', wants 'one white rose', an emblem with connotations opposed to those of the red rose (*BC*, 41). In Mr Lyon's house, she felt herself to be 'Miss Lamb, spotless, sacrificial' (*BC*, 45). At the beginning of 'The Tiger's Bride', 'the lovely land where the lemon trees grow', visited by the beautiful young narrator, is described as being like 'the blessed plot where the lion lies down with the lamb' (*BC*, 51) – thus, a place where one of the emblems of terror renounces violence and lives at peace, in contrast to Blake's conception that 'Opposition is True Friendship'.

The ensuing course of events for innocent heroines involves an encounter with terror and with the violent energy of sexuality as symbolised by the male beast. In 'The Courtship of Mr Lyon', the transition to this encounter is signalled by the dish containing 'sandwiches of thick-cut roast beef, still bloody' (*BC*, 43). The failure fully to engage in this marriage of contraries leads to impasse, to thwarted development. Thus, when in 'The Courtship of Mr Lyon', Beauty has returned to her home and forgotten about her feral lover, we are told that she 'was learning, at the end of her adolescence, how to be a spoiled child' (*BC*, 48) and that 'her face was acquiring, instead of beauty, a lacquer of the invincible prettiness that characterizes certain pampered, exquisite, expensive cats' (*BC*, 49). Such a state is reminiscent of Blake's idea of innocence, for he hints in the *Songs* as well as 'Tiriel' and *The Book of Thel*, that this state has the potential, if arrested, to become false, to become the enemy of maturation.

But it is not only the young female heroine who may recoil from the fearful encounter of honest sexuality. In 'The Tiger's Bride' the Beast's 'sole desire is to see the pretty young lady unclothed nuder without her dress' (*BC*, 58), on the understanding that she is a virgin, but the young narrator remarks, 'I wished I'd rolled in the hay with every lad on my father's farm, to disqualify myself from this humiliating bargain. That he should want so little was the reason why I could not give it' (*BC*, 61). Confirmation that this littleness constitutes the failed encounter is provided by the mechanical servants who populate the Beast's house: 'We surround ourselves [...] for utility and pleasure, with simulacra' (*BC*, 60). Fortunately for both Beauty and the Beast, the latter cannot quell his true nature: 'The tiger will never lie with the lamb; he acknowledges no pact that is not reciprocal. The lamb must learn to run with the tigers' (*BC*, 64). This accords with Blake's 'Without contraries is no progression', and Beauty's willing participation in the adventure is confirmed by her acquisition of 'beautiful fur' (*BC*, 67). But the fur is revealed by the licking of the Beast's tongue which 'ripped off skin after successive skin', and this indicates another way of thinking about the process: that the 'bestial' has always been within Beauty and the opposition of Beauty and the Beast, at least as applied to essentialised notions of gender, is a false mythology.

Nor does Carter wish to support the unredeemed de Sade: the loveless, egotistical and ultimately solitary pursuit of sexual gratification in which the other becomes merely an object. The short story 'The Bloody Chamber' is placed at the beginning of the collection of that name as if to emphasise this point, amid so much that tends to show the value of liberating the sublime energies of sexuality. The point is underscored by the fact that the cruel Marquis, clearly modelled on de Sade, is rejected in favour of the blind young piano-tuner. Yet there is a play on the notion of erotic pain: 'To see him, in his lovely, blind humanity, seemed to hurt me very piercingly, somewhere inside my breast' (*BC*, 31). The aspect of sexuality that is, in Blake's phrase, 'like the lion's tooth' shares with the more tender side of love the quality of being a trespass on the self. But the former leads only to the solitary hell de Sade depicts unless relieved by the latter. As for the tigerish female, she appears, appropriately enough, in the relatively straightforward form of the mother who, having 'disposed of a man-eating tiger' on her eighteenth birthday, is fit to dispatch the Marquis too (*BC*, 40).

The reminder that contraries should find no easy reconciliation, either for Blake or Carter, is pertinent to the interpretation of *The Passion of New Eve*. Carter reminds us of the Blakean connections of Mother's realm of Beulah by quoting Blake himself on his own realm of Beulah: 'There is a place where contrarieties are equally true.' But, as is well known to Blakeans, Beulah, though an estimable place, is inferior to Eden, which is the true home of imagination. This is confirmed by Blake, not only when he says that Beulah is a place of rest for 'The Sons of Eden', but also when he explains the slightly cryptic phrase about contrarieties being equally true: as he says of Beulah, 'It is a pleasant lovely Shadow / Where no dispute can come' (*Milton*, 30, 2–3). But Blake's ideal is productive contention, as in the phrase 'Opposition is true Friendship' quoted above. Its pleasant, temporary truce is a sign of Beulah's inferiority. Carter builds further negativity into this sense of uncontested essentialisms. The word Mother itself should arouse our suspicions, and these are confirmed by the hymn of praise to the Goddess in her different versions (*PNE*, 61–62). It is true, of course, that Mother 'was her own mythological artefact'. But the very fact that she has to inscribe the artefact in the relative permanence of altered flesh is another sign that what she is constructing is an essentialist notion of the female: 'And she had made herself! Yes, made herself! She was her own mythological artefact; she had reconstructed her flesh painfully, with knives and with needles, into a transcendental form as an emblem' (*PNE*, 60). This bears on a certain ambiguity, to which we have already alluded, about the idea of constructed myth. If myths are lies, that is because they are constructed by the reigning ideology. But constructedness can also be liberating if it permits free transformations which can effect critique. However, Mother's desire to give permanent form to mythological artefact renders her suspect.

However, this is not to say that there is no poetic justice in her emasculation of Evelyn: on the contrary, Carter is representing one inevitable result of the war of the essentialised sexes. In this light, it might seem that Tristessa, the transvestite, as such possessing more obviously 'constructed' sexuality, would be a more positive role-model than Mother, but this is not the case. Tristessa's acting out of the male dream of Woman ('he had been the perfect man's woman'; *PNE*, 128), complete with mournful tears ('Our Lady of the Sorrows'; *PNE*, 122), reveal that the best that Tristessa can do, unlike Mother, is raise the question of the artifice of sexual representations. For a long time, as Linden Peach puts it, 'Evelyn fails to make a distinction between transvestism and female masquerade. In other words, he fails to distinguish between a man dressed as a woman and a man dressed as a woman masquerading as Woman.[46]

The uncertainty of Evelyn's fate at the end of *The Passion of New Eve* seems appropriate. What kind of conception of human individuals would both profit by the critique of mythological representation and at the same time offer the erotic poetry of play and artifice? The conception seems unstable. In the end, Carter wants to validate loving and tender sexual relationships, and these, as with the young Marquise and her piano-tuner in 'The Bloody Chamber', or Fevvers and Walser in *Nights at the Circus*, seem to embody a realm of authenticity, beyond the masks and costumes. Yet this is not a realm where one feels that the masks and costumes are ever fully abandoned: that would be a return to false innocence. This dilemma is a common postmodernist one, to be found also in the work of Carter's friend and fellow-Blakean, Iain Sinclair. The dilemma is that whereby representations (frequently epitomised as myth) are seen to be pervasively falsifying, but are also valued and appreciated for their imaginatively transforming potential in the hands of the creative artist and in the playfulness of true lovers. In the case of both Carter and Sinclair, Blake offers a template crafted by one who seemed to be the first artist in the English tradition to be aware of this tension in ways of conceiving myth.

The possibility that Blake's own mythology can be seen in a negative way is conveyed by the not unfriendly parody to be found in the depiction of the Shaman in the latter chapters of *Nights at the Circus*:

> The Shaman was the pedant of pedants. There was nothing vague about his system of belief. His type of mystification necessitated hard, if illusory, fact, and his mind was stocked with concrete specifics. With what passionate academicism he devoted himself to assigning phenomena their rightful places in his subtle and intricate theology. (*NC*, 252–53)

The Shaman's people live in a 'dream', his dream:

> Their dream was foolproof. An engine-turned fabrication. A closed system. Foolproof because it *was* a closed system. The Shaman's cosmogony, for all its complexity of forms, impulses and states of being perpetually in flux, was finite because it was a human invention and possessed none of the implausibility of authentic history. (*NC*, 253)

Even the geography of this invented universe is 'mystically four-dimensional' (*NC*, 253), like Blake's 'Fourfold universe'.

Yet of course, nowhere does the influence of Blake show itself more strongly than in this very capacity to question whether all myths, even one's own, even Blake's, are in danger of becoming a 'system' in the malign sense of the word. This is the final subtlety in the endeavour to create myths while believing that myths lie.

11
Salman Rushdie, Myth and Postcolonial Romanticism

The phenomenon whereby postcolonial literature conducts a special relationship with canonical British Romanticism is worthy of study in itself. Katie Trumpener has revealed the way in which, in a closely parallel phenomenon, the Irish national novel, from the Romantic period downwards, contributes the idea of a specifically national bardic inspiration to emerging colonial and postcolonial literatures. As far as British Romanticism is concerned, one needs to estimate the influence of Wordsworth on Derek Walcott; one needs to ask why Wordsworth is recited in Anita Desai's *In Custody*, or why David Malouf's *Remembering Babylon* takes its epigraphs from Blake and Clare, or why Ben Okri appropriates a phrase of Blake for his *Mental Fight* – or why Salman Rushdie's *Satanic Verses* weaves the influence of Blake's *The Marriage of Heaven and Hell* into an already complex handling of the uncanonical verses supposedly dictated by the devil to Muhammad and subsequently excised. A general answer would have to do with the ironic discovering of what purports to be a universal and liberating message of truth in the sacred texts of the imperial power, a message, which, moreover, can be represented as consonant with the truths conveyed more locally, for instance, in the Urdu and Persian poetry which are the classics of North India. In the case of Blake, there is also the fact of his emphasis on conflict, on contrariety, to be considered.

The contrary expressed by Blake in terms of his emblems of Lamb and Tyger is an influence on Okri's character Black Tyger (spelt thus) in *The Famished Road*. It would be easy, too easy perhaps, to emphasise the importance of contrariety and struggle in the ideas Blake bequeathed to a postcolonial context. But just as important is the sense of mythology as dramatising aspects of the self. This is certainly true for Blake's influence on Wilson Harris, and is specifically addressed by Okri in *Mental Fight*:

> We are, in ways small and great
> The figures, the myths and legends
> That we ourselves have invented.
> Our dreams are self-portraits.
>
> Our myths, our heroic legends,
> Are the concealed autobiography
> Of the human race.[1]

Okri even addresses the Blakean idea of the 'mind-forg'd manacles' producing mental illusions, which, because products of the imagination, are still both powerful and dangerous:

> O the nightmare visions
> Of Breughel and Bosch,
> The infernos of druggies
> The neurotic hades
> Are but the mental productions
> Of illusions gone utterly wrong.[2]

Both of these quotations from Okri possess a strong resonance with the central ideas of *Satanic Verses*.

This is not to deny that contraries are also important to it. They are also (and this is very much to our purpose) an important presence in a volume of poems which Rushdie acknowledges as an influence on *The Satanic Verses*. As he says, 'the "Gagari" poems of "Bhupen Gandhi" are, in fact, echoes of Arun Kolatkar's collection *Jejuri*'.[3] This book, consisting of a sequence of poems which first appeared in 1974 in *Opinion Library Quarterly*, was published in 1976 and proceeded to win the Commonwealth Poetry Prize the following year.[4] Its title is the name of a small Hindu town full of temples, many of them dilapidated or completely ruined. The boundary between temples and other buildings seems to have been completely eroded, so that a cowshed can be mistaken for a temple ('Manohar').[5] This erosion itself becomes part of the subject-matter: 'That's no doorstep. / It's a pillar on its side' ('The Doorstep').[6] God is everywhere, in any case, the more so when a ruined temple becomes home to a mongrel bitch and her litter of puppies. 'No more a place of worship this place / is nothing less than the house of god' ('Heart of Ruin').[7] But one does not require the image of the temple to feel the omnipresence of god; ordinary stones will do well enough: 'what is god / and what is stone / the dividing line / if it exists / is very thin / at jejuri' ('A Scratch').[8] The crops in this stony field are also god: 'there is no crop / other than god / and god is harvested here'. A Blakean note is struck in a couple of the poems which complicates the pantheistic blurring of boundaries. 'Ajamil and the Tigers' is a re-writing of Blake's 'Night' from *Songs of Innocence*, the song in which the angels try to keep 'wolves and tygers' away from the flock, and the lion and the lamb lie down together in heaven. In Kolatkar's poem, the tiger people and their king are constantly thwarted by the new sheepdog of Ajamil, 'the good shepherd'. The sheepdog finally ties up all the tigers. When they pretend that they have come in peace, Ajamil pretends to believe them, makes a truce with them, and offers them 'lamb chops and the roast'. Ajamil knows that 'even tigers have got to eat some time'. The result is that 'well fed tigers and fat sheep drink from the same pond'. The story is more hard-headed and practical than Blake's emblematic poem, but its message is nevertheless quite a Blakean one: the tiger will not lie down with the sheep unless its tigerish nature is recognised. The recognition of contraries is submitted to parallel but more archetypal handling in 'A Song for Vaghya'. The singer's song states that the only word he knows is 'God', and he knows it 'backwards' – 'dog', of course – but also conveying a sense that seems opposed to God, like the Satanic or like the 'tygerish' aspects of Blake's *Experience* or *Hell*: 'I know it as fangs / inside my flanks. / But I also know it / as a lamb / between my teeth'.[9]

In *Satanic Verses*, Rushdie refers to the controversy which had been aroused on the Hindu religious right by *Jejuri* when he mentions 'Bhupen Gandhi' and his books about 'the "little temple town" of Gagari'. But the most significant part of the reference consists of a discussion which occurs among members of India's liberal cultural elite: the film-maker George Miranda, his new girlfriend Swatilekha, Bhupen Gandhi himself, and Salahuddin. Swatilekha accuses Bhupen of having been 'seduced by religion into a dangerous ambiguity' (*SV*, 536). He retorts that there is nothing ambiguous about saying that 'the only crop of Gagari is the stone gods being quarried from the hills', which sounds like a reference to going hungry. But he continues that 'I have spoken of herds of legends, with sacred cowbells tinkling.' Swatilekha, however, feels there is not enough 'clarity' in such 'metaphors' (*SV*, 537). She has a theory: society is 'orchestrated' by '*grand narratives*: history, economics, ethics'. But with the corruption of the state, people are thrown back on the oldest of the grand narratives, religious faith. Bhupen replies that 'We can't deny the ubiquity of faith. If we write in such a way as to pre-judge such belief as in some way deluded or false, then are we not guilty of elitism, of imposing our world-view on the masses?' But Swatilekha prefers a black-and-white view: 'Secular versus religious, the light versus the dark. Better you choose which side you are on.'

Lyotard, the originator of this kind of usage of the phrase 'grand narrative' himself purports to show that in the postmodern such narratives are broken up and replaced by 'communication circuits' where the traffic is organised by 'language games'.[10] Rushdie's novel, with its ludic interweaving of narratives about the contemporary with fictional transformations of history, and with its magic-realist blending of the fantastic and the verisimilitudinous, is clearly aligned with language games rather than grand narratives. Furthermore, there is an ethical and spiritual dimension to this alignment, for *The Satanic Verses* validates an erosion of purist and puritanical notions of goodness, and nurses a particular hostility to the patriarchal monotheism which is represented as nurturing these noxious tendencies in their most virulent form. At the same time, not least because of its use of spiritual imagery and scriptural narratives (both canonical and non-canonical) it can hardly be said to be unambiguously hostile to religion. Its stance is therefore quite closely aligned to that of Bhupen Gandhi – and to that of Kolatkar's poems, including their Blakean attribution of contrary aspects to the divine. Thus, it is also suspicious of the supposedly enlightened, monologic liberal discourse of Swatilekha.

The Marriage of Heaven and Hell is the Blake text which makes a crucial contribution to the thinking of *The Satanic Verses*. In chapter V, Gibreel picks up Allie Cone's copy of *The Marriage* and when she wakes up, reads from Proverbs of Hell, 'The lust of the goat is the bounty of God.' He then continues with the passage about how the world will be consumed in fire at the end of six thousand years, and that this would come to pass by an improvement in sensual enjoyment. This is the prelude to love-making, but not before we have registered Blake's reminder that 'I have always found that Angels have the vanity to speak of themselves as the only wise' – a remark specifically appropriate to the Angel Gibreel, who in the end succumbs to fear of women and sexuality, as part of the morality which induces his eternal self to dictate the cononical Koran to Muhammad.

The wisdom which Angels seek to conceal or evade is portrayed as evaded or handled hypocritically at the very inception of Islam. Gibreel's early interests are listed like a concise compendium of the imaginative breadth of which spirituality is capable, but they have written into them this sense of Islam's limitations: he studies 'the metamorphic myths of Greece and Rome, the avatars of Jupiter, the boy who became a flower, the spider-woman, Circe, everything; and the theosophy of Annie Besant, and unified field theory, and the incident of the Satanic verses in the early career of the Prophet, and the politics of Muhammad's harem after his return to Mecca in triumph' (*SV*, 24). The phrases about the Satanic verses and Muhammad's harem are put in this company to remind one of the polytheistic context of the growth of Islam, the act of repression involved in excluding the old gods and goddesses, and the connected fact, as Rushdie implies, of a dubious attitude to woman. Shortly afterwards, we learn that, in Gibreel's dreams, 'he was tormented by women of unbearable sweetness and beauty', and we make the link between the mind that is open to desire of woman, and the essentially polytheistic imagination which occupies its days.

The episode of the Satanic verses is the core around which these ideas cluster. The historical source of this story is the annalist Tabari, who relates how Muhammad unexpectedly praises the goddesses who had been worshipped in Mecca alongside Allah, including the great goddess, Al-Lat. As Rushdie quotes it, 'Have you thought upon Lat and Uzza, and Manat, the third, the other? [...] They are the exalted birds, and their intercession is desired indeed' (*SV*, 114). This declaration pleases the crowd in Mecca, of which these goddesses are the patron deities, and also pleases Hind, the powerful woman whose family of origin own the temples and profit by the cults. Hind epitomises the war between the God (Allah) and the Goddess (Al-Lat) in terms which, the novel suggests, we should sympathise with, despite the material interest:

If you are for Allah, I am for Al-Lat. And she doesn't believe your God when he recognizes her. Her opposition to him is implacable,

irrevocable, engulfing. The war between us cannot end in truce!
Yours is a patronizing, condescending lord. Al-Lat hasn't the slightest
wish to be his daughter. She is his equal, as I am yours. (*SV*, 121)

The sympathy, of course, should be qualified, for this struggle leads to
an unending war of the sexes. Yet Hind's words accurately identify
the dangerous and sterile assumption of male superiority. And, like
Blake in *The Marriage of Heaven and Hell*, she believes that there is no
reconciliation of such stark contraries.

But the chief parallel with *The Marriage* is in the large governing
idea of an alternative, satanic scripture:

Those who restrain desire, do so because theirs is weak enough to
be restrained; and the restrainer or reason usurps its place & governs
the unwilling.

And being restrain'd, it by degrees becomes passive, till it is only
the shadow of desire.

The history of this is written in Paradise Lost, & the Governor or
Reason is call'd Messiah.

And the original Archangel, or possessor of the command of the
heavenly host, is call'd the Devil or Satan, and his children are
call'd Sin & Death.

But in the Book of Job, Milton's Messiah is call'd Satan.

For this history has been adopted by both parties. (*MHH*, 5–6; *E*)

And subsequently, as if to put matters straight, Blake announces com-
batively: 'I have also the Bible of Hell, which the world shall have
whether they will or no.'

The 'Satanic verses' are not the only alternative Abrahamic scripture
referred to in the novel: there is also a reference to the story briefly
summarised in the Book of Genesis whereby 'the sons of God' had
visited ' the daughters of men':

And it came to pass, when men began to multiply on the face of
the earth, and daughters were born to them,

That the sons of God saw the daughters of men that they were
fair; and they took them wives of all that they chose [...]

The giants were in the earth in those days, and also after that,
when the sons of God came in unto the daughters of men, and

they bare children to them: the same were the mighty men which were of old, the men of renown. (Genesis 6: 1–4)

God sees, however, that these 'mighty men' are in fact very wicked. This is the story of which a fuller account is given in the apocryphal Book of Enoch, which had been lost to Europe until James Bruce, the explorer who sought the sources of the Nile, brought a copy back from Ethiopia, giving a brief account of it in his *Travels*, published in 1790. The tradition had not, however, been lost to Islam, and this is one reason for Rushdie's inclusion of the reference.

The Ethiopian Book of Enoch emphasises the evil nature of the congress between sons of God and daughters of men.[11] Rushdie has it that 'a number of angels [...] had been flung out of Heaven because they had been *lusting after the daughters of men*, who in due course gave birth to an evil race of giants' (*SV*, 321). From one point of view, the particular value of this alternative tradition to Rushdie resides in the way it shows lust for woman invading the portals of heaven. This is a central point: ultimately it defines the nature of the choice Gibreel sees as confronting him: 'He saw now the choice was simple; the infernal love of the daughters of men, or the celestial adoration of God. He had found it possible to choose the latter; in the nick of time' (*SV*, 321). From another point of view, it reinforces the reference to *The Marriage of Heaven and Hell*, where Blake speaks of 'The Giants who formed this world into its sensual existence, and now seem to live in it in chains' (Plates 15–17). At least in Blake's terminology, the word 'sensual' can be ambiguous.

Ultimately, Muhammad erases the 'Satanic verses' by invoking the superiority of the male child: 'Shall He [Allah] have daughters and you sons? [...] That would be a fine division' (*SV*, 124). The original words are ascribed to the intervention of Shaitan (Satan). But Rushdie believes, with Blake, that what the faithful call evil is necessary to existence, and that its repression leads to a malaise which he takes pains to record and symbolise. Thus, when Chamcha engages in a 'violent outburst' against Gibreel, the horns on his head diminish, a visual representation of emergence from the repression that has distorted humanity. In a similar kind of reflex action, it is said that, 'When the progenitor, the creator is revealed as satanic, the child will frequently grow prim' (*SV*, 67). Even earlier forms of the Abrahamic tradition had recognised this. As the ghost of Rekha Merchant reminds Gibreel, having mocked his self-identification as an Archangel,

> This notion of separation of functions, light versus dark, evil versus good, may be straightforward enough in Islam – *O children of Adam, let not the Devil seduce you, as he expelled your parents from the garden, pulling off from them their clothing that he might show them their shame* – but go back a bit and you see that it's a pretty recent fabrication. (*SV*, 323)

She cites Amos ('Shall there be evil in the city and the lord hath not done it?') and Deutero-Isaiah ('I form the light and create darkness'). Even the very name, Mahound, which is the darkly evocative name by which the Christian West once identified Muhammad – 'the dream-tag the farangis hung around his neck' (*SV*, 93) – is intended to suggest the moral uncertainty that afflicts all humanity, including the Prophet.

The Manichean aspect of the Islamic tradition is undermined by the 'moral fuzziness' of England, which Gibreel half-humourously, half-seriously, blames upon the weather:

> 'When the day is not warmer than night', he reasoned, 'when the light is not brighter than the dark, when the land is not drier than the sea, then clearly a people will lose the power to make distinctions, and commence to see everything – from political parties to sexual partners to religious beliefs – as much-the-same, nothing-to-choose, give-or-take. What folly! For truth is extreme, it is *so* and not *thus*, it is *him* and not *her*: a partisan matter, not a spectator sport. (*SV*, 354)

England brings contraries into unstable interaction with each other, while Gibreel wishes for a stark separation in which the good stands out clearly. But it is especially London, Blake's city, which has this destabilising effect: Gibreel ends by apostrophising it: 'City [...] I am going to tropicalize you.' He has already castigated it: 'O most slippery, most devilish of cities!' Earlier Gibreel has felt its streets 'coiled around him, writhing like serpents'. The city 'had grown unstable again, revealing its true, capricious, tormented nature, its anguish of a city that had lost its sense of itself and wallowed, accordingly, in the impotence of its selfish, angry present of masks and parodies' (*SV*, 320). This is the vision of London which precipitates Gibreel's sense of having escaped the 'infernal love' of 'the daughters of men' (*SV*, 321). In pursuit of salvation for London, Gibreel wanders through the streets, like Blake's wanderer in his 'London':

> I wander thro' each charterd street
> Near where the charterd Thames does flow
> And mark in ev'ry face I meet
> Marks of weakness marks of woe

One of the ideas in this stanza is that of mapping, and Gibreel 'would redeem this city: Geographer's London, all the way from A to Z' (*SV*, 322). But he finds that 'the city in its corruption refused to submit to the dominion of the cartographers, changing shape at will and without warning, making it impossible for Gibreel to approach his quest in the systematic manner he would have preferred' (*SV*, 327). In other words, he is more aligned with the systematic spirit Blake is implicitly criticising, than with the lost freedom represented by the flowing Thames. Even so, he can feel the suffering around him in the 'wasteland' or in 'a grand colonnade built of human flesh and covered in skin that bled when scratched' – compare Blake's 'soldier's sigh' that 'Runs in blood down palace walls', also from 'London'. Unfortunately, his patriarchal religion is no salve for the genuinely exploitative depredations of capitalism.

This is a point to reflect upon, for it is possible to put together the sense of corruption and the idea of 'masks and parodies' in such a way that one can understand Gibreel's unease. The empty parodies confected in a city that has lost its moral bearings are not true guides to creative endeavour. But Rushdie's account is an ambivalent one, his postmodernism an ambivalent phenomenon. The problem with London, its nurturing of 'masks and parodies', is not unambiguously a problem. For these can indeed be aligned also with artifice and creative self-fashioning. Long before this point we had read of Changez Chamchawala's opinion that 'a man untrue to himself becomes a two-legged lie' (*SV*, 48) and the inference is drawn that 'A man who sets out to make himself up is taking on the Creator's role [...] he's unnatural, a blasphemer, an abomination of abominations' (*SV*, 49).

But this propensity is deeply embedded in the book's themes and is linked to its narrative adventurousness. The idea of self-transformation is inscribed in the fact of being an Indian in London, in Saladin's denial of Bombay, in being a film actor, in being at one and the same time the Archangel Gibreel and the Gibreel who lived in London. But these are also all acts of imagination: Rushdie makes explicit quite early on his linking of action and imagination when Gibreel reflects on his 'damn fool nickname, *angel*' and then on 'Motherfucking dreams, cause of all the trouble in the human race, movies, too, if I was God I'd cut the imagination out of people' (*SV*, 122) – which is what he wishes, in the end, to do in the name of God. Perhaps, indeed, the most powerful act of imagination is precisely to imagine one's gods or God, and feel that one has actually been in the divine presence. And this is precisely what Gibreel does, having recalled Blake's account in *The Marriage of Heaven and Hell* of how Blake's Isaiah described the encounter: '*I saw no God, nor heard any, in a finite organical perception; but my senses discover'd the infinite in every thing*' (*SV*, 305 – quoted from *The Marriage*, Plate 12). But Rushdie is careful to distinguish, as well as to compare, Gibreel's vision and that of Blake: 'For Blake's Isaiah, God had simply been an immanence, an incorporeal indignation; but Gibreel's vision of the Supreme Being was not abstract in the least' (*SV*, 318). This definiteness is a malignant sign, but Blake is only representing the perversion of something excellent: the creative powers of imagination pondered by Allie Cone, when she remembers Blake's question from *The Marriage*: '*does a firm perswasion that a thing is so, make it so?*' To which Blake has Isaiah reply, '*All poets believe that it does. & in ages of imagination this firm perswasion moved mountains*' (*SV*, 338 – quoted from *The Marriage*, Plate 12).

12
Conclusion

Blake enters the twentieth century for many writers as the exponent of a poetic style which was seen as direct and forceful, but also suggestive, in a way which accorded with certain tendencies in Modernism. This allowed him to operate as a congenial mentor, and set him apart from other Romantic poets even for one who entertained grave doubts about him, namely T.S. Eliot, though in his case it could be said that part of his intention was to isolate the radical elements in Blake's aesthetic from what still seemed to him to be sullied by bad Romantic attitudes: in this, of course, he also had the ulterior motive of discouraging such attitudes in his contemporaries. But Blake's stance as a kind of revolutionary, and rebel against bourgeois morality, does him no harm.

In the postmodern, the increasing sense of the impossibility of constructing a grand narrative, as well as the sense of loss that impossibility may entail, leads to a growing interest in Blake as myth-maker. The appropriateness of regarding him in this light resides in his being self-conscious about his own construction of myth, and also in his creating different versions of his mythology. Blake's status as a rebel reinforces the sense of his honesty in constructing his myth: his attempt to avoid the way in which myths can so easily become (as Sinclair and Carter put it) 'lies', his feeding this very attempt back into the myth. This is the explanation for Blake's extraordinary standing at the beginning of the twenty-first century.

Appendix

Iain Sinclair on Blake (email to author)

Really, all I can say is that [Blake] remains fundamental to any mapping of London. That, by choice, I walk through Bunhill Fields at the slightest excuse. (It's about twenty minutes from here, at the border of the old city.) Whatever sense of geography I have developed begins with a reading of the prophetic books of 'Jerusalem'. The use of Blakean avatars in 'Suicide Bridge' was instinctive rather than schematic. I liked the idea of taking names that had emerged from the mundane, the treason trial, and been absorbed into a grander mythological scheme, and then returning them once more, confused and shaken, to the vortex of the contemporary city. Blake as inhabitant, citizen, nonconformist, realist/visionary, self-publisher, married man, [or] walker is a presence I would consider before writing anything about London.

Notes

1 Introduction: Blake between romanticism, modernism and postmodernism

1. Richard Ellmann, *Oscar Wilde* (London: Hamish Hamilton, 1987), 40.
2. Edwin John Ellis and William Butler Yeats, eds, *The Works of William Blake, Poetic, Symbolic and Critical*, 3 vols (London: Bernard Quaritch, 1893).
3. W. B. Yeats, *The Poems: A New Edition*, 2nd edn (London and Basingstoke: Macmillan, 1989), 9. Subsequent references given as *YP*, followed by page number, in brackets in the main text.
4. Hazard Adams, *Blake and Yeats: The Contrary Vision* (Ithaca NY: Cornell University Press, 1955), 240–43; and see Margaret Rudd, *Divided Image: A Study of William Blake and W.B. Yeats* (London: Routledge and Kegan Paul, 1953), 35–56, for a discussion of Yeats's idea of 'the quarrel with ourselves' which draws on the idea of contraries.
5. A. E. Housman, *The Name and Nature of Poetry* (Cambridge: Cambridge University Press, 1933), 40.
6. Ibid., 45.
7. Ibid., 49.
8. David Gascoyne, *Collected Poems 1988* (Oxford: Oxford University Press, 1988), 54–55, 145–46.
9. Roger Fry, *Vision and Design* (Harmondsworth: Penguin, 1961), 174–75.
10. Bernard Shaw, *Three Plays for Puritans*, ed. Michael Billington (Harmondsworth: Penguin Books, 2000), 26.
11. Ibid., 43.
12. Ibid., 43.
13. Stephen Spender, *World Within World*, 2nd edn (London: Faber, 1977; 1st edn 1951), 34.
14. W. H. Auden, *The English Auden: Poems, Essays and Dramatic Writings 1927–1939* (London: Faber, 1077), 394–408.
15. Michael Horovitz, ed., *Children of Albion: Poetry of the Underground in Britain* (Harmondsworth: Penguin, 1969), 316.
16. Ibid., 219.
17. Adrian Mitchell, *Tyger: A Celebration Based on the Life and Work of William Blake* (London: Jonathan Cape, 1971).
18. Ted Hughes, *Cave Birds: An Alchemical Cave Drama* (London: Faber, 1978), 56.
19. Maud Ellmann, *The Poetics of Impersonality: T. S. Eliot and Ezra Pound* (Brighton: Harvester, 1987).

2   Zoas and moods: myth and aspects of the mind in Blake and Yeats

1. Keith Thomas, *Religion and the Decline of Magic: Studies in Popular Beliefs in Sixteenth- and Seventeenth-Century England* (London: Weidenfeld & Nicholson, 1971), 271, 378; Christopher Hill, *The World Turned Upside Down*, 2nd edn (Harmondsworth: Penguin, 1976), 287–305; Henry J. Cadbury, 'Early Quakerism and Uncanonical Lore', *Harvard Theological Review*, 40 (1947), 204–05.
2. See *The House of Death*. Colour Print. Tate Gallery. Illustration of *Paradise Lost*, XI, 491–92.
3. Jean Seznec, *The Survival of the Pagan Gods*, trans. B. Sessions (New York: Pantheon Books, 1953), 237.
4. Ibid., 238.
5. Robert James, *A Medicinal Dictionary*, 2 vols (London, 1743–45) II, 'Mania'.
6. Ibid.
7. Ibid.
8. Morton D. Paley, *Energy and the Imagination: A Study in the Development of Blake's Thought* (Oxford: Clarendon Press, 1970), 95.
9. Jean H. Hagstrum, 'Blake and the Sister-Arts Tradition', in *Blake's Visionary Forms Dramatic*, David V. Erdman and John E. Grant, eds (Princeton: Princeton University Press, 1970), 88.
10. Cf. a quotation from Conrad in Michael Levenson, *A Geneaology of Modernism* (Cambridge: Cambridge University Press, 1984), 2, and compare with this the use of the word 'mood' by T. E. Hulme, quoted in Levenson, *A Geneaology of Modernism*, 44.
11. Compare the contrast between the prophet and 'the enchanter' in Margaret Rudd, *Divided Image: A Study of William Blake and W.B. Yeats* (London: Routledge and Kegan Paul, 1953), 1–34.
12. Hazard Adams, *The Book of Yeats's Poems* (Tallahasee: Florida State University Press, 1990).
13. W. B. Yeats, *Essays and Introductions* (London: Macmillan, 1961), 195. Hereafter, *EI*.
14. W. B. Yeats, *The Poems: A New Edition*, ed. Richard Finneran, 2nd edn (Basingstoke: Macmillan, 1989), 56. Future references are given in the main text as YP followed by the page number.
15. Levenson, *A Geneaology of Modernism*, 1–2.
16. Stan Smith, *The Origins of Modernism: Eliot, Pound, Yeats and the Rhetorics of Renewal* (Hemel Hempstead: Harvester Wheatsheaf, 1994), 177–78.
17. Cairns Craig, *Yeats, Eliot, Pound and the Politics of Poetry* (London: Croom Helm, 1982), 72–111.
18. Michael Bell suggested the connection of this poem with the earlier image of the ladder. See also the discussion in Edward Larrissy, *Yeats the Poet: The Measures of Difference* (Hemel Hempstead: Harvester Wheatsheaf, 1994), 193.

3 Eliot between Blake and Yeats

1. T. S. Eliot, *The Sacred Wood: Essays on Poetry and Criticism* (London: Methuen, 1960; reprint of 2nd edn 1928), 151. Subsequent references given as *SW*, followed by page number in the main text.
2. T. S. Eliot, *Inventions of the March Hare*, ed. Christopher Ricks (London: Faber, 1996), xxvii.
3. David Goldie, *A Critical Difference: T. S. Eliot and John Middleton Murry in English Literary Criticism, 1919–1928* (Oxford: Oxford University Press, 1998), 81.
4. T. S. Eliot, *The Use of Poetry and the Use of Criticism*, 2nd edn (London: Faber, 1964; 1st edn 1933.), 140.
5. W. B. Yeats, *The Wind Among the Reeds* (London: John Lane, 1899), see notes 65–108.
6. W. B. Yeats, *Essays and Introductions* (London: Macmillan, 1961), 114.
7. William Blake, *Milton*, 6: 1–5; David V. Erdman, ed., *The Complete Poetry and Prose of William Blake*, newly rev. edn (New York: Doubleday, 1988), 99. Subsequent references given as *E*, followed by page number in the main text.
8. T. S. Eliot, *The Complete Poems and Plays* (London: Faber, 1969), 70.
9. Helen Gardner, *The Composition of Four Quartets* (London: Faber, 1978), 85.
10. Leon Surette, *The Birth of Modernism: Ezra Pound, T. S. Eliot, W. B. Yeats and the Occult* (Montreal and Kingston: McGill-Queen's University Press, 1993).
11. Bernard Bergonzi, 'Eliot's Cities', *T. S. Eliot at the Turn of the Century*, ed. Marianne Thormählen (Lund: Lund University Press, 1994), 59–76 (p. 61).
12. Hugh Kenner, *The Invisible Poet: T. S. Eliot* (London: Methuen, 1965; 1st edn 1959), 110.
13. T. S. Eliot, 'The Mysticism of William Blake', *The Nation & Athenaeum* (17 September 1927), 779.
14. William Blake, 'Illustrations of the Book of Job', IX (1825). Repr., in *Blake's Job: A Commentary*, ed. Andrew Wright (Oxford: Clarendon Press, 1972), 26.
15. J. Middleton Murry, *William Blake* (London: Jonathan Cape, 1936; 1st edn 1933), 17, 269.
16. See Goldie, *A Critical Difference*, 108.
17. Gardner, *Composition*, 18.
18. Harold Bloom, *The Anxiety of Influence: A Theory of Poetry* (New York: Oxford University Press, 1973), 14, 15.

4 Blake and oppositional identity in Yeats, Auden and Dylan Thomas

1. John Kelly and Eric Domville, eds, *The Collected Letters of W.B. Yeats*, I, *1865–1895* (Oxford: Clarendon Press, 1986), 50.
2. R. F. Foster, *W.B. Yeats: A Life*, I, *The Apprentice Mage* (Oxford: Oxford University Press, 1997), 99.

3. Ibid.
4. Quoted in Allen R. Grossman, *Poetic Knowledge in the Early Yeats: A Study of the Wind Among the Reeds* (Charlottesville NC: University Press of Virginia, 1969), 130.
5. George Mills Harper, *The Making of Yeats's A Vision: A Study of the Automatic Script*, I (London and Basingstoke: Macmillan, 1987), xiii, 10–11.
6. Ibid., xiii–xiv.
7. Ibid., 144.
8. Ibid., 16.
9. John G. Blair, *The Poetic Art of W. H. Auden* (Princeton: Princeton University Press, 1965), 16.
10. W. H. Auden, *The Enchafèd Flood, or The Romantic Iconography of the Sea* [1950] (New York: Vintage Books, 1967).
11. Ibid., 53.
12. James Fenton, 'Blake Auden and James Auden', *The Strength of Poetry* (Oxford: Oxford University Press, 2001), 209–27.
13. Blair, *Poetic Art*, 26.
14. Michael Roberts, 'Not This Time?', *The Spectator*, 100 (26 July 1940), 301–02 (p. 301).
15. Fenton, *Strength of Poetry*, 213.
16. Quoted in Herbert Greenberg, *Quest for the Necessary: W. H. Auden and the Dilemma of Divided Consciousness* (Cambridge MA: Harvard University Press, 1968), 56.
17. Ibid., 21.
18. William Plomer, 'Review of W. H. Auden', *The Orators, Sunday Referee* (22 May 1932), 6.
19. Stephen Spender, 'Five Notes on W. H. Auden's Writing', in *W.H. Auden: The Critical Heritage*, ed. John Haffenden (London: Routledge and Kegan Paul, 1983), 102–10 (p. 104).
20. Richard Hoggart, *Auden: An Introductory Essay* (London: Chatto and Windus, 1965), 36.
21. Ibid., 35–36.
22. Ibid., 120.
23. Fenton, *Strength of Poetry*, 224.
24. Ibid., 225.
25. Auden, *Enchafèd Flood*, 81.
26. W. H. Auden, *Collected Longer Poems* (London: Faber and Faber, 1968), 84.
27. Dylan Thomas, 'To Pamela Hansford Johnson' [15 October 1933], in *The Collected Letters of Dylan Thomas*, ed. Paul Ferris (London: Dent, 1985), 25.
28. Dylan Thomas, 'Poetic Manifesto', in *Dylan Thomas: Early Prose Writings*, ed. Walford Davies, (London: J. M. Dent & Sons Ltd, 1971), 154–60.
29. Ibid., 156.
30. Ibid., 156, 157.
31. Ibid., 157–58.
32. Ibid., 159.

33. Ralph Maud, ed., *Poet in the Making: The Notebooks of Dylan Thomas* (London: J.M. Dent & Sons, 1968), 33.

34. Don McKay, 'Crafty Dylan and the Altarwise Sonnets: "I build a flying tower and I pull it down" ', *University of Toronto Quarterly*, 55 (1985–86), 375–94 (p. 381).

35. Dylan Thomas, *Portrait of the Artist as a Young Dog* (London: Dent, 1940), 21.

36. Ibid., 35.

37. James J. Balakier, 'The Ambiguous Reversal of Dylan Thomas's "In Country Sleep" ', *Papers on Lauguage and Literature*, 32:1 (1996), 21–44 (p. 41).

38. John Goodby, ' "Very profound and very box-office": The Later Poems and *Under Milk Wood*', in *Dylan Thomas*, John Goodby and Chris Wigginton, eds (Basingstoke: Palgrave, 2001), 192–220 (p. 207).

5   Blake and Joyce

1. James Joyce, *Stephen Hero* (London: Jonathan Cape, 1944), 216.

2. James Joyce, *Occasional, Critical, and Political Writing*, ed. Kevin Barry (Oxford: Oxford University Press, 2000), 28. Subsequent references in the text as *OCPW*, followed by page number.

3. James Joyce, *Chamber Music* (London: Jonathan Cape, 1907), 20.

4. Richard Ellmann, *James Joyce*, 2nd edn (Oxford: Oxford University Press, 1983), 364.

5. Stanislaus Joyce, *My Brother's Keeper* (New York: Viking Press, 1958), 171.

6. Ellmann, *James Joyce*, 124.

7. James Joyce, *A Portrait of the Artist as a Young Man* (London: Jonathan Cape, 1964), 192.

8. Robert F. Gleckner, 'Joyce's Blake: Paths of Influence', in *William Blake and the Moderns*, Robert J. Bertholf and Annette S. Levitt, eds (Albany: SUNY Press, 1982), 135–63 (p. 139).

9. Ibid., 140–44.

10. C. P. Curran, *James Joyce Remembered* (New York: Oxford University Press, 1968), 9.

11. Joyce, *My Brother's Keeper*, 33.

12. Curran, *James Joyce Remembered*, 35; Joyce, *My Brother's Keeper*, 99.

13. See discussion at Gleckner, 'Joyce's Blake: Paths of Influence', 136.

14. Ibid.

15. Ibid.

16. Ibid., 137–38.

17. Ellmann, *James Joyce*, 146.

18. Joyce, *My Brother's Keeper*, 112.

19. James Joyce, *Ulysses*, The Corrected Text, ed. Hans Walter Gabler (Harmondsworth: Penguin, 1986), 31.

20. Enrico Terrinoni, 'Blakean Ghosts and Shadows in "Proteus" ', *Romantic Joyce: Joyce Studies in Italy (8)*, ed. Franca Ruggieri (Rome: Bulzoni Editore, 2003), 47–56 (p. 52).

21. Morton D. Paley, 'Blake in Nighttown', quoted in Gleckner, 'Joyce's Blake', 149.
22. James Joyce, *Finnegans Wake*, intro. Seamus Deane (Harmondsworth: Penguin, 1992), 563.

6 'Deposits' and 'rehearsals': repetition and redemption in *The Anathémata* of David Jones: a comparison and contrast with Blake

1. David Blamires, *David Jones: Artist and Writer* (Manchester: Manchester University Press, 1971), 1, 4.
2. Robert Lowth, *Lectures on the Sacred Poetry of the Hebrews* (London: J. Johnson, 1787), translated from the Latin of 1759.
3. Compare Walter Benjamin, 'The Work of Art in the Age of Mechanical Reproduction', in *Illuminations*, ed. Hannah Arendt, trans. Harry Zohn (London: Collins, 1973), 219–53.
4. See Gershom G. Scholem, *Walter Benjamin: The Story of a Friendship* (London: Faber, 1982).
5. Gershom G. Scholem, *Major Trends in Jewish Mysticism*, rev. 2nd edn (New York: Schocken, 1946), 237–39, 260–68.
6. See *Marriage*, Plate 4, 34, and *Urizen*, Plates 2–3, p. 70. For the influence of Kabbalah on Blake, see Morton D. Paley, *Energy and the Imagination: A Study of the Development of Blake's Thought* (Oxford: Clarendon Press, 1970), 14, 69, 94.
7. Nerval compares the revival of memories of childhood in the middle of life to the effect of a palimpsest: 'Les souvenirs d'enfance se ravivent quand on a atteint la moitié de la vie. C'est comme un manuscrit palimpseste dont on fait reparaître les lignes par des procédés chimiques', *Les Filles du feu, Les chimères* (Paris: Gallimard, 1965), 61.
8. Soren Kierkegaard, *The Concept of Dread*, trans. Walter Lowie (Princeton, 1944), 16. Discussed by Lorraine Clark, *Blake, Kierkegaard, and the Spectre of Dialectic* (Cambridge: Cambridge University Press, 1991), 103.
9. David Jones, *The Anathémata*, 2nd edn (London: Faber, 1972; 1st edn 1952), 73–4. Subsequent references given as *Ana* in text, followed by page number.
10. Saunders Lewis, 'Epoch and Artist', *Agenda*, 5 (David Jones Special Issue, Spring–Summer, 1967), 112–15 (p. 115).
11. David Jones, *The Dying Gaul* (London: Faber, 1978), 216. Future references given in text as *DG*, followed by page number.
12. Henri d' Arbois de Jubainville, *The Irish Mythological Cycle and Celtic Mythology*, trans. Richard Irvine Best (Dublin: O'Donoghue & Co., 1903), 190: Finn (Middle Irish 'Find') is reborn as Mongan.
13. David Jones, *Epoch and Artist* (London: Faber, 1959), 168. Future references are given in the text as *E&A*, followed by the page number.
14. Jones's engravings for Coleridge's poem were executed in 1928. They are reproduced by Clover Hill Editions, London, in 1964, in their edition of the poem.

7   Blake, postmodernity and postmodernism

1. Jean-François Lyotard, *The Postmodern Condition: A Report on Knowledge*, trans. Geoff Bennington and Brian Massumi (Manchester: Manchester University Press, 1986). Translated from *La Condition postmoderne: rapport sur la savoir* (1979). The point about Kant is developed in an essay included in an appendix, 'Answering the Question: "What is Postmodernism?" ', 71–82.
2. Paul Hamilton, 'From Sublimity to Indeterminacy: New World Order or Aftermath of Romantic Ideology', in *Romanticism to Postmodernism*, ed. Edward Larrissy (Cambridge: Cambridge University Press, 1999), 13–28 (p. 27).
3. Lyotard, *Postmodern Condition*, 81.
4. Ibid., 78.
5. Ibid., 81.
6. William H. Galperin, *The Return of the Visible in British Romanticism* (Baltimore: Johns Hopkins University Press, 1993), 244–70, especially 244–56.
7. Ibid., 257–70.
8. Nicholas M. Williams, *Ideology and Utopia in the Poetry of William Blake* (Cambridge: Cambridge University Press, 1998), 209–19.
9. Ibid., 212.
10. Leslie A. Marchand, ed., *Byron's Letters and Journals*, 12 vols (London: Murray, 1973–82), III, 220.
11. Ira Livingston, *Arrow of Chaos: Romanticism and Postmodernity*. Theory Out of Bounds Series, vol. 9 (Minneapolis and London: University of Minnesota Press, 1997), 14.
12. Ibid., 2.
13. Ibid., xi.
14. Hazard Adams, 'Blake and the Postmodern', in *Essays for S. Foster Damon*, ed. Alvin H. Rosenfeld (Providence: Brown University Press, 1969), 3–17 (p. 7).
15. Ibid., 17.
16. Northrop Frye, *The Stubborn Structure: Essays on Criticism and Society* (London: Methuen, 1970). These points are well supported by a reading of the essay 'The Instruments of Mental Production', 3–21. Adams's reference to Frye is on page 8 of 'Blake and the Postmodern'.
17. See Maurice Merleau-Ponty, 'On the Phenomenology of Language' and 'From Mauss to Claude Lévi-Strauss', *Signs*, trans. Richard C. McCleary (Evanston: Northwestern University Press, 1964), 84–97, 114–25.
18. Adams, 'Blake and the Postmodern', 9.
19. Annette S. Levitt, ' "The Mental Traveller", in *The Horse's Mouth*: New Light on the Old Cycle', in *William Blake and the Moderns*, Robert J. Bertholf and Annette S. Levitt, eds (Albany: State University of New York Press, 1982), 186–211 (p. 187).
20. Joyce Cary, *The Horse's Mouth*, 2nd edn (London: Michael Joseph, 1951; 1st edn 1944), 52.

21. Ibid., 190.
22. Peter J. Conradi, *Iris Murdoch: A Life* (London: Harper-Collins, 2001), 295: on Murdoch's friendship with Cary, and on their circle.
23. Peter J. Conradi, *The Saint and the Artist: A Study of the Fiction of Iris Murdoch*, 2nd edn with new foreword by John Bayley (London: Harper Collins, 2001), 372.
24. Robert J. Bertholf, 'Robert Duncan: Blake's Contemporary Voice', in *William Blake and the Moderns*, Bertholf and Levitt, eds, 92–110 (p. 94).
25. Robert Duncan, *Derivations: Selected Poems 1950–1956* (London: Fulcrum Press, 1968), 9.
26. Robert Duncan, *Roots and Branches* (London: Jonathan Cape, 1970), 51.
27. Ibid., 50.
28. Barry Miles, *Ginsberg: A Biography* (London: Virgin, 2000), 208.
29. Paul Portugés, *The Visionary Poetics of Allen Ginsberg* (Santa Barbara: Ross-Erikson, 1978), 23.
30. Allen Ginsberg, *Howl and Other Poems* (San Francisco: City Lights Books, 1956), 29. Subsequent references given as *HOP*, followed by page numbers in brackets in the text.
31. Alicia Ostriker, 'Blake Ginsberg, Madness, and the Prophet as Shaman', in *Wiliam Blake and the Moderns*, Bertholf and Levitt, eds, 113–31 (p. 121).
32. Ibid., 120, 121.
33. David Trotter, *The Making of the Reader: Language and Subjectivity in Modern American, English and Irish Poetry* (Basingstoke: Macmillan, 1984), 200–01.
34. Ibid., 202.
35. Shirley Dent and Jason Whittaker, *Radical Blake: Influence and Afterlife from 1827* (Basingstoke and New York: Palgrave Macmillan, 2002), 165.
36. Nicholas M. Williams, 'Eating Blake, or An Essay on Taste: The Case of Thomas Harris's *Red Dragon*', *Cultural Critique*, 42 (1999), 143–70 (p. 155).
37. Ibid., 140–47.
38. Ibid., 146.
39. Ibid., 147.
40. Ibid., 149.
41. Subject of a conference in the School of English, University of Leeds, July 2005.
42. Iain Sinclair, *Suicide Bridge: A Book of the Dead Hamlets: May 1974 to April 1975* (London: Albion Village Press, 1975), 8–9.
43. Dent and Whittaker, *Radical Blake*, 61.
44. For thoughts on 'deconstructive materialism' see Marjorie Levinson, *Wordsworth's Great Period Poems: Four Essays* (Cambridge: Cambridge University Press, 1986), 10.
45. Edward Larrissy, *William Blake* (Oxford: Blackwell, 1985), 42–55.
46. Livingston, *Arrow of Chaos*, 180.
47. Ibid., 105.
48. Graham Pechey, '1789 and After: Mutations of "Romantic" Discourse', in *1789: Reading Writing Revolution*, Francis Barker *et al.*, eds (Colchester: University of Essex, 1982), 52–66.
49. Ibid., 70–109.

50. Graham Pechey, 9.
51. Williams, *Ideology and Utopia*, 219.
52. Ibid.
53. Livingston, *Arrow of Chaos*, 79.
54. Ibid., 73.
55. Stephen Leo Carr, 'Illuminated Printing: Toward a Logic of Difference', in *Unnam'd Forms: Blake and Textuality*, Nelson Hilton and Thomas A. Vogler, eds (Berkeley and Los Angeles: University of California Press, 1986), 177–96.
56. Ibid., 187.
57. Robert Essick, 'How Blake's Body Means', in *Unnam'd Forms*, Nelson and Vogler, eds, 197–217, 204; Robert Viscomi, *Blake and the Idea of the Book* (Princeton: Princeton University Press, 1993), 163–76.
58. Essick, 'How Blake's Body Means', 202.
59. Carr, 'Illuminated Printing', 188.
60. Edward Larrissy, 'Spectral Imposition and Visionary Imposition: Printing and Repetition in Blake', in *Blake in the Nineties*, Steve Clark and David Worrall, eds (Basingstoke: Macmillan; New York: St Martin's Press, 1999), 75.
61. Williams, 'Eating Blake', 145.
62. Ibid., 150.

8 Joyce Cary: getting it from the horse's mouth

1. Quoted in Alan Bishop, *Joyce Cary: Gentleman Rider* (Oxford: Oxford University Press, 1989), 87.
2. Annette S. Levitt, ' "The Mental Traveller" in *The Horse's Mouth*: New Light on the Old Cycle', in *William Blake and the Moderns*, Robert J. Bertholf and Annette S.Levitt, eds (Albany: SUNY Press, 1982), 186–211 (p. 211, n. 20). The annotated text is a reprint of 1942.
3. Bishop, *Joyce Cary*, 87.
4. Joyce Cary, *The Horse's Mouth*, Carfax Edition, (London: Michael Joseph, 1951), 46. First published 1944. Subsequent references (to the Carfax Edition) are given in the text as *HM*, followed by the page number.
5. Compare Dennis Hall, *Joyce Cary: A Reappraisal* (New York: St Martin's Press, 1983), 74.
6. Bishop, *Joyce Cary*, 258.
7. Bishop, *Joyce Cary*, 254.
8. See Hall, *Joyce Cary*, 148, for a memorable epitome of Cary's universe.

9 Two American disciples of Blake: Robert Duncan and Allen Ginsberg

1. Burton Hatlen, 'Robert Duncan's Marriage of Heaven and Hell: Kabbalah and Rime in *Roots and Branches*', in *World, Self, Poem: Essays on Contemporary Poetry from the 'Jubilation of Poets'*, ed. Leonard M. Tramick (Kent, Ohio: Kent State University Press, 1990), 207–27 (pp. 207–09).

2. Ibid., 209.
3. Ibid.
4. Ibid., 212–13.
5. Robert Duncan, *Roots and Branches* (London: Jonathan Cape, 1970), 5, 4. Subsequent references are given as *RB* in the text, followed by page number.
6. Robert Peters and Paul Trachtenberg, 'A Conversation with Robert Duncan (1976)', *Chicago Review*, 44:1 (1998), 92–116 (p. 92).
7. Ibid., 94.
8. Robert Duncan, *Bending the Bow* (London: Jonathan Cape, 1971), 51. Future references are given in the text as *BB*, followed by the page number.
9. Peters and Trachtenberg, 'A Conversation', 99.
10. Robert Duncan, *The Truth and Life of Myth: An Essay in Essential Autobiography* (New York: House of Books, 1968), 24.
11. Robert Duncan, *The Opening of the Field* (London: Jonathan Cape, 1969), 76.
12. Quoted in Robert J. Bertholf, 'Robert Duncan: Blake's Contemporary Voice', in *William Blake and the Moderns*, Robert J. Bertholf and Annette S. Levitt, eds (Albany: SUNY Press, 1982), 92–110 (p. 101).
13. Ibid., 94.
14. Duncan, *Truth and Life of Myth*, 24.
15. Duncan, *Opening of the Field*, 11.
16. Ibid., 13.
17. Bertholf, 'Robert Duncan', 94.
18. Robert Duncan, *Derivations: Selected Poems 1950–1956* (London: Fulcrum Press, 1968), 41.
19. Duncan, *Truth and Life of Myth*, 15–16.
20. Duncan, *Opening of the Field*, 11.
21. Duncan, *Truth and Life of Myth*, 15.
22. Robert Duncan, *As Testimony: The Poem and the Scene* (San Francisco: White Rabbitt Press, 1964; 2nd impression 1966), 9–10.
23. Duncan, *The Opening of the Field*, 42.
24. Ibid., 43.
25. Bertholf, 'Robert Duncan', 98–99.
26. Duncan, *Truth and Life of Myth*, 8.
27. Robert Duncan, *The Sweetness and Greatness of Dante's Divine Comedy* (San Francisco: Open Space, 1965), unpaginated.
28. Duncan, *Truth and Life of Myth*, 40.
29. Allen Ginsberg, *Collected Poems 1947–1980* (New York: Harper & Row, 1984), 354. Future references given in the text as *CP* followed by page number.
30. Allen Ginsberg, 'Notes Written on Finally Recording Howl', in *A Casebook on the Beat* (New York: Thomas Y. Crowell, 1961), 28.
31. Paul Portugés, *The Visionary Poetics of Allen Ginsberg* (Santa Barbara: Ross-Erikson, 1978), 23.
32. Anon.,*Writers at Work: The Paris Review Interviews*, 3rd series (New York: Viking Press, 1967), 308–10.
33. Ibid., 311.

34. Allen Ginsberg, *Selected Poems 1947–1945* (Harmondsworth: Penguin Books, 1997), 378.
35. Ibid., 316–17.
36. Alicia Ostriker, 'Blake, Ginsberg, Madness and the Prophet as Shaman', *William Blake and the Moderns*, Robert J. Bertholf and Annette S. Levitt, eds (Albany: SUNY Press, 1982), 111–31 (p. 112).
37. Ibid.

10 Postmodern myths and lies: Iain Sinclair and Angela Carter

1. Andrew Crozier and Tim Longville, *A Various Art* (Manchester: Carcanet, 1987), 12.
2. Peter Barry, *Contemporary British Poetry and the City* (Manchester: Manchester University Press, 2000), 165.
3. Charles Olson, *The Maximus Poems* (New York: Jargon/Corinth Books, 1960).
4. Charles Olson, *A Bibliography on America For Ed Dorn* (San Francisco: Four Seasons Foundation, 1964), 13.
5. Charles Olson, *Selected Writings*, ed. Robert Creeley (New York: New Directions, 1966), 24.
6. Iain Sinclair, *Lud Heat: A Book of the Dead Hamlets* (London: Albion Village Press, 1975), 42; Iain Sinclair, *Lud Heat and Suicide Bridge* (London: Granta Books, 1995), 57. References to *Lud Heat* are to both these editions, as the first edition contains photographs absent from the more readily available joint edition of *Lud Heat* and *Suicide Bridge*. Subsequent references to *Lud Heat* will be in the form *LH* followed by page number, and *LHSB* followed by page number in brackets in the text.
7. Iain Sinclair, *Lights Out for the Territory* (London: Granta Books, 1997), 274.
8. Edward Dorn, *The Collected Poems, 1956–1974: Enlarged Edition* (San Francisco: Four Seasons Foundation, 1983), 91.
9. Ibid., 191.
10. Ibid., 198–99.
11. Ibid., 87.
12. Quoted by Peter Middleton in 'Dorn', *Poetry Information*, 20 and 21 (Winter, 1979–80), 18–30 (p. 24).
13. Edward Dorn, *Slinger* (Berkeley: Wingbow Press, 1975), F58R (unpaginated).
14. Thomas Pynchon, *Gravity's Rainbow* (London: Picador, 1975; 1st edn 1973), 144.
15. Iain Sinclair, *White Chappell: Scarlet Tracings* (London: Paladin, 1987), 49.
16. Ibid., 50.
17. Simon Perrill, 'A Cartography of Absence: The Work of Iain Sinclair', *Comparative Criticism*, 19 (1997), 309–39.
18. Sinclair, *White Chappell*, 50.
19. Barry, *Contemporary British Poetry*, 172.
20. Sinclair, *White Chappell*, 159.
21. Ibid., 161.

22. Ibid., 162.
23. Paul March-Russell, 'The Politics of Time and Form in Douglas Oliver's *A Salvo for Africa*', *English*, 53:207 (2004), 203–18 (p. 204).
24. Shirley Dent and Jason Whittaker, *Radical Blake: Influence and Afterlife from 1827* (Basingstoke and New York: Palgrave Macmillan, 2002), 63.
25. Iain Sinclair, *Downriver (Or, The Vessels of Wrath): A Narrative in Twelve Tales* (London: Vintage, 1995), 385. First published 1991.
26. Dent and Whittaker, *Radical Blake*, 64.
27. Perrill, 'A Cartography', 312.
28. Lorna Sage, *Angela Carter* (Plymouth: Northcote House/British Council, 1994), 29.
29. Lorna Sage, 'Introduction', in *Flesh and the Mirror: Essays on the Art of Angela Carter*, ed. Lorna Sage (London: Virago, 1994), 1–23 (p. 12).
30. Angela Carter, *Expletives Deleted* (London: Chatto & Windus, 1992), 73.
31. Angela Carter, 'Little Lamb Get Lost', in *Shaking a Leg: Journalism and Writings*, ed. Jenny Uglow (London: Chatto & Windus, 1997), 305–09 (p. 305).
32. Ibid., 306.
33. Guido Almarsi, 'In the Alchemist's Cave: Radio Plays', in *Flesh and the Mirror*, 216–29 (p. 220).
34. Angela Carter, 'Notes from the Front Line', in *Shaking a Leg*, 38.
35. Edward Larrissy, ' "Self-Imposition", Alchemy, and the Fate of the "Bound" in Later Blake', in *Historicizing Blake*, Steve Clark and David Worrall, eds (Basingstoke: Macmillan, 1994), 59–72 (p. 63).
36. Angela Carter, *The Passion of New Eve* (London: Victor Gollancz, 1977), 13. Future references are given in the text as *PNE* followed by the page number.
37. Sage, *Angela Carter*, 38–39.
38. Angela Carter, *The Sadeian Woman* (London: Virago, 1979), 36.
39. Ibid., 24.
40. Carter, *Shaking a Leg*, 38.
41. Sage, *Angela Carter*, 2–3, 26–28, 31.
42. Roland Barthes, *Mythologies*, trans. Annette Lavers (London: Jonathan Cape, 1972), 56–57, 142.
43. Angela Carter, 'William Burroughs', in *Shaking a Leg*, 463–65 (p. 465).
44. Angela Carter, *The Bloody Chamber* (London: Virago, 1979), 17. Subsequent references in the text as *BC*, followed by page number.
45. Angela Carter, *Nights at the Circus* (London: Virago, 1984), 9. Subsequent references in the text as *NC* followed by page number.
46. Linden Peach, *Angela Carter* (Basingstoke: Macmillan, 1998), 115.

11 Salman Rushdie, myth and postcolonial romanticism

1. Ben Okri, *Mental Fight* (London: Phoenix, 1999), 5.
2. Ben Okri, 13.

3. Salman Rushdie, *The Satanic Verses* (London: Random House, 1988), 549. Future references to this work are given in the text as *SV* followed by the page number.
4. Arun Kolatkar, *Jejuri* (Bombay: Clearing House, 1976).
5. Ibid., 20.
6. Ibid., 13.
7. Ibid., 12.
8. Ibid., 28.
9. Ibid., 34.
10. Jean-François Lyotard, *The Postmodern Condition: A Report on Knowledge*, trans. Geoff Bennington and Brian Massumi, foreword by Fredric Jameson (Manchester: Manchester University Press, 1986), 15.
11. See the discussion in John Beer, 'Blake's Changing View of History: The Impact of *The Book of Enoch*', in *Historicizing Blake*, Steve Clark and David Worrall, eds (Basingstoke: Macmillan, 1994), 159–78 (pp. 161–64).

Bibliography

Adams, Hazard, *Blake and Yeats: The Contrary Vision* (Ithaca: Cornell University Press, 1955).

——, *The Book of Yeats's Poems* (Tallahasee: Florida State University Press, 1990).

——, 'Blake and the Postmodern', in *Essays for S. Foster Damon*, ed. Alvin H. Rosenfeld (Providence: Brown University Press, 1969), 3–17.

Almarsi, Guido, 'In the Alchemist's Cave: Radio Plays', in *Flesh and the Mirror: Essays on the Art of Angela Carter*, ed. Lorna Sage (London: Virago, 1994).

Anon. *Writers at Work: The Paris Review Interviews*, 3rd series (New York: Viking Press, 1967), 308–10.

Arbois de Jubainville, Henri d', *The Irish Mythological Cycle and Celtic Mythology*, trans. Richard Irvine Best (Dublin: O' Donoghue & Co., 1903).

Auden, W. H., *Collected Longer Poems* (London: Faber and Faber, 1968).

——, *The Enchafèd Flood, or The Romantic Iconography of the Sea*, 1st edn 1950 (New York: Vintage Books, 1967).

Balakier, James J., 'The Ambiguous Reversal of Dylan Thomas's "In Country Sleep" ', *Papers on Language and Literature*, 32:1 (1996), 21–44.

Barry, Peter, *Contemporary British Poetry and the City* (Manchester: Manchester University Press, 2000).

Barthes, Roland, *Mythologies*, trans. Annette Lavers (London: Jonathan Cape, 1972).

Beer, John, 'Blake's Changing View of History: The Impact of *The Book of Enoch*', in *Historicizing Blake*, Steve Clark and David Worrall, eds (Basingstoke: Macmillan, 1994), 159–78.

Benjamin, Walter, 'The Work of Art in the Age of Mechanical Reproduction', in *Illuminations*, ed. Hannah Arendt, trans. Harry Zohn (London: Collins, 1973), 219–53.

Bergonzi, Bernard, 'Eliot's Cities', in *T. S. Eliot at the Turn of the Century*, ed. Marianne Thormählen (Lund: Lund University Press, 1994), 59–76.

Bertholf, Robert J. and Annette S. Levitt, eds, *William Blake and the Moderns* (Albany: SUNY Press, 1982).

Bertholf, Robert J., 'Robert Duncan: Blake's Contemporary Voice', in *William Blake and the Moderns*, Bertholf and Levitt, eds, q.v., 92–110.

Bishop, Alan *Joyce Cary: Gentleman Rider* (Oxford: Oxford University Press, 1989).

Blair, John G., *The Poetic Art of W. H. Auden* (Princeton: Princeton University Press, 1965).

Bloom, Harold, *The Anxiety of Influence: A Theory of Poetry* (New York: Oxford University Press, 1973).

Cadbury, Henry J., 'Early Quakerism and Uncanonical Lore', *Harvard Theological Review*, 40 (1947), 204–05.

Carr, Stephen Leo, 'Illuminated Printing: Toward a Logic of Difference', in *Unnam'd Forms: Blake and Textuality*, Nelson Hilton and Thomas

A. Vogler, eds (Berkeley and Los Angeles: University of California Press, 1986), 177–96.

Carter, Angela, *The Bloody Chamber* (London: Virago, 1979).

Carter, Angela, *Expletives Deleted* (London: Chatto & Windus, 1992).

——, *Nights at the Circus* (London: Virago, 1984).

——, *The Passion of New Eve* (London: Victor Gollancz, 1977).

——, *The Sadeian Woman* (London: Virago, 1979).

——, *Shaking a Leg: Journalism and Writings*, ed. Jenny Uglow (London: Chatto & Windus, 1997).

Cary, Joyce, *The Horse's Mouth*, Carfax Edition (London: Michael Joseph, 1951). First published 1944.

Clark, Lorraine, *Blake, Kierkegaard, and the Spectre of Dialectic* (Cambridge: Cambridge University Press, 1991).

Conradi, Peter J., *Iris Murdoch: A Life* (London: Harper-Collins, 2001).

——, *The Saint and the Artist: A Study of the Fiction of Iris Murdoch*, 2nd edn, with new foreword by John Bayley (London: Harper-Collins, 2001).

Craig, Cairns, *Yeats, Eliot, Pound and the Politics of Poetry* (London: Croom Helm, 1982).

Crozier, Andrew and Tim Longville, eds, *A Various Art* (Manchester: Carcanet, 1987).

Curran, C. P., *James Joyce Remembered* (New York: Oxford University Press, 1968).

Davies, Walford, ed., *Dylan Thomas: Early Prose Writings* (London: J.M. Dent & Sons Ltd, 1971).

Dent, Shirley and Jason Whittaker, *Radical Blake: Influence and Afterlife from 1827* (Basingstoke and New York: Palgrave Macmillan, 2002).

Dorn, Edward, *The Collected Poems, 1956–1974: Enlarged Edition* (San Francisco: Four Seasons Foundation, 1983).

——, *Slinger* (Wingbow Press, Berkeley, 1975).

Duncan, Robert, *As Testimony: The Poem and the Scene* (San Francisco: White Rabbitt Press, 1964; 2nd impression 1966).

——, *Bending the Bow* (London: Jonathan Cape, 1971).

——, *Derivations: Selected Poems 1950–1956* (London: Fulcrum Press, 1968).

——, *The Opening of the Field* (London: Jonathan Cape, 1969).

——, *Roots and Branches* (London: Jonathan Cape, 1970).

——, *The Sweetness and Greatness of Dante's Divine Comedy* (San Francisco: Open Space, 1965).

——, *The Truth and Life of Myth: An Essay in Essential Autobiography* (New York: House of Books, 1968).

Eliot, T. S., *The Complete Poems and Plays* (London: Faber, 1970).

——, *Inventions of the March Hare*, ed. Christopher Ricks (London: Faber, 1996).

——, *The Sacred Wood: Essays on Poetry and Criticism* (London: Methuen, 1960). Reprint of 2nd edn (1928).

——, *The Use of Poetry and the Use of Criticism*, 2nd edn (London: Faber, 1964; 1st edn 1933).

——, The Mysticism of William Blake', *The Nation & Athenaeum* (September 17, 1927), 779.

Ellis, Edwin John and William Butler Yeats, eds, *The Works of William Blake, Poetic, Symbolic and Critical*, 3 vols (London: Bernard Quaritch, 1893).

Ellmann, Maud, *The Poetics of Impersonality: T. S. Eliot and Ezra Pound* (Brighton: Harvester, 1987).

Ellmann, Richard, *James Joyce*, 2nd edn (Oxford: Oxford University Press, 1983).

——, *Oscar Wilde* (London: Hamish Hamilton, 1987).

Erdman, David V. and John E. Grant, eds, *Blake's Visionary Forms Dramatic* (Princeton: Princeton University Press, 1970).

Essick, Robert, 'How Blake's Body Means', in *Unnam'd Forms: Blake and Textuality*, Nelson Hilton and Thomas A. Vogler, eds (Berkeley and Los Angeles: University of California Press, 1986), 197–217.

Fenton, James, 'Blake Auden and James Auden', *The Strength of Poetry* (Oxford: Oxford University Press, 2001), 209–27.

Foster, R. F, *W. B. Yeats: A Life*, I, *The Apprentice Mage* (Oxford: Oxford University Press, 1997).

Fry, Roger, *Vision and Design* (Harmondsworth: Penguin, 1961).

Frye, Northrop, *The Stubborn Structure: Essays on Criticism and Society* (London: Methuen, 1970).

Galperin, William H., *The Return of the Visible in British Romanticism* (Baltimore: Johns Hopkins University Press, 1993).

Gardner, Helen, *The Composition of* Four Quartets (London: Faber, 1978).

Gascoyne, David, *Collected Poems 1988* (Oxford: Oxford University Press, 1988).

Ginsberg, Allen, 'Notes Written on Finally Recording Howl', *A Casebook on the Beat* (New York: Thomas Y. Crowell, 1961).

——, *Collected Poems 1947–1985* (Harmondsworth: Penguin, 1995).

——, *Howl and Other Poems* (San Francisco: City Lights Books, 1956).

Gleckner, Robert F., 'Joyce's Blake: Paths of Influence', in *William Blake and the Moderns*, Bertholf and Levitt, eds, q.v., 135–63.

Goldie, David, *A Critical Difference: T. S. Eliot and John Middleton Murry in English Literary Criticism, 1919–1928* (Oxford: Oxford University Press, 1998).

Goodby, John, ' "Very profound and very box-office": the Later Poems and *Under Milk Wood*', in *Dylan Thomas*, John Goodby and Chris Wigginton, eds (Basingstoke: Palgrave, 2001), 192–220.

Greenberg, Herbert, *Quest for the Necessary: W. H. Auden and the Dilemma of Divided Consciousness* (Cambridge MA: Harvard University Press, 1968).

Grossman, Allen R., *Poetic Knowledge in the Early Yeats: A Study of* The Wind Among the Reeds (Charlottlesville, NC: University Press of Virginia, 1969).

Hagstrum, Jean H., 'Blake and the Sister-Arts Tradition', *Blake's Visionary Forms Dramatic*, in *Blake's Visionary Forms Dramatic*, Erdman and Grant, eds, q.v., 82–91.

Hall, Dennis, *Joyce Cary: A Reappraisal* (New York: St Martin's Press, 1983).

Hamilton, Paul, 'From Sublimity to Indeterminacy: New World Order or Aftermath of Romantic Ideology', in *Romanticism to Postmodernism*, ed. Edward Larrissy (Cambridge: Cambridge University Press, 1999), 13–28.

Harper, George Mills, *The Making of Yeats's A Vision: A Study of the Automatic Script* (London and Basingstoke: Macmillan, 1987).

Hatlen, Burton, 'Robert Duncan's Marriage of Heaven and Hell: Kabbalah and Rime in *Roots and Branches'*, in *World, Self, Poem: Essays on Contemporary Poetry from the 'Jubilation of Poets'*, ed. Leonard M. Tramick (Kent, Ohio: Kent State University Press, 1990), 207–27.

Hill, Christopher, *The World Turned Upside Down*, 2nd edn (Harmondsworth: Penguin, 1976).

Hoggart, Richard, *Auden: An Introductory Essay* (London: Chatto and Windus, 1965).

Horovitz, Michael, *Children of Albion: Poetry of the Underground in Britain* (Harmondsworth: Penguin, 1969).

Housman, A. E., *The Name and Nature of Poetry* (Cambridge: Cambridge University Press, 1933).

James, Robert, *A Medicinal Dictionary* (London) 2 vols, 1743–45.

Jones, David, *The Anathémata*, 2nd edn (London: Faber, 1972). 1st edn 1952.

——, *The Dying Gaul* (London: Faber, 1978).

——, *Epoch and Artist* (London: Faber, 1959).

James Joyce, *A Portrait of the Artist as a Young Man* (London: Jonathan Cape, 1964).

——, *Chamber Music* (London: Jonathan Cape, 1907).

——, *Finnegans Wake*, intro Seamus Deane (Harmondsworth: Penguin, 1992).

——, *Occasional, Critical, and Political Writing*, ed. Kevin Barry (Oxford: Oxford University Press, 2000).

——, *Stephen Hero* (London: Jonathan Cape, 1944).

——, *Ulysses*, The Corrected Text, ed. Hans Walter Gabler (Harmondsworth: Penguin, 1986), 31.

Joyce, Stanislaus, *My Brother's Keeper* (New York: Viking Press, 1958).

Kelly, John and Eric Domville, eds, *The Collected Letters of W. B. Yeats*, I, *1865–1895* (Oxford: Clarendon Press, 1986).

Kenner, Hugh, *The Invisible Poet: T. S. Eliot* (London: Methuen, 1965). 1st edn 1959.

Kierkegaard, Soren, *The Concept of Dread*, trans. Walter Lowie (Princeton: Princeton University Press, 1944).

Kolatkar, Arun, *Jejuri* (Bombay: Clearing House, 1976).

Larrissy, Edward, *William Blake* (Oxford: Blackwell, 1985).

——, *Yeats the Poet: The Measures of Difference* (Hemel Hampstead: Harvester, 1994).

——, ' "Self-Imposition", Alchemy, and the Fate of the "Bound" in Later Blake', in *Historicizing Blake*, Steve Clark and David Worrall, eds (Basingstoke: Macmillan, 1994), 59–72.

——, 'Spectral Imposition and Visionary Imposition: Printing and Repetition in Blake', in *Blake in the Nineties*, Steve Clark and David Worrall, eds (Basingstoke: Macmillan; New York: St Martin's Press, 1999), 61–77.

Levenson, Michael, *A Geneaology of Modernism* (Cambridge: Cambridge University Press, 1984).

Levinson, Marjorie, *Wordsworth's Great Period Poems: Four Essays* (Cambridge: Cambridge University Press, 1986).

Levitt, Annette S., ' "The Mental Traveller" in *The Horse's Mouth*: New Light on the Old Cycle', in *William Blake and the Moderns*, Bertholf and Levitt, eds, q.v., 186–211.

Lewis, Saunders, 'Epoch and Artist', *Agenda*, 5 (David Jones Special Issue, Spring-Summer, 1967), 112–15.

Livingston, Ira, *Arrow of Chaos: Romanticism and Postmodernity*. Theory Out of Bounds Series, vol. 9 (Minneapolis and London: University of Minnesota Press, 1997).

Lowth, Robert, *Lectures on the Sacred Poetry of the Hebrews* (London, 1787), translated from the Latin of 1759.

Lyotard, Jean-François, *The Postmodern Condition: A Report on Knowledge*, trans. Geoff Bennington and Brian Massumi (Manchester: Manchester University Press, 1986). Translated from *La Condition postmoderne: rapport sur la savoir* (1979).

Marchand , Leslie A., ed., *Byron's Letters and Journals*, 12 vols (London: Murray, 1973–82).

March-Russell, Paul, 'The Politics of Time and Form in Douglas Oliver's *A Salvo for Africa*', *English*, 53:207 (2004), 203–18.

Maud, Ralph, ed., *Poet in the Making: The Notebooks of Dylan Thomas* (London: J. M. Dent & Sons, 1968).

McKay, Don, 'Crafty Dylan and the Altarwise Sonnets: "I build a flying tower and I pull it down" ', *University of Toronto Quarterly*, 55 (1985–86), 375–94.

Merleau-Ponty, Maurice, 'On the Phenomenology of Language' and 'From Mauss to Claude Lévi-Strauss', *Signs*, trans. Richard C. McCleary (Evanston: Northwestern University Press, 1964), 84–97, 114–25.

Middleton, Peter, 'Dorn', *Poetry Information*, 20 and 21 (Winter, 1979–80), 18–30.

Miles, Barry, *Ginsberg: A Biography* (London: Virgin, 2000).

Mitchell, Adrian, *Tyger: A Celebration Based on the Life and Work of William Blake* (London: Jonathan Cape, 1971).

Murry, J. Middleton, *William Blake* (London: Jonathan Cape, 1936). 1st edn 1933.

Nerval, Gérard de, *Les Filles du feu, Les chimères* (Paris: Gallimard, 1965).

Okri, Ben, *Mental Fight* (London: Phoenix, 1999).

Olson, Charles, *A Bibliography on America For Ed Dorn* (San Francisco: Four Seasons Foundation, 1964).

——, *The Maximus Poems* (New York: Jargon/Corinth Books, 1960).

——, *Selected Writings*, ed. Robert Creeley (New York: New Directions, 1966).

Ostriker, Alicia, 'Blake Ginsberg, Madness, and the Prophet as Shaman', in *William Blake and the Moderns*, Bertholf and Levitt, eds, q.v., 111–31.

Paley, Morton D., *Energy and the Imagination: A Study of the Development of Blake's Thought* (Oxford: Clarendon Press, 1970).

Peach, Linden, *Angela Carter* (Basingstoke: Macmillan, 1998).

Pechey, Graham, '1789 and After: Mutations of "Romantic" Discourse', in *1789: Reading Writing Revolution*, ed. Francis Barker *et al.* (Colchester: University of Essex, 1982), 52–66.

Perrill, Simon, 'A Cartography of Absence: The Work of Iain Sinclair', *Comparative Criticism*, 19 (1997), 309–39.

Peters, Robert and Paul Trachtenberg, 'A Conversation with Robert Duncan (1976)', *Chicago Review*, 44:1 (1998), 92–116.

Plomer William, 'Review of W.H. Auden, *The Orators'*, *Sunday Referee* (22 May, 1932), 6.

Portugés, Paul, *The Visionary Poetics of Allen Ginsberg* (Santa Barbara: Ross-Erikson, 1978).

Pynchon, Thomas, *Gravity's Rainbow* (London: Picador, 1975), 144. 1st edn 1973.

Roberts, Michael, 'Not This Time?', *The Spectator*, 100 (26 July 1940) 301–02, (301).

Rudd, Margaret, *Divided Image: A Study of William Blake and W. B. Yeats* (London: Routledge and Kegan Paul, 1953).

Rushdie, Salman, *The Satanic Verses* (London: Random House, 1988).

Sage, Lorna, *Angela Carter* (Plymouth: Northcote House/British Council, 1994), 29.

——, *Flesh and the Mirror: Essays on the Art of Angela Carter* (London: Virago, 1994).

Scholem, Gershom G., *Major Trends in Jewish Mysticism*, 2nd rev. edn (New York: Schocken, 1946).

——, *Walter Benjamin: The Story of a Friendship* (London: Faber, 1982).

Seznec, Jean, *The Survival of the Pagan Gods*, trans. B. Sessions (New York: Pantheon, 1953).

Shaw, Bernard, *Three Plays for Puritans*, ed. Michael Billington (Harmondsworth: Penguin Books, 2000).

Sinclair, Iain, *Downriver (Or, The Vessels of Wrath): A Narrative in Twelve Tales* (London: Vintage, 1995), 385. First published 1991.

——, *Lights Out for the Territory* (London: Granta Books, 1997).

——, *Lud Heat and Suicide Bridge* (London: Granta Books, 1995).

——, *Lud Heat: A Book of the Dead Hamlets* (London: Albion Village Press, 1975).

——, *Suicide Bridge: A Book of the Dead Hamlets: May 1974 to April 1975* (London: Albion Village Press, 1975).

——, *White Chappell: Scarlet Tracings* (London: Paladin, 1987).

Smith, Stan, *The Origins of Modernism: Eliot, Pound, Yeats and the Rhetorics of Renewal* (Hemel Hempstead: Harvester, 1994).

Spender, Stephen, *World Within World*, 2nd edn (London: Faber, 1977). 1st edn 1951.

——, 'Five Notes on W. H. Auden's Writing', in *W. H. Auden: The Critical Heritage*, ed. John Haffenden (London: Routledge and Kegan Paul, 1983), 102–10.

Surette, Leon, *The Birth of Modernism: Ezra Pound, T.S. Eliot, W.B. Yeats and the Occult* (Montreal and Kingston: McGill-Queen's University Press, 1993).

Terrinoni, Enrico, 'Blakean Ghosts and Shadows in "Proteus"', in *Romantic Joyce: Joyce Studies in Italy (8)*, ed. Franca Ruggieri (Rome: Bulzoni Editore, 2003), 47–56.

Thomas, Dylan, *The Collected Letters of Dylan Thomas*, ed. Paul Ferris (London: Dent, 1985).

——, *Portrait of the Artist as a Young Dog* (London: Dent, 1940).

Thomas, Keith, *Religion and the Decline of Magic: Studies in Popular Beliefs in Sixteenth- and Seventeenth-Century England* (London: Weidenfeld & Nicolson, 1971).

Trotter, David, *The Making of the Reader: Language and Subjectivity in Modern American, English and Irish Poetry* (Basingstoke: Macmillan, 1984).

Viscomi, Robert, *Blake and the Idea of the Book* (Princeton: Princeton University Press, 1993).

Williams, Nicholas M., *Ideology and Utopia in the Poetry of William Blake* (Cambridge: Cambridge University Press, 1998).

——, 'Eating Blake, or An Essay on Taste: The Case of Thomas Harris's *Red Dragon*', *Cultural Critique*, 42 (1999), 143–70.

Wright, Andrew, ed., *Blake's Job: A Commentary* (Oxford: Clarendon Press, 1972).

Yeats, W. B., *Essays and Introductions* (London: Macmillan, 1961).

——, *The Poems: A New Edition*, 2nd edn, ed. Richard J. Finneran (London and Basingstoke: Macmillan, 1989).

——, *The Wind Among the Reeds* (London: John Lane, 1899).

Index

Bloom, Harold, 16, 36
body and mind/soul, dualism, 12,
     48, 55
Boehme, Jakob, 38, 66–67, 138
Bonnard, Pierre, 86
The Book of Thel, 141
The Book of Urizen, 12–13, 41, 91, 132
The Book of Yeats's Poems, by Hazard
     Adams, 24
Bornstein, George, 14
Bourdieu, P., 94
bourgeois morality, 9, 16
Brautigan, Richard, 128
British Union of Fascists, 106
Bruce, James, 152
Bryant, Jacob, 19, 21
Buddhism, 94, 121
Bunyan, John, 7, 101, 102
     Pilgrim's Progress, 102
Burlington Magazine (1904), by Roger
     Fry, 6
Burnt Norton, by T.S. Eliot, 32, 35
Burton, Robert,
     Anatomy of Melancholy, 22
Byron, George Gordon, 45, 64, 82
     Childe Harold, 81

Camus, Albert, 103
canon-formation, 1
Cape Goliard, 125
capitalist system, capitalism, 9, 71,
     95, 126, 131
The Captive and the Free, by Joyce
     Cary, 102
Carr, Stephen Leo, 98
Carroll, Lewis, 136
Cartari, Vincenzo
     Imagini delli Dei de gl'Antichi, 20
Carter, Angela, 12, 13–14, 82,
     136–45
     Bloody Chamber, 141
     Nights at the Circus, 139, 140–41,
          144
     The Passion of New Eve, 138–39,
          142–43
     The Sadeian Woman, 139

Cary, Joyce, 86–87
     The Captive and the Free, 102
     The Horse's Mouth, 85, 100–7
     To be a Pilgrim, 102
Cassady, Neal, 115
Catling, Brian, 134
Celt, Celtic, 4, 59–60, 61, 62, 70,
     75, 130
Certeau, Michel de, 94
Cézanne, Paul, 6, 86, 106
Chamber Music, by James Joyce, 58
chaos theory, 83, 85, 86, 96, 98
Chaucer, Geoffrey, 104
Childe Harold, by George Gordon,
     Lod Byron, 81
*Children of Albion: Poetry of the
     Underground in Britain*, by
     Michael Horovitz, 10
Christ, 74–76
Christian, Christianity, 10, 34, 41,
     46, 48
     Catholic orthodoxy, 77
     iconography, 19
     Judeo-Christian, 108
Clare, John, 146
Clark, Lorraine,
     *Blake, Kierkegaard, and the Spectre of
          Dialectic*, 73
Coleridge, Samuel Taylor, 15, 80, 82
     The Rime of the Ancient Mariner, 77
Collected Poems, by W.B. Yeats, 39, 40
Collins, William, 22
colouring approach, 98
Cone, Allie, 149, 155
Conrad, Joseph
     The Nigger of the Narcissus, 25
consciousness, 115, 127, 128, 135,
     139
conservatism, 102, 106
*Constructive Vision and Visionary
     Deconstruction*, by Peter
     Otto, 96
continuity, 73
contrariety, 41, 43, 110, 141, 146
corruption, 132
cosmic polarities, 41